RICHARD BAUMAN is Director of the Center for Intercultural Studies in Folklore and Oral History at the University of Texas.

FOR THE REPUTATION
OF TRUTH

FOR THE REPUTATION OF TRUTH

POLITICS, RELIGION, AND CONFLICT
AMONG THE PENNSYLVANIA QUAKERS
1750–1800

Richard Bauman

THE JOHNS HOPKINS PRESS, Baltimore and London

The Johns Hopkins Press, Baltimore, Maryland 21218
The Johns Hopkins Press Ltd., London

Library of Congress Catalog Card Number 79-143626

ISBN-0-8018-1178-3

To
G.K., Z.B., and J.B.,
who are not Quakers, but who have kept
a peace testimony of their own

CONTENTS

PREFACE

In terms of the history of its development, this book is a very long tail wagging the dog of its next-to-the-last chapter, for my initial interest in the Pennsylvania Quakers concerned their missionary activity among the Allegheny Seneca, an undertaking which began in 1798 and which serves to bring the present study to a close. Some of the Friends who were involved in this venture and some of the later commentators upon it drew a comparison between the work among the Iroquois and the much earlier activities of Friends among the Indians during the 1750s, a time, it appeared, when Indians were at the center of Quaker affairs in Pennsylvania. Considering this a necessary part of my research into the background of the missions to the Seneca, I began to investigate the events and activities of the fifties. The background soon became foreground, and this book is the result.

The central political event of the mid-eighteenth century, according to most views of Quaker history, was the so-called withdrawal from the Assembly in 1756, when six Friends resigned their seats in the House and were later followed by enough of their brethren to bring to a close the period when acknowledged Friends constituted a majority of the representatives in the Quaker colony. The ostensible reason for this act, rightly considered a turning point in the political history of the Pennsylvania Quakers, was the incompatibility of the Quaker religious testimony with participation in government. A problem of this kind will always catch an anthropologist's eye, for it represents a case of role conflict, or role strain in Goode's terms, "the felt difficulty in fulfilling role obligations" caused by mutually inconsistent sets of behavioral expectations or obligations.[1]

I found the situation at mid-century of additional interest because the missionary activity of the 1790s, the source of my first interest in the Quakers, was undertaken to a large degree under government auspices. The question arose of why the Quakers of the 1750s found religion and participation in government incompatible, while those of the 1790s were willing and even eager to work under government sponsorship. How had the conflict been reconciled? What other changes had taken place? I thus became more involved with the situation of role conflict and its reconciliation than with the missionary venture among the Iroquois.

Looking further into the political events of the mid-eighteenth century, it soon became apparent that not all the Quakers who held public office at the time experienced or reacted to these events in the same way. A significant number of Friends never withdrew from office at all, and some of those who did withdraw returned to office shortly thereafter. There were in fact a good many Quakers in public office in Pennsylvania up to the time of the Revolution. It seemed apparent that role strain was not a universal factor among the Quakers in government, and so it became necessary to find out which Quakers experienced role conflict, which did not, and why. This called for a definition of the roles and situations at issue in terms of the participants' own view of the dimensions involved—for an understanding of political and religious role expectations, goals, and ways of understanding events and the consequences of action as they appeared to the Quakers themselves. This is what I have attempted to achieve in the analysis which follows.

Role conflict, however, is only one aspect of the study, for the

[1] William J. Goode, "A Theory of Role Strain," *American Sociological Review*, 25 (1960) : 483.

different cognitive and behavioral orientations which manifested themselves among Friends individually also had much to do with the organization of the Quakers as a corporate body, the Philadelphia Yearly Meeting of the Society of Friends (see Appendix I). Much of the political energy of an important segment of politically significant Friends was channeled through the Yearly Meeting and its subordinate agencies, and the political behavior of all Friends was a Meeting concern. In fact, the same forces which generated role conflict within individual Friends also provoked social conflict within the membership of the Society as members were faced with the same sets of discrepant role expectations but opted for different courses of action, thus precipitating cleavage within the Society.

Another dimension was thus added to the study—namely, a determination of the distribution of political and religious styles within the organizational structure of the Philadelphia Yearly Meeting and the effects of this distribution on the corporate actions of the Society. The key questions here included how the actions of the organization articulated with those of the individual members of all types, and how the organization monitored and reacted to its own actions, the behavior of its members, and the environment.

The analytical perspective employed on both levels, the individual and the social, is an essentially processual and ecological one, in the sense advanced by Beals and Siegel in *Divisiveness and Social Conflict*: "We view conflict not simply as a domain in itself, but also as a manifestation of the inherent properties of culturally based behavior in its continuing interaction with the environment. In this sense our approach is ecological. It explicitly relates the dynamics of external conditions—the multifold operations of the environment—to customary adaptations of belief systems and social structure."[2] The Quakers are viewed, individually and as a group, in interaction with their behavioral environment,[3] reacting

---

[2] Alan R. Beals and Bernard J. Siegel, *Divisiveness and Social Conflict* (Stanford, Calif., 1966), p. vii.

[3] A. Irving Hallowell, *Culture and Experience* (Philadelphia, 1955), pp. 175–82.

and adapting to situations of stress from the environment and to the consequences of their own behavior over the span of half-a-century. Particular external events, or crises, which figured especially prominently in Quaker experience provide points of reference for the course of the study.

In its final form, then, the study is a processual analysis, within a framework of role conflict and social conflict, of social change on two interrelated levels, the individual and the social. For individual Quakers, the change was in the content of their political and religious roles as members of the Society of Friends in Pennsylvania. The Philadelphia Yearly Meeting, on the other hand, underwent change in structure, composition, and political role within the larger political community.

For the sake of conceptual clarity, and because it differs from the usage of historians who have treated the same period, a word should be said concerning the sense in which political behavior is conceived in this work. The terms and concepts I have employed are widely debated in the literature,[4] and I do not intend these remarks to be my own personal entries in the theoretical lists of political anthropology, but only to give a sense of the conceptual organizing principles which I have found useful for the purposes of this study.

Reduced to its least common denominator, we may identify as political all behavior which is aimed at influencing the setting and pursuit of the public goals of a group, including efforts made to achieve positions or states which are viewed as affording influence over these goals, as well as activities directed at influencing the kinds of political behavior in which other members of the group engage.[5] Social boundaries at all levels of integration delimit fields of political interaction, and political processes may be studied at any of these levels. There is some conceptual utility, however, in

---

[4] I have drawn upon F. G. Bailey, *Strategems and Spoils* (Oxford, 1969); David Easton, *A Framework for Political Analysis* (Englewood Cliffs, N.J., 1965) and *A Systems Analysis of Political Life* (New York, 1965); and Victor Turner, Mark Swartz, and Arthur Tuden, *Political Anthropology* (Chicago, 1966).

[5] Turner, Swartz, and Tuden, *Political Anthropology*, p. 7.

distinguishing political systems having to do with "whole societies" or segments thereof,[6] for which the term *political community* may be reserved.

In heterogeneous societies, made up of subgroups characterized by varying degrees of institutional divergence,[7] the members may be viewed as belonging to a common political community insofar as they participate to some degree in a common structure and set of processes for the establishment and pursuit of over-all public goals, however tight or loose the ties may be, and however the political labor may be divided.[8] The political community which is relevant to this study is the colony of Pennsylvania, a clearly delimited administrative unit which was the focus of a large proportion of the political energies of the members of the Philadelphia Yearly Meeting during the period under review. During and after the Revolution, a portion of this energy was redirected to the emergent national system, so this will have to be taken into consideration as well, but the emphasis throughout will be on behavioral factors, and the expansion of the community will not be a major consideration. It is the individual and corporate political behavior of Quakers within the larger community which will be the principal focus of attention.

Because the case which is treated in this work—the political activity of an eighteenth-century American religious group in a heterogeneous society—may appear to be far removed from the usual sphere of anthropological interest, and terms such as "household," "lineage," "clan," "village," "tribe," "headman," and "chief"—to which political anthropologists are habituated—are absent from its pages, it may be useful to state explicitly at the outset that the analytical framework has been consciously derived with reference to a particular segment of the anthropological literature, and that the work is intended, among other things, as a

---

[6] Cf. Easton, *A Framework for Political Analysis*, p. 38, and Bailey, *Strategems and Spoils*, p. 23.

[7] M. G. Smith, *The Plural Society in the British West Indies* (Berkeley and Los Angeles), p. 82.

[8] Easton, *A Systems Analysis of Political Life*, p. 177.

contribution to that literature. To be specific, the present study deals with essentially the same problems as Max Gluckman's Introduction to "The Village Headman in British Central Africa,"[9] Lloyd Fallers' *Bantu Bureaucracy*,[10] and A. L. Epstein's *Politics in an Urban African Community*[11]—namely, role conflict in the political sphere, and the effect of external factors on political behavior and social structure in a heterogeneous milieu. Parallels and divergences will be discussed where appropriate in the study.

Similarities and differences in the methodological sphere, however, may be usefully outlined here. The most obvious factor is that the historical dimension is prominent in the latter two works as well as the present one. Of the three, it is least fully developed in Fallers' book, although his work is subtitled *A Century of Political Evolution among the Basoga of Uganda*. Much of the historical material in *Bantu Bureaucracy* is merely a chronicle of events linking traditional Busoga with the modern Busoga of the early 1950s, when Fallers conducted his fieldwork. The historical material of greatest analytical interest concerns the incompatibility of the role expectations of corporate lineage and state bureaucracy as a source of role conflict in traditional Busoga, to which a parallel is subsequently developed in modern Busoga. The perspective is not processual or developmental, then, but comparative, with two historical stages of the same society being compared.

Epstein's framework is much closer to that of the present study, in that development over time is central to his analysis and he has found it useful, as I have, to organize his analysis around a succession of crisis points. The principal difference between our approaches lies in the greater prominence given in the present analysis to the feedback of information concerning past action and its effect upon subsequent action.

One general difference between my approach and that of Fallers and Epstein reflects the nature of our respective source materials.

[9] In Max Gluckman, *Order and Rebellion in Tribal Africa* (London, 1963), pp. 146–52.
[10] 2nd ed. (Chicago, 1965).
[11] (Manchester, 1958).

The availability of personal documents produced by politically significant individuals and relating to events as they happened over a considerable span of time made it possible for me to follow the careers of those individuals more closely than might an anthropologist who spends a relatively short time in the field and must rely on life history material for this kind of time depth on the individual level. Likewise, the fullness of the organizational documents provided an unbroken record of the affairs of the Pennsylvania Quakers as a corporate group. This, in fact, is one of the principal advantages of basing a study of this kind on documentary historical materials from literate societies—namely, that these materials provide a record of events as they happened and as they engendered other events over a far greater span of time than can be comprehended by ethnographic field research. The importance of personal and organizational documents for the kind of analysis I have carried out has led me to quote perhaps more extensively from my sources than seems to be fashionable in contemporary historical writing. Matters of fashion, however, are of less concern to me than providing the reader with as much as possible of the primary evidence on which my analysis is based.

For the historians who may read this book, no rationalization of the subject matter will be necessary, but some points concerning the approach I have taken may be in order. Although the work has been conceived and pursued within an anthropological frame of reference, I would suggest that the approach is consistent with the objectives of an increasing number of historians as well. In his contribution to *The Reinterpretation of American History*, for example, Jack P. Greene has written: "For early America, the most visible elements of [political] culture—the formal concepts of political thought and the external forms of institutional development—have received a considerable amount of attention from historians during the past seventy-five years. What has been until recently almost completely ignored and what, it now appears, is vastly more important, is that elusive and shadowy cluster of assumptions, traditions, conventions, values, modes of expression, and habits of thought and belief that underlay those visible elements."[12] I believe that my analysis contributes to precisely this objective, but goes one step beyond it as well, in attempting to integrate the aspects of political culture which Greene catalogs with the behavior of the historical actors involved and with the processes of change which occurred.

E. E. Evans-Pritchard, an anthropologist who has been more concerned with history than most of his colleagues, has cited Maitland to the effect that anthropology must choose between being history and being nothing, adding for his own part that he accepts the dictum, "though only if it can also be reversed— history must choose between being social anthropology or being nothing."[13] In these terms, in which I too concur, this study has covered its tracks—it at least escapes the danger of being nothing. Whether it contributes *something* to either or both disciplines must remain for the reader to judge.

[12] "Changing Interpretations of Early American Politics," in *The Reinterpretation of Early American History*, ed. Ray Allen Billington (San Marino, Calif., 1966), p. 172.
[13] E. E. Evans-Pritchard, "Anthropology and History," in his *Social Anthropology and Other Essays*, paperback ed. (New York, 1964), p. 190.

ACKNOWLEDGMENTS

In his vital and stimulating book *The Image*, Kenneth Boulding has noted a melancholy academic truth: "Society owes an enormous debt to those marginal men who live uneasily in two different universes of discourse. Society is apt to repay this debt by making them thoroughly uncomfortable and still more marginal" (p. 146). I do not flatter myself that society owes me any enormous debts of gratitude, but I can certainly attest to the sense of marginality which comes of working at the intersection of two fields which many others would prefer to keep separate. It is therefore with a special sense of gratitude that I acknowledge my own personal and scholarly debt to those whose encouragement, support, aid, and counsel made it possible for me to pursue the course of study and research which has culminated in the present work.

I wish particularly to thank Anthony N. B. Garvan and Murray G. Murphey of the University of Pennsylvania American Civilization Department, and Anthony F. C. Wallace of the Anthropology Department, for their willingness to confront and overcome all the academic inertia and bureaucratic impedimenta generated by my desire to work simultaneously in both departments, and, perhaps more important, for believing in the validity of the perspective I sought to develop under their guidance. I am grateful also to Lee Benson of the History Department for developing my awareness,

ACKNOWLEDGMENTS

both "by conduct and conversation," as the Quakers would say, of the importance of bringing the theoretical perspective of the social and behavioral sciences to bear upon the materials of history, and, still more, for providing a strong source of encouragement at the inception of this study and throughout its duration.

In addition, it is my pleasant duty to acknowledge the generous assistance of the directors and staffs of a number of libraries and archives, who, through their unfailing courtesy, cooperation, and interest, have facilitated my research to a degree which any scholar would cherish. I wish especially to thank Mrs. Alice Allen of the Department of Records, Philadelphia Yearly Meeting; Dr. Frederick B. Tolles, Miss Dorothy Harris, and the staff of the Friends Historical Library, Swarthmore College; Dr. Edwin Bronner, Mrs. Betty Tritle, and the staff of the Quaker Collection, Haverford College; and Mr. J. Harcourt Givens and the staff of the Manuscript Room, Historical Society of Pennsylvania.

My colleague Richard N. Adams took the time during an extraordinarily busy period in his own affairs to read and comment on an earlier draft of this study, to the benefit, I believe, of the final version. I wish also to express my appreciation to Mrs. Frances Terry for her skill and patience in typing both drafts of the manuscript in the midst of her other duties.

Finally, I offer my heartfelt thanks to my wife, Louise, whose devoted confidence helped me to make some of my earliest intellectual commitments, whose trust has sustained me ever since through the zigs and zags of an unorthodox academic career, and whose selfless support, both spiritual and material, has made this as much her work as mine.

FOR THE REPUTATION
OF TRUTH

I

POLITICAL BEHAVIOR BEFORE 1750

Personally and painfully familiar with the effects of religious persecution and political disability, and passionately devoted to the ideals of toleration, William Penn was determined to make clear from the outset that his colony on the Delaware was to be free "for all mankind," a haven not only for his Quaker co-religionists but for all who wished to settle there. While civil and religious liberty were to be extended to all, however, Penn left no room for doubt that Pennsylvania was planned and founded "more especially" for the Quakers, as a refuge from persecution in Britain and as a "holy experiment" in government in which his brethren could enjoy that freedom of conscience which he valued above all other political considerations.[1]

During the first two decades of the colony's existence, when Friends still constituted a majority of the population and Penn's own involvement in the affairs and development of his province was at its height, the lines dividing the secular government of Pennsylvania from the Quaker meeting structure were often obscure and at times nonexistent. Even after the turn of the eighteenth century, when the Quakers were outnumbered by other denominations and the secular political realm had become clearly

[1]'Edward C. O. Beatty, *William Penn as Social Philosopher* (New York, 1939), pp. 45 and 158.

1

demarcated from the religious both in organization and practice, the Quakers continued to look upon predominance in government as a natural perquisite of their historical position and continuing importance in the colony. Penn's injunction, written during the political campaign of 1679 in England, might well have served them as a guide: "There is nothing more to your Interest, then [sic] for you to understand your *Right* in *Government*, and to be constantly Jealous over it; for your *Well-being* depends upon its Preservation."[2]

Within the Society, there was no question of the appropriateness of Quakers serving in government. When Quaker magistrates in Pennsylvania encountered difficulties because of laws passed in England requiring the taking or administering of oaths by judicial officials, the general reaction was not resignation to the inappropriateness of Quakers filling these offices, but a persistent political effort to remove the disabilities.

At no time during the first half of the eighteenth century did the Yearly Meeting undertake to define a political role for the Quakers in Pennsylvania, except for the caution, issued in 1710, against deviation from Quaker principles in the conduct of office. This advice was prompted by the partisan wrangling and manipulation which characterized relations between the two political factions into which the Quakers had split, a Whiggish, liberal, country-based party led by David Lloyd, and a conservative, urban party led by James Logan. Although many a Quaker officeholder compromised or sacrificed his testimony in succeeding years, the Yearly Meeting issued no further advice on participation in government until 1758.

The partisan rift within the Society ultimately healed by about 1725 or 1730, by which time the Quakers were well outnumbered in Pennsylvania. Divided or unified, however, they continued to control the elective offices of the colony throughout the period, by virtue of their wealth, social position, and historical pre-eminence, with the support of the German pietists, who valued Quaker tol-

[2] Edwin B. Bronner, *William Penn's "Holy Experiment"* (New York, 1962), p. 10, italics in the original.

2

eration and pacifism, and sustained by a system of legislative apportionment which favored the eastern areas of the province where Quakers predominated. In a day when recruitment to political office was largely a function of wealth, social position, and local influence, the powerful Quaker merchants and landowners were able to settle election tickets among themselves, their subsequent election being almost a foregone conclusion. The time of the Yearly Meeting, which brought Friends together shortly before the fall elections, was particularly appropriate for such machinations, although the meetings themselves were never given over to these proceedings.

During the period under review, the nature and degree of participation by politically active Quakers in meeting affairs was determined by individual factors of socialization and temperament. Such government leaders as Thomas Lloyd (1640–95), the elder Isaac Norris (1671–1735), the elder Israel Pemberton (1684–1754), and John Kinsey (1693–1750) were equally influential in the service of their church, while David Lloyd (1656–1731) and James Logan (1674–1751) had comparatively little to do with Society affairs.[3] In either case, the realm of activity to which an individual devoted his efforts was a matter of personal concern; activity in government did not, per se, prejudice one's standing in the church, for holding office was not yet considered a threat to Quaker principles.

Nevertheless, from the 1690s on, there was one major issue which confronted the Quakers in Pennsylvania periodically which did represent a serious challenge to their continued participation in government, though the challenge was not always recognized as such. This was the problem of military defense.[4] Owing in large part to the enlightened Indian policy of its founder, Pennsylvania was spared the ordeal of the Indian wars to which its sister

---

[3] Isaac Sharpless, *Political Leaders of Provincial Pennsylvania* (Philadelphia, 1919).

[4] The best discussion of this problem appears in Hermann Wellenreuther, "The Political Dilemma of the Quakers in Pennsylvania, 1681–1748," *Pennsylvania Magazine of History and Biography*, 94 (1970) : 135–72.

colonies were frequently subjected. Beginning in 1689, however, with the outbreak of King William's War, the province was periodically called upon by the imperial government to mobilize its defenses and to furnish military assistance to other colonies or to the crown.

As early as 1693, in response to demands for military aid, the Pennsylvania Assembly resorted to the expedient of providing the funds, while stipulating against their direct application to warlike purposes. By 1709, the standard evasion was that the money would become part of the queen's general revenue, to be appropriated subsequently at her discretion. The prevailing view in the Pennsylvania Assembly was that this practice was consistent with Quaker principles, or at least was not in violation of any, in that it was perfectly correct to give money to the queen for the support of her government, the uses to which it was subsequently put "being not our part, but hers." The grant of 1709 was followed two years later by an even larger one, also allotted "for the queen's use."

None of the American colonies during this period, even those where the religious scruples of the inhabitants were not a factor, displayed a ready willingness to deliver up money for the defense of other provinces or the advancement of distant imperial ambitions. In this respect, Pennsylvania was no exception, but the government of the Quaker colony was in a uniquely vulnerable position. The grant of 1693 was made only after the king had seized the government of the colony from Penn the preceding year, in large part because of Pennsylvania's failure to accede to demands for contributions to imperial defense. As the only sure means of winning military appropriations from the province, proposals were actually made for the exclusion of Quakers from government in times of war. Threatened with this prospect, the Quaker legislators evinced a greater willingness to meet the crown's demands. The government was subsequently restored to the Proprietor, but apprehensions of royal seizure persisted and were a major factor in motivating the appropriations of 1701, 1709, and 1711.

The Quakers' dilemma was eased somewhat in 1701 when the provincial lieutenant governor, Andrew Hamilton, took into his

4

own hands the task of commissioning officers and raising a defense force within the colony, as he was empowered to do under the terms of the charter granted to Penn by the crown. This relieved the assemblymen of the necessity of passing a militia bill, which they were conscientiously unwilling to do, on the grounds that they would thereby be compelling others to fight, something they could no more do than make war themselves. On the other hand, though, they did not feel themselves compelled to *prevent* people who did not share their religious scruples from engaging in military activities, a distinction which often proved useful. As we shall see, these very expedients were firmly rejected by many members of the succeeding generation in Pennsylvania as constituting outright compromise of the Quaker religious testimony, but it is most important to note that such moral reservations were not in evidence during this early period.

After the War of the Spanish Succession was concluded by the Treaty of Utrecht, Pennsylvania enjoyed almost three decades of peace, during which the problems of military aid and imperial defense faded from view. In 1739, however, with the War of Jenkins' Ear imminent, the issue was revived in all its vigor.

The difficulty was first raised when Governor George Thomas, at the behest of the Proprietors, urged the Assembly to make provision for the defense of Pennsylvania, including the raising of a militia. Noting that many of the inhabitants of the province were Quakers, whose principles against the bearing of arms were well known, the legislators asserted their scruples against violating the conscience of Friends by compelling them to participate in military exercises. To exempt Quakers from measures calling upon others to fight would be equally inadmissible, for it was both inconsistent with the peace testimony and partial to one segment of the population. The Assembly recognized the rights of those who felt called upon to defend themselves by force of arms, and suggested to the governor that it was within his power to enlist troops on his own initiative. For their own part, they would continue to trust in the protection of Divine Providence, which had shielded the province from war since its founding, but they would not interfere with the military activities of others so long as the rights of conscience were respected.

There followed several exchanges between the governor and the Assembly in which a number of important points were scored by both parties. Thomas contended that, as representatives of all the people, Quaker assemblymen were obliged to protect the province from invasion. He suggested further that, "as the world is now circumstanced, no purity of heart or set of religious principles will protect us from the enemy," advancing the Quakers' own code of criminal law in Pennsylvania and the earlier wartime appropriations of money for the crown's use as evidence of their implicit recognition of this fact. The Assembly in turn discounted the possibility of invasion, rejected the analogy between police and military power, suggested that the earlier appropriations had not been of any real benefit, and expressed confidence that their refusal to furnish the requested legislation would bring no ill effects to the province. In his final reply, the governor, in his frustration, felt compelled to ask his opponents, "If your principles will not allow you to pass a bill for establishing a militia, if they will not allow you to secure the navigation of a river by building a fort, if they will not allow you to provide armies for the defence of the inhabitants, if they will not allow you to raise men for his Majesty's service for distressing an insolent enemy, is it calumny to say your principles are inconsistent with the ends of government?"[5] This question was asked with increasing frequency in the ensuing years, by Quakers and non-Quakers alike.

After the initial exchange in the fall of 1739, the Assembly continued to thwart Governor Thomas' attempts to implement his defense program, and to retain most of its popular support while doing so. In the election of 1741, for example, although his partisans gained control of the Philadelphia city government, the results of the Assembly contest so aroused the governor that he addressed a strong letter to the Board of Trade attacking the Quaker Assembly for its intransigence and for increasing the Quaker majority in

---

[5] Sharpless, *Political Leaders of Provincial Pennsylvania*, p. 168.

the face of his suggestion that Friends withdraw from office, and recommending their exclusion therefrom. The Assembly covered its flanks, however, by voting three thousand unsolicited pounds for the king's use.

After the hotly contested and violent election of the following year resulted in another overwhelming defeat for the governor's supporters, more voices were added to the campaign for the exclusion of Quakers from the Assembly. Two hundred sixty-five prominent persons signed a petition charging the Assembly with failure to provide for the defense of the colony and appealing to Parliament for laws to curb the Quaker hegemony.

Despite its initial lack of success, these years represented an important period of crystallization and growth for the anti-Quaker opposition, which formerly had been a negligible factor in provincial politics. Thus a word or two concerning the background of the emerging party will be useful at this point.

On the death of William Penn in 1718, the colony passed to his three sons, none of whom shared his father's intense ideological commitment to Pennsylvania or his dedication to Quakerism; two of them, in fact, became converts to the Church of England. Their principal concern apparently was the troubled state of the family's finances, and they looked upon Pennsylvania chiefly as a potential source of profit. The intangible part of their father's legacy passed to his brethren in Pennsylvania, however, and constituted a formidable obstacle to the financial ambitions of the new Proprietors.

Throughout his adult life, Penn was a dedicated and energetic defender of civil liberties, as strong dissenters tended to be, and he fostered the spirit of Whiggism in his colony. In 1687, for the edification of the colonists, he compiled and published *The Excellent Privilege of Liberty and Property*, a collection of constitutional documents including, among others, the Magna Charta, Edward I's Confirmation of the Charters, an abstract of his own patent from the king, and his Frame of Government for Pennsylvania. The purpose, as he explained it in his preface, was to "raise up noble resolutions in all the Freeholders . . . not to give away anything of Liberty and Property that at present they do, (or of right as loyal

7

English subjects ought to) enjoy, but take up the good example of our ancestors, and understand that it is easy to part with or give away great privileges, but hard to be gained if once lost."[6]

That he need not have been concerned on this account, however, soon became abundantly clear, as the politicians in Pennsylvania turned the Proprietor's principles back upon him and jealously contended for privileges and concessions at every turn. During the years of partisan schism, even the conservative faction professed a devotion to the ideals of liberty and property, though they tended to stress the latter somewhat more than the former.

By the time Penn's sons succeeded to his estate, the Pennsylvania Assembly had secured to itself a comparatively high degree of power and was able, as we have seen, to frustrate the Proprietary program with relative ease. On the other hand, notwithstanding its control of the provincial government, the Quaker party was effectively barred from the administrative branch because the Proprietors retained control of the colony's appointive offices, which also served them as a base for attracting supporters to their interests. Thus, while the Quaker party retained overwhelming electoral support and was able to maintain its legislative control, the anti-Quaker opposition came to center on support for the Proprietors and their appointed governors.

The earliest anti-Quaker opposition had been mounted principally by Anglicans, but the nascent Proprietary party of the early 1740s included increasing numbers of Presbyterians, as well as back-country Lutherans and members of the German Reformed church, who did not share the pacifist principles of their pietist countrymen and were strongly concerned about the security of the frontier against the threat of Indian attack. The leader of the party in these years, and for many years thereafter, was William Allen, a tremendously wealthy and capable Presbyterian who had earlier held a number of provincial offices and was at the time recorder of the province and a member of the Assembly, in which he served

---

[6] Frederick H. Tolles, *Meeting House and Counting House*, 2nd ed. (New York, 1963), pp. 12–13.

until the Revolution. In 1750 he secured the office of chief justice as well.

On the popular level, additional developments were taking place at this time which affected the growth and character of the opposition forces in the succeeding period. Perhaps the most important of these was initiated by the arrival of George Whitefield in Philadelphia in 1739, bearing with him the torch of religious revival. The Quakers themselves were largely untouched by the fervors of the Great Awakening, but the period witnessed a tremendous increase in religious awareness and sectarian self-consciousness, particularly among the lower- and middle-class Presbyterians.[7] These developments were a vital factor in the emerging alignment of religious denominations in partisan coalitions and relationships. During the next thirty-five years, they contributed as well to the growth of a general political "public" in Pennsylvania, one concerned and informed about political issues and taking an ever-increasing part in their determination.[8] Although it could not be foreseen in 1740, the tide of Quaker rule in Pennsylvania had begun to ebb.

At the same time that the external opposition to Quaker rule was coalescing and gaining strength, important developments were taking place within the Society of Friends which tended in some of the same directions. The Assembly policy notwithstanding, there was a tangible division among the Quakers with respect to the military and related political issues of the period.

The spokesman for one faction within the Philadelphia Yearly Meeting was the now aged James Logan, Proprietary secretary in Pennsylvania and, in earlier years, leader of the conservative, Proprietary faction of Quakers. In 1741, disturbed by the rapid growth and intensification of the Assembly's opposition to the Proprietary

---

[7] Carl and Jessica Bridenbaugh, *Rebels and Gentlemen*, 2nd ed. (New York, 1962), p. 19.

[8] Dietmar Rothermund, *The Layman's Progress* (Philadelphia, 1961), pp. 83 and 113–14.

appointees and program, he addressed a highly significant letter to the Yearly Meeting then sitting. In it, he asserted his personal conviction of the justifiability of defensive warfare while acknowledging that this was contrary to an orthodox interpretation of the peace testimony. He went on to advance the following principal points, most of which corresponded fairly closely to the views expressed by Governor Thomas two years earlier. Pointing out that Friends comprised, at most, one-third of the population, Logan defended the right of the other people to laws for their protection. He suggested that the prosperity of the colony made it more than ever vulnerable to attack, and urged those of his brethren with scruples against defense to withhold themselves from candidacy for public office and to decline to serve if elected.[9]

Although Logan's position was supported by others in the Meeting, on the recommendation of the committee to which it had been assigned for preliminary consideration, and in accordance with standard Yearly Meeting procedure, it was denied a general hearing. The actual disposition of the Meeting representatives cannot be known with absolute certainty, but several factors are suggestive in this regard. The fact that Logan chose to address the Yearly Meeting concerning the position of the Quaker Assembly is an indication that he perceived a strong correspondence between the two bodies with regard to their positions on the issues raised. It is significant in this connection that the clerk of the Yearly Meeting was John Kinsey, Speaker of the Assembly and leader of the Quaker party, and therefore closely implicated in the actions and policies of the House. As clerk, it was Kinsey's task to appoint the committee which would consider Logan's letter, and this provided him with a simple and effective means of foreclosing debate from the outset.

In opposition to the defense faction among the political activists was a group conspicuously led by the younger Israel Pemberton, a vigorous and talented young merchant whose astuteness in trade and family connections had secured him a considerable fortune.

[9] James Logan, "James Logan on Defensive War," *Pennsylvania Magazine of History and Biography*, 6 (1882) : 402–11.

His grandfather was one of the earliest Quaker settlers in Pennsylvania, and his father had enjoyed a long and useful career in politics and in service to his church.

Friends who sided with Pemberton, in contradistinction to Kinsey and his followers, rejected not only the idea of a militia but also the compromise implicit in granting money ostensibly for the king's general use, but obviously for war. In 1744, Pemberton challenged Kinsey's power by attempting to set up a slate of more strictly pacifist candidates for the Assembly in the Quaker stronghold of Philadelphia (now Montgomery) County, but, like Logan, he was defeated. The Kinsey ticket, unopposed by Proprietary candidates, was easily elected. Nevertheless, Pemberton persisted in his opposition to the compromisers and defense adovcates within the Society. In 1748 he initiated a campaign against a group of Friends who contributed to the fitting out of a privateer to defend the city against a rumored French invasion, and the following year he led the movement against Thomas Penn's proposal that the Assembly share with the Proprietors the expense of building a fort in the Ohio valley to keep out the French.

With the death of Kinsey in 1750, Pemberton's power increased. In that year he assisted in setting up the Assembly ticket, and was himself elected to a seat in the House in an election which aroused considerable excitement in the Quaker party, but in which the Proprietary party mounted no opposition. He also succeeded Kinsey as clerk of the Yearly Meeting, but the speakership of the Assembly passed to Isaac Norris II, son of the elder Isaac Norris and son-in-law of James Logan. The elder Norris had been instrumental in carrying through the Assembly the grant of two thousand pounds for the queen's use in 1709, and was the author of the argument that the way in which the money was spent was "her part, not ours." Although his father and father-in-law were supporters of the Proprietary interest, the younger Norris identified himself with the Quaker party in opposition to the now Anglican and Presbyterian Proprietary party. Some of his views on defense corresponded to those of Logan, as we shall see, but as party leader he upheld the Kinsey position.

11

In an analysis which equates the political with the partisan, the above would suffice as a description of mid-eighteenth-century political alignments among the Pennsylvania Quakers, but a wider conceptualization of the political field calls for further examination of the modes of Quaker political behavior which were characteristic of the period. One viewpoint in particular, overshadowed by the stormy contests of the governor and the Assembly, is of crucial significance in the light of later developments.

Late in 1748, toward the end of King George's War, rumors reached Philadelphia that a fleet of six French privateers was fitting out in the West Indies for an attack on the city the following spring. The province had been raised to a state of agitation by the presence of enemy vessels in Delaware Bay the preceding summer, and upon hearing of the prospective invasion the new governor, Anthony Palmer, summoned the Assembly to ready the city's defenses. Specifically, he urged the legislature to fit out a privateer and to complete the construction of a shore battery below the city, which had been started earlier on private initiative but subsequently bogged down for lack of funds. The Assembly refused to act on Palmer's request, despite the high degree of public concern and the suggestion of some members that the projects might be financed by a grant for the king's use. In the end the privateer was privately financed, and a number of Quakers were among the contributors.

John Churchman, a revered Quaker minister from Chester County, was in the city on a religious visit at the time the governor summoned the Assembly. "One night as I lay in my bed," he wrote, "it came very weightily upon me to go to the house of assembly, and lay before the members thereof the danger of departing from trusting in that divine power which had hitherto protected the inhabitants of our land in peace and safety. . . . It seemed to be a very difficult time, many, even of our Society, declaring their willingness that a sum of money should be given to the king, to show our loyalty to him, and that they were willing to part with their substance for his use, though as a people, we had a testimony to bear against wars and fightings." After a period of painful hesita-

tion, Churchman took the unprecedented step of presenting himself at the House, and, solely in the role of a concerned individual,
asked to be allowed to address the Assembly. At first Kinsey suggested that he wait until the close of the session, after which the
Quaker members could remain to hear him out; but Churchman
persisted, maintaining that what he had to say was as much for the
ears of non-Friends as for his fellow Quakers, whereupon he was
admitted. He recorded the event in his journal as follows:

> . . . There was a great awe over my mind when I went in, which I
> thought in some measure spread, and prevailed over the members
> beyond my expectation, after a silence of perhaps ten or twelve
> minutes, I felt as though all fear of man was taken away, and my
> mind influenced to address them in substance after the following
> manner.

> *"My Country-men, and fellow Subjects, Representatives of the
> Inhabitants of this Province,*

> Under an apprehension of the difficulties before you, I feel a
> strong sympathy with you, and have to remind you of a just and
> true saying of a great minister of Jesus Christ in his day, *The
> powers that be, are ordained of God.* Now if men in power and
> authority, in whatsoever station, would seek unto God . . . for wis-
> dom and counsel to act simply for him that ordained the power,
> and permitted them to be stationed therein, that they should be his
> ministers; such will be a blessing under God to themselves and
> their country; but if those in authority do suffer their own fears
> and the persuasion of others, to prevail with them to neglect such
> attention, and so make, or enact laws in order to their own protec-
> tion and defence by carnal weapons and fortifications, styled
> human prudence, he who is superintendent, by withdrawing the
> arm of his power, may permit those evils they feared to come sud-
> denly upon them, and that in his heavy displeasure. May it with
> gratitude be ever remembered how remarkably we have been pre-
> served in peace and tranquility for more than fifty years! no inva-
> sion by foreign enemies, and the treaties of peace with the natives,
> wisely began by our worthy proprietor William Penn, preserved
> inviolate to this day.

13

"Tho' you now represent, and act for a mixed people of various denominations as to Religion; yet remember the Charter is the same as at first; beware therefore of acting to oppress tender Consciences, for there are many of the Inhabitants whom you now represent, that still hold forth the same religious principles with their predecessors, who were some of the first adventurers into this, at that time wilderness land, who would be greatly grieved to see warlike preparations carried on, and encouraged by a law consented to by their brethren in profession, or others, contrary to the Charter, still conscientiously concluding, that the reverent and true fear of God, with an humble trust in his ancient arm of Power, would be our greatest defence and safety; and they who hold different principles and are settled in this government, can have no just cause of reflection if warlike measures are forborne, because they knew the Charter framed, and the peaceable Constitution, and have ventured themselves therein.

"We may observe by sundry laws enacted in Parliament, when the Reformation was but newly begun in England, our mother country, there seemed to be wisdom from above to influence their minds; may you be rightly directed at this time, many of whom do fully believe in the immediate influence of Christ, the wisdom of God, which is truly profitable to direct! It is not from disrespect to the King or Government that I speak after this manner, for I am thankful in heart, that the Lord in mercy hath vouchsafed, that the throne of Great Britain should be filled with our present benevolent Prince, King George the second; may his reign be long and happy!"[10]

John Churchman's speech is notable in several respects, some of which will be discussed in detail below. For the present, we may note Churchman's insistence upon the primacy of the Quakers in Pennsylvania. In the context of an overwhelming Quaker majority in the Assembly, his statement must be viewed as an entreaty to his co-religionists to be directed solely by Quaker principles, under divine guidance, disregarding "their own fears and the persuasion

[10] John Churchman, *An Account of the Gospel Labours and Christian Experiences of . . . John Churchman*, The Friends' Library, vol. 6 (Philadelphia, 1842), pp. 200–201.

of others"—namely, the Proprietary leaders and their own non-Quaker constituents, who at that time outnumbered the Quakers in the province by about four to one! His appeal to the charter exemplified the mythical view of the colony's history held by many Quakers of the period, for none of the charters framed by Penn, including the one of 1701 which was then in effect, made any reference at all to this aspect of military affairs. On the other hand, the royal charter granting Penn the government of Pennsylvania conferred upon him all the powers of war, and he made clear to his lieutenant governors, all but one of whom were non-Quakers, their power to act under these provisions. Churchman's position stands in direct contrast to that of Logan; he was unwilling to make any concession to the mixed population of the province, or to countenance any compromise of the Quaker testimony to worldly considerations. This view was to have far-reaching effects upon the whole pattern of Quaker political behavior in the half-century that followed.

An additional and fundamental aspect of Churchman's behavior during these same years casts further light on subsequent events. We may recall that, whatever their ideological differences, Logan, Kinsey, and Pemberton all oriented their programs and activities toward the sphere of political office as the locus of power and influence. Churchman's orientation was completely antithetical to theirs in this respect: he was prompted to personal action by an individual concern for the Quaker testimony; he sought no personal power or position. It is illuminating to note that, when he was afforded access to political office and was urged by other Friends to avail himself of the opportunity, he declined to do so.

As I sat in a week-day meeting in the winter of 1748, I felt great weakness and poverty attending my mind, which occasioned a deep inquiry into the cause. After a time of inward waiting, the humbling divine presence was felt in reverent profound silence, yet the gentle operation of the divine power caused an inward trembling, and the following was uttered in a language intelligible to the inward man; "gather thyself from all the cumbers of the world, and be thou weaned from the popularity, love, and friend-

15

ship thereof." I believed this to be the voice of the holy One of Israel, as a merciful warning to prepare for my final change, or to stand ready for some service which would separate me from temporal business and the nearest connections in life; and from that time I endeavoured to settle my affairs, and contract my little business as well as I could. In the summer following I met with an unexpected trial, for without my knowledge my name was put in the new commission for justices of the peace, and endeavours were used to persuade me to be qualified in order to act in that station; and some of my particular friends told me it seemed providential, and they thought it was my place to accept thereof, as I might be helpful by way of example, to some in the commission who were Friends. For a short time I was exceedingly straitened, but my eye being fixed on the Lord for counsel, it pleased him in great condescension once more to revive the sentence before mentioned, "gather thyself from all the cumbers of the world," &c., which settled the point, and I became easy in mind, and humbly thankful to my blessed Instructor who had called me for other services.[11]

These passages from John Churchman's journal have been quoted at length because the experiences and attitudes they record, once analyzed and understood, afford insight into a mode of political behavior which was shortly to have tremendous impact upon the Society of Friends in Pennsylvania. Comparatively few Friends who were in a position to do so would have done as Churchman did in rejecting office in 1749, but within one decade many more were to adopt a similar course.

While an extensive analysis will be more illuminating after the outward events of the early 1750s have been summarized, it is useful at this point to enumerate certain salient aspects of Churchman's experiences, which will become still clearer in the light of subsequent discussion. Most important are the following: (1) the concern that the Quaker testimony, particularly the peace testimony, be strictly upheld; (2) complete attendance and reliance upon God for personal direction and support, with a concomitant rejection of "human prudence" and "the cumbers of the world";

[11] *Ibid.*, p. 203.

(3) a direct, personal, inward experience of the Divine Presence, attained through introspective attentiveness to the movings of one's mind in an attitude of silent, passive humility; (4) the belief that the dispensations of "the great Superintendent" may be influenced by the behavior of men.

At first glance, the kind of orientation which has been illustrated in the experience of John Churchman might easily appear to be apolitical, and so it has been considered by most students of Quaker history. The designation "political" is usually reserved for direct engagement in the processes of government, and analyses of Quaker politics in eighteenth-century Pennsylvania are confined almost wholly to participation in election campaigns, voting, and officeholding. We will defer until a later chapter our discussion of the truly political significance of these essentially religious attitudes, beliefs, and activities. The next major task will be to analyze the circumstances and events of the crucial years of the mid-1750s, as the diverse orientations toward involvement in politics which characterized the various members of the Society at mid-century coalesced into overt patterns of political commitment and brought to the surface a series of tensions which ultimately wrought a substantial transformation in the place of the Quakers in American society.

II

THE CRISIS OF THE MID-1750s

The 1750s have been appropriately treated by historians as a major turning point in the political history of the Pennsylvania Friends. The Quakers entered the decade in full control of the Assembly and the minor offices of the colony, apparently convinced of the appropriateness of their political position, and left it with their Assembly majority forever broken, with severe doubts about their political future, and with widespread misgivings concerning the propriety of any Quaker involvement in politics whatsoever. At the very center of this transformation was the political crisis of the mid-1750s.

The problem which occupied the center of the partisan arena in the early 1750s was that of paper money.[1] The issue's history in Pennsylvania had been long and was bound up with the recurrent colonial dilemma of imbalance between the outflow of specie to England and the growing demands of business at home. Money grew especially tight in Pennsylvania in the late 1740s, and the resulting clamor for relief brought the issue to the fore once again.

The Home Government was generally disposed against the

---

[1] Two important discussions of this period are John J. Zimmerman, "Benjamin Franklin and the Quaker Party, 1755–1756," *William and Mary Quarterly*, 17 (1960) : 291–313, and Ralph L. Ketcham, "Conscience, War, and Politics in Pennsylvania, 1755–1757," *William and Mary Quarterly*, 20 (1963) : 416–39.

colonists' reliance upon paper money, fearing excesses which might lead to inflation, and preferring payments in specie in any case. In 1748 the problem was under consideration in the House of Commons, and Thomas Penn accordingly instructed Governor Hamilton not to approve any further issues of paper, pending the outcome of parliamentary deliberations. The Assembly disregarded Penn's directive, however, and proceeded to pass a money bill, which the governor thereupon refused to sign.

Parliament finally acted on the matter in 1751, with a bill forbidding the use of legal-tender bills of credit in New England, but making no mention of any of the other colonies. Thereafter, Penn's instructions, usually encumbered with numerous subordinate provisions, stipulated that no sizable issues of paper money were to be approved in Pennsylvania without a suspending clause to allow for the approval of the Home Government ministry before actual implementation of the bill.

These instructions, and Hamilton's compliance, provoked the ire of the Assembly, and there followed a period of increasingly bitter wrangling as the House sent up bill after bill which failed to conform to Penn's stipulations, and the governor refused each one in succession. Popular indignation reached a height in 1753, when Hamilton refused a bill because it lacked a suspending clause. The Royal Order of 1740, in which suspending clauses were invoked, did not apply to Pennsylvania, and the colonists interpreted the inclusion of this requirement in the governor's instructions as a clear indication that the Proprietors were intent upon preventing any issuance of paper money whatsoever.

At about this time, a complicating factor arose in the form of an imminent war with France precipitated by that country's imperial ambitions in the Ohio valley. With the outbreak of open hostilities, and the resultant call for defense preparations by the Proprietors, the Assembly gained a highly effective lever with which to exert pressure upon the opposition forces—namely, refusal to grant money for defense unless provisions for paper currency were accepted. As the demands of the war grew more urgent, the Assembly increased its pressure on the Proprietors by including in a tax bill for the financing of the war a provision for the taxation of the vast Proprietary estates, whose exemption from such levies had long been a popular grievance. The Proprietors were no more willing to accept this measure than they were to approve a money bill which did not conform to their stipulations. Both sides looked upon the controversy as one involving a question of basic principle —whether the ultimate control of financial matters was to rest in the hands of the Proprietors or with the representatives of the people—and neither was predisposed to make concessions.

The people themselves, caught up between the two contending parties, were largely disregarded by both. Particularly on the frontier, threatened constantly by the Indians who had attached themselves to the French interest, there was rising fear and concern among the settlers at the failure of those in power to render them protection against the enemy. With the war the most immediate threat, popular concern over Whig financial principles declined very rapidly, but the Proprietors and the assemblymen, removed from the rigors of the frontier, would not yield.

Fostered by the Proprietary propagandists, a public outcry arose against the Assembly for not taking steps to alleviate the crisis. The Assembly was, in fact, the natural target for popular indignation, for it did lie within the power of the House to make immediate provision for the protection of the frontier.

The main line of attack mounted by the opposition placed the blame for the Assembly's inaction on the Quakers, alleging their sole concern to be the maintenance of their political power. They were charged on the one hand with cloaking their parsimony under the guise of religious principle, and on the other with deliberately passing unacceptable defense bills in order to retain the support of the people, who were too ignorant in matters of government to realize why the bills must be refused by the governor.[2]

One of the primary objectives of the Proprietary party was to nullify the Quaker-German alliance on which the continued dominance of the Quakers depended. The Anglican Reverend William

[2] William Smith, *A Brief State of the Province of Pennsylvania* (1755; reprint ed., London, 1865), pp. 15, 17, 22–23.

21

Smith, the most able penman in the Proprietary camp, addressed a large part of his telling pamphlet, *A Brief State of the Province of Pennsylvania* (1755), to this end, advocating a series of strongly restrictive anti-German measures which would have resulted in the complete political disablement of that group. More alarming was his proposal that an oath of allegiance to the king and a "Test or Declaration that they will not refuse to defend their Country against all his Majesty's Enemies" be required of all assemblymen as qualifications for assuming their seats, measures which would effectively have barred Quakers from public office. The potential influence of the *Brief State* was discounted by Assembly leaders in Pennsylvania,[3] but the pamphlet was widely read in England, to the considerable disadvantage of the Friends. The campaign for their exclusion from the Assembly gained more ground after the commencement of Indian attacks on the frontier in October, 1755, and prompted a group of aroused Pennsylvanians to address petitions against the Quakers and their German allies to the Home Government in England.

The Norris wing of the Quaker party was disturbed by the anti-Quaker tenor of the attacks against the Assembly. Their concern, however, was prompted not so much by a regard for the reputation of the church as by the apprehension that the charges were obscuring the issues which they felt were really at stake, the rights of liberty and property.

Norris himself subscribed to the Logan position on defensive war, believing that the principle of pacifism was inapplicable in a world which held forth no real prospect of a general peace. Therefore, he deemed it necessary, while the Quakers held a share in the government, for the Assembly to tax the people and contribute to the support of military defense. He allowed that his sentiments on the question differed from those of most of his fellows in the Assembly,[4] but he went along with the tactic of earmarking military appropriations "for the king's use," which accomplished the

---

[3] Isaac Norris to Robert Charles, 30/iv/55, 16/vi/56, INLB, 1 : 70, 2 : 71.
[4] Isaac Norris to John Fothergill, 25/v/55, INLB, 1 : 76–77.

same purpose in the long run. Outside the House, and independent of his position as leader of the Quaker party, Norris initiated a subscription of ten thousand pounds (contributing seven hundred pounds from his own funds) for the aid of Colonel Johnson in his attack on Crown Point in order to demonstrate the invalidity of the opposition charges.[5] On another occasion, he noted that by April, 1754, Pennsylvania had already victualed the Virginia and Eastern expeditionary forces, paid the officers traveling through the province, conveyed their baggage and engaged to clear the road to Fort Duquesne, and was likely to incur further expenses of at least two thousand pounds that year, all without the assistance of the governor or the acceptance of a single law passed by the Assembly for these supports. These actions, he maintained, should make it abundantly clear that the disputes were not a Quaker cause, but the cause of liberty and of the rights guaranteed to the people by the charter and laws of the province.[6]

Norris, in fact, looked upon the Quakers in Pennsylvania primarily from a political point of view: they were the keystone of a partisan alliance of various political groups (identified in denominational terms) which, in the interests of liberty, was concerned with keeping the Presbyterians (the Proprietary party) out of power.[7] In effect, Norris was meeting the opposition on its own terms in this regard, by himself identifying the Quakers as a political body; far from defending the Quaker peace testimony, he endeavored to prove that the Quaker majority in the Assembly was not actuated by it!

Although Norris had no difficulty at this time in maintaining control of the Quaker majority and thus of the House, there was a contingent within his party, in which Israel Pemberton figured prominently, which opposed his policies in the matter of defense. Pemberton did not choose to keep his seat in the Assembly after his first term (1750–51), but he did retain a degree of influence

---

[5] Theodore Thayer, *Pennsylvania Politics and the Growth of Democracy* (Philadelphia, 1953), p. 43.
[6] Isaac Norris to Robert Charles, 30/iv/55, 24/v/55, INLB, 1 : 70, 75.
[7] *Ibid.*, 29/iv/55, INLB, 1 : 70–71.

within the party, and his position continued to be represented. James Pemberton, Israel's younger brother, wrote about the election of 1755, "It is with some Reluctance several of us enter again on the Service the Disposition of our S[peake]r whose Conduct we cannot in all respects approve renders the Task the more disagreeable which together with the Prospect of Warr gives me great Concern."[8]

The war reached the frontiers of Pennsylvania soon after the election, whereupon the Norris faction and the Proprietary representatives, with Benjamin Franklin acting as the principal mediator between them, cooperated in voting for defense appropriations and for Franklin's bill providing for a volunteer militia. The views of the more strictly pacifist members were expressed in the few dissenting votes cast against these measures and against the Assembly's rejection of an address by twenty-three pacifist Quakers setting forth their reservations against paying taxes to be used for war.[9]

Through the assiduous efforts of the Proprietary party's London agents, and in the absence of any attempt at public refutation by the Quaker party, the anti-Quaker charges made by Smith and others came to be generally credited in England, where no distinction was made between the acts of the Assembly and the policy of Friends as a body.[10] The prevailing conclusion was that, having accepted a public trust which they could not discharge, the Quakers in Pennsylvania were unfit for participation in government; owing the people protection, they would not even let them protect themselves. The campaign reached the point where bills were prepared to exclude the Quakers from office by an act of Parliament dissolving the Assembly then sitting, and instituting as qualifications for assumption of office an oath of allegiance to the king and a pledge to aid in defending against his enemies. The supporters of these measures contended that the Quakers' numbers, wealth, and love

---

[8] James Pemberton to Richard Partridge, 7/x/55, PP, 11 : 9½.
[9] See below, pages 29–30.
[10] John Fothergill to Israel Pemberton, 8/v/56, EC, 2 : 13.

of power would continue to assure them of a majority unless they were totally excluded from office in this manner.

At this point, a group of influential English Friends was able to intercede with Lord Granville, president of the Privy Council, who undertook to prevent enactment of the proposed measures on the condition that the Quakers voluntarily abstain from offering themselves as candidates or accepting seats in the Assembly for as long as conditions of war prevailed in America. The suggestion was also made that the Quakers unite as a body in support of other candidates who were not principled against war.[11]

The English Friends enjoined the compliance of their Pennsylvania brethren with these conditions in the strongest terms, warning them that the honor, reputation, and welfare of the whole Society stood as security for their good behavior. In addition, not trusting to letters alone in a matter of this importance, the London Meeting for Sufferings resolved to send two of its members to Pennsylvania to help carry through its recommendations.

Meanwhile, the pacifists in the Assembly, already uneasy about serving under Norris, believed that their position had become still more untenable when Governor Morris issued a declaration of war against the Indians on April 10, 1756, and instituted a bounty on Indian scalps. This was the first declaration of war ever issued by the government of Pennsylvania, and it therefore assumed a greater symbolic significance in the view of those who were strongly concerned for the integrity of the Quaker testimony than might otherwise have been the case. The visiting minister, Samuel Fothergill, described the effect of the declaration. "But as it now appears that we can scarcely keep the Truth and its testimony inviolate, and retain those places [in government], many stand up on the Lord's side and declare they have none on earth in comparison with the God of their fathers."[12]

---

[11] Hinton Brown to James Pemberton, 11/iii/56, PP, 11 : 55; John Fothergill to Israel Pemberton, 16/iii/56, EC, 2 : 10.

[12] Samuel Fothergill to Ann Fothergill, 28/iv/56, in George Crosfield, *Memoirs of the Life and Gospel Labours of Samuel Fothergill, with Selections from his Correspondence* (Liverpool, 1843), pp. 255–56 (hereafter cited as *Life of Fothergill*).

The most dramatic consequence of this dilemma facing Friends in office was that by mid-June, four months before the arrival of the Friends from England, six Quakers—James Pemberton, Joshua Morris, William Callender, William Peters, Peter Worral, and Francis Parvin—resigned from the Assembly. They gave as their reason the fact that many of their constituents seemed to believe that the present situation of public affairs called upon the Assembly for service of a military nature, with which they could not comply, concluding it most conducive to the peace of their own minds and the reputation of their religious profession to resign.[13] In the ensuing special election, the vacant seats were filled by non-Quaker members of the Quaker party. It is likely that some Quakers at least worked for the election of non-Quakers, but most declined to vote entirely.[14]

The leaders of the Quaker party were generally pleased by the outcome of this sequence of events. Benjamin Franklin expressed relief that "all the stiff rump except one that would be suspected of opposing the service from religious motives, have voluntarily quitted the Assembly,"[15] and Isaac Norris was confident— mistakenly, as it turned out—that Quaker principles would no longer obscure the real partisan issues.[16]

The regular election of 1756 was held five days before the arrival of John Hunt and Christopher Wilson, the emissaries from the London Meeting for Sufferings. With only private letters as a basis for action, and anticipating that the message from London might be different in content, those Friends most interested in preserving the integrity of the testimony avoided becoming involved in the election (beyond preventing a majority of Friends from being elected to the Assembly) by declining to vote themselves and by influencing others to do likewise. A number of potential candidates withdrew from the contest. Nevertheless, twelve

---

[13] *Votes and Proceedings of the House of Representatives of the Province of Pennsylvania* (Harrisburg: Pennsylvania Archives, 8th ser., 1931–35), 5 : 4246 (hereafter cited as *Votes*).

[14] Israel Pemberton to John Fothergill, 26/vi/56, EC, 2 : 14.

[15] Quoted in Thayer, *Pennsylvania Politics*, p. 56.

[16] Isaac Norris to Robert Charles, 16/vi/56, INLB, 2 : 70.

Quakers were elected to seats in the House—that is, twelve who were acknowledged members of the Society; the opposition claimed the number to be sixteen.[17] The disparity in the figures stems from the fact that many Friends who had been disowned by the Society, or were not recognized as members for some other reason, continued to consider themselves Quakers or retained the behavioral characteristics of Quakers, such as qualifying for their seats by affirmation instead of by oath.

When Hunt and Wilson arrived, they joined with a committee of Friends to treat with the Quakers who had been elected and endeavor to persuade them to decline their seats. Isaac Norris was the first to be called on, because his resignation would have influenced most of the others to follow this course, but the committee's efforts with the Speaker were unsuccessful.[18] In the end, four more Friends were prevailed upon not to take their seats, leaving a total of eight in the thirty-six-member House; before the first Friends resigned, there had been twenty-six acknowledged Quakers in the Assembly. This was the first time in the history of the province that Quakers did not constitute a majority of the membership, and they were never again to do so.

Although no election returns have been preserved to establish the fact with certainty, all available evidence indicates that defeat at the polls was not a factor in the sharp decline in the number of Quakers elected. All sides are agreed that the Quakers would have had no difficulty in keeping their seats, for the Quaker party retained its overwhelming majority. The opposition was still too weak and faction-ridden to gain a victory at the polls, so the retreat from office must therefore be attributed to decisions made among Friends.

The total number of representatives who cast dissenting votes in any or all of the Assembly ballots mentioned above (tax bill, militia bill, rejection of pacifist Friends' address) was nine. Six of

---

[17] James Pemberton to Samuel Fothergill, xi/56, PP, 34 : 43.
[18] *Ibid*.

these were the ones who resigned their seats; one remained in the Assembly for a number of years after 1756.[19] This means that as many as eleven Quaker members of the 1755–56 House—for only two of whom we have prior evidence of dissatisfaction with the majority policy of the Quaker party—withdrew from the Assembly by declining to run or refusing their seats once elected. We will now attempt to determine their possible grounds for doing so.

One obvious factor influencing their decision was the bargain made by the English Friends with Lord Granville. Indeed, from this perspective, those who withdrew in 1756 may be looked upon as helping to protect the *future* political position of the Quakers, for remaining in office at this time would in all likelihood have resulted in their permanent exclusion thereafter.[20] On the other hand, at least one other factor must be considered as well, one which assumes critical importance in the remainder of this study and must therefore be discussed in some detail.

In the early months of 1755, when Pennsylvania was on the threshold of war, a visiting English minister, Catherine Payton, and some other concerned Friends, took it upon themselves to call together their co-religionists in the Assembly and warn them of the difficulties and spiritual pitfalls which would attend their efforts to uphold the peace testimony while acceding to the people's demands for military action. This unusual interview was cited by the Proprietary partisans as evidence of Quaker unwillingness to defend the province,[21] but Catherine Payton strongly defended the action, maintaining that she was merely obeying her calling as a minister, and not, as alleged, improperly intermeddling in the affairs of government. On the contrary, she insisted, she and her companions had purposely avoided any direct concern or interest in the partisan issues of the moment.[22]

Later, after the Indians had attacked the frontier, and the

---

[19] *Votes*, 5 : 4104, 4164, 4174, 4246.
[20] Ketcham, "Conscience, War and Politics," p. 431.
[21] William Smith, *A Brief View of the Conduct of Pennsylvania for the Year 1755* (London, 1756), p. 61.
[22] Catherine Phillips, *Memoirs of the Life of Catherine Phillips* (Philadelphia, 1798), pp. 141–42.

Assembly was considering a large defense appropriation and tax bill, the most influential of the English ministers then visiting Pennsylvania, Samuel Fothergill, held a similar interview with the Quaker assemblymen, once again to impress upon them the inconsistency of their actions in the light of their Quaker profession.[23] The following day, a group of twenty-three Friends presented to the Assembly, on behalf of themselves and others, a highly significant address concerning the proposed tax. Because of its pivotal importance, the document is quoted here in full; its significance, and that of the epistle quoted after it, will be discussed further in a later chapter.

The consideration of the Measurers [sic] which have lately been pursued, and are now proposed, having been weightily impressed on our Minds, we apprehend that we should fall short of our Duty to you and to ourselves, and to our Brethren in religious Fellowship, if we did not in this Manner inform you that although we shall at Times heartily and freely contribute, according to our Circumstances, either by the Payment of Taxes, or in such other Manner as may be judged necessary, towards the Exigencies of Government; and sincerely desire that due Care may be taken, and proper Funds provided, for raising Money to cultivate our Friendship with our Indian Neighbours, and to support such of our Fellow-Subjects who are or may be in Distress, and for such other like benevolent purposes: Yet as the raising Sums of Money, and putting them into the Hands of Committees, who may apply them to Purposes inconsistent with the peaceable Testimony we profess, and have borne to the World, appears to us in its Consequences to be destructive of our religious Liberties, we apprehend many among us will be under the Necessity of suffering rather than consenting thereto by the Payment of a Tax for such Purposes, and thus the Fundamental Part of our Constitution may be essentially affected, and that free Enjoyment of Liberty of Conscience, for the Sake of which our Fore fathers left their native Country, and settled this, then a Wilderness, by Degrees be violated.

23 Samuel Fothergill to Susanna Fothergill, 6/xi/55, in Crosfield, *Life of Fothergill*, p. 219.

We sincerely assure you we have no temporal Motives for thus addressing you, and could we have preserved Peace in our Minds, and with each other, we should have declined it, being unwilling to give you any unnecessary Trouble, and deeply sensible of your Difficulty in discharging the Trust committed to you irreproachably in these perilous Times, which hath hath [sic] engaged our fervent Desires, that the immediate Instructions of supreme Wisdom may influence your Minds, and that being preserved in a steady Attention thereto, you may be enabled to secure Peace and Tranquility to yourselves and those you represent, by pursuing Measures consistent with our peaceable Principles; and then we trust we may continue humbly to confide in the Protection of that Almighty Power, whose Providence has heretofore been as Walls and Bulwarks round about us.[24]

Despite the plea of the petitioners, however, the bill was passed by the Assembly, and a week later the legislators voted to reject the address, both with the above-noted dissenting votes of a small group of Quaker representatives. Isaac Norris was highly displeased by the address, and denounced it strongly for providing fuel for the arguments of the anti-Quaker opposition.[25]

The Assembly's tax bill, like its predecessors, was rejected by the governor, but a compromise tax measure and a militia bill were passed and signed later in the month, once again arousing the concern of Friends who were conscientiously scrupled against all aspects of war. On December 16, some of the members of a joint committee appointed by the Yearly Meeting to consider the tax question issued an Epistle of Tender Love and Caution to Friends in Pennsylvania, setting forth the pacifist position.

We Salute you in a fresh Renewed sense of our Heavenly Fathers Love, Which hath Graciously overshadowed us in several Weighty & solid Conferences we have had together, with many other Friends, upon the present Scituation of the affairs of the Society in this Province, and in that Love we find our Spirits

[24] *Votes*, 5 : 4102.
[25] Isaac Norris to Robert Charles, 27/xi/55, INLB, 1 : 90–91.

Engaged to acquaint you that under a Solid Exercise of mind to seek for Council & Direction from the High Priest of our Profession, who is the Prince of Peace, we believe he hath Renewedly favoured us with Strong and lively Evidence that in his due and Appointed time, the Day which hath Dawn'd in these latter Ages foretold by the Prophet, wherein Swords Should be Beaten into plowshares, & Spears into Pruning Hooks, Shall Gloriously Rise higher & higher, and the Spirit of the Gospel which teaches to love Enemies, prevail to that Degree, that ye Art of War, Shall be no more Learn'd; and that it is his Determination to Exalt this Blessed day in this our Age, if in the Depth of Humility we Receive his Instructions and Obay his voice, and being painfully Apprehensive that the large Sum granted by the late Act of Assembly for the Kings Use is principally intended for purposes inconsistent with our peaceable Testimony, we therefore think, that as we Cannot be Concern'd in Wars & Fightings So neither ought we to Contribute thereto by paying the Tax, Directed by ye said Act, though Suffering be the Consequence of our Refusal, which we hope to be Enabled to bear with Patience, and the some part of the Money to be Raised by the said Act, is said to be for Such Benevolent Purposes as Supporting our Friendship with our Indian Neighbours & Relieving the Destress of our Fellow Subjects, who have Suffered in the present Calamities, for whom our Hearts are Deeply, and we Affectionately & with Bowels of tenderness Sympathize with them therein, And we could most Chearfully contribute to those Purposes if they were not so Mixed that we cannot in the Manner proposed Shew our hearty Concurrence therewith, without at the same time assenting to, or allowing ourselves in Practi[c]es which we apprehend Contrary to the Testimony which the Lord hath given us to bear, for his Name & Truths Sake; and haveing the Health & Prosperity of the Society at hart We Earnestly Exhort Friends to wait for the appearing of the true Light, and Stand in the Council of God, that we may know him to be the Rock of Salvation, and place of our Refuge for Ever

And Beware of the Spirit of the world which is Unstable and often Draws into dark and timerous Reasonings, least the God thereof Should be Suffered to blind the Eye of the mind, and such not knowing the sure Foundation of the Rock of Ages, may partake of the terrors & fears that are not known to the Inhabitants of that place where the Sheep & Lamb of Christ ever had a quiet Habitation, which a Remnant have to say to the praise of his Name, they have been bless'd with a measure of in this day of Distress, and as our Fidelity to the present Government, and our willingly paying all Taxes for Purposes which do not Interfere with our Consciences & may Justly Exempt us from the Imputation of Disloyalty, So we Earnestly Desire that all who by a deep & quiet Seeking for Directions, from the holy Spirit are or Shall be Convinced, that he Calls us as a people to this Testimony may dwell under ye Guidance of the same Divine Spirit, & manifest by the meekness and humility of their Conversation that they are really under that Influence, and therein may know true Fortitude and Patience to bear that and Every other Testimony committed to them Faithfully & Uniformly, and that all Friends may know their Spirits Clothed and Covered with true Charity the Bond of Christian Fellowship Wherein we again tenderly Salute You and Remain

Your Friends and Brethren[26]

In terms of the epistle and the earlier address, Quakers in the Assembly who supported the tax measures were, from a strict point of view, contributing to the persecution of their fellow Quakers who were principled against paying the taxes, for all such measures carried penalties for noncompliance. Historically, unrestricted liberty of conscience had always been one of the highest of Quaker values, and in succeeding years the above charge became the most wide-ranging and generally applicable argument against any kind of officeholding by Quakers, especially in connection with positions which did not in themselves involve more clear-cut violations of Quaker discipline.[27]

Thus, simultaneous with the development of a campaign by outsiders against Quakers in office, a movement with the same objective was gaining strength within the Society. In the early stages, some members confined their opposition to political service

[26] John Pemberton *et al.* to Friends in Pennsylvania, 16/xii/55, MS 851, Quaker Collection, Haverford College Library, Haverford, Pa.

[27] Israel Pemberton to John Fothergill, 17/xii/55, EC, 2 : 8; James Pemberton to Samuel Fothergill, xi/56, PP, 34 : 43.

in times of war,[28] but others advocated a wholesale withdrawal of Friends from office while universal righteousness was so conspicuously lacking in the world.[29] Samuel Fothergill went so far as to express the hope that current circumstances would issue in the Quakers' "dismission from government, their connexion with which hath been of great dis-service of later times to the real end of our being raised up as a peculiar people, to bear our testimony to Him whose kingdom is in peace and righteousness."[30] The engagement of the English Friends with Lord Granville forestalled the dismissal of the Quakers from government by external agency, but the campaign for self-exclusion within the Society continued to gain momentum.

Although the problems surrounding taxation and officeholding were linked by, and derived from, a concern on the part of certain Friends for a stricter and more faithful adherence to the peace testimony, this concern was in itself a symbol and symptom of a more general one, the need for a thoroughgoing reformation of behavior within the Society in all its aspects. The crisis of the mid-1750s brought the demand for religious reform fully into the political sphere, and it was this movement which ultimately provided the guidelines for the reorientation of Quaker political behavior in the decades to follow.

The importance of the reform movement in the political turmoil which characterized Pennsylvania Quakerdom during and after the withdrawal from the Assembly has been recognized by others, but its true significance within the Society and its precise effect upon Quaker political behavior have not been properly analyzed or understood. The next chapter will endeavor to fill that gap, for much of our subsequent analysis depends upon an understanding of the ideological positions, world views, and behavior patterns of the reformist and non-reformist factions in the years which followed 1755.

[28] Anthony Benezet to Jonah Thompson, 24/iv/56, in George S. Brookes, *Friend Anthony Benezet* (Philadelphia, 1937), p. 220.

[29] John Churchman to Israel Pemberton, 20/xi/56, PP, 11 : 146.

[30] Samuel Fothergill to Ann Fothergill, 28/iv/56, in Crosfield, *Life of Fothergill*, p. 255.

III

THE GROWTH OF THE REFORM MOVEMENT

Every social group, whatever its size or composition, is characterized by certain criteria which constitute the minimum essential qualifications for membership. This does not refer to the various rules, norms, laws, obligatory customs, and the like, by which members of the group control, or attempt to control, each other's behavior, but rather to those rock-bottom basic qualities or attributes without which no individual can even begin to be held accountable for his behavior in terms of whatever other norms the group may observe. For example, to cite a clear-cut but un-Quakerly illustration, an individual must be an adult male and have taken the oath of induction into the United States Army before he becomes subject to the myriad of rules and regulations which all members of the army are expected to observe and obey. Without these conditions (periods of martial law aside), the army code of discipline would have no direct bearing on his behavior, but, with them, he is completely subject to its control.

Clearly, the potential inventory of individual criteria and combinations of criteria which may constitute a basis for group formation is almost limitless, and this is one of the chief factors accounting for the difficulty of theorizing about groups. Another difficulty stems from the fact that the essential criteria of persistent corporate groups may change over time, even while the group persists in terms of continuity of membership and name.

In the very earliest years of the Society of Friends, admission to the Quaker fold demanded personal convincement and a true inward change of nature, a personal reformation.[1] The First Professors of the faith insisted that no one should enter the fellowship who was not there by the conscious act of his own faith, a first-hand spiritual experience of the indwelling Light of Christ, which was the life, power, and spirit of God at work in the human heart and brought to bear upon the human soul. This experience was the *sine qua non* of early Quakerism, that from which all else followed. The first Friends believed their fellowship to be grounded in a common experience of spiritual life and a common witness to a common body of Truth, for illumination by the Light brought the worshipping Friend into union with the Divine and, through Him, with all others who were attuned to the Light. To be sure, it was expected that the essential experience would naturally be accompanied by certain outward behavioral characteristics and transformations, but these were considered voluntary and implicit; they did not call for rules.

For the first generation of Quakers, all of whom entered the church through personal convincement in the above manner, commitment to the direct personal experience of the Inner Light was inseparable from a particular kind of cognitive orientation toward events and behavior in the outside world. In terms of Kenneth Boulding's illuminating concept, their relational image—that is, their picture of the universe around them as a system of regularities—was dominated by the agency of God.[2] For the Inner Light was actually a medium of communication and direction (through which the attentive soul might come to know God's will) manifested positively in a strong inward sense that a certain action be taken to meet a particular situation, or negatively in the conviction that a course of action which had been contemplated be eschewed. That is, the true Friend initiated action under God's direction and

---

[1] In the discussion which follows, I have drawn upon William C. Braithwaite, *The Second Period of Quakerism*, 2nd ed. (Cambridge, 1961); Howard H. Brinton, *Guide to Quaker Practice*, 2nd ed. (Wallingford, Pa., 1952); and Rufus M. Jones, *The Later Periods of Quakerism*, 2 vols. (London, 1921).

[2] Kenneth Boulding, *The Image* (Ann Arbor, 1956), p. 47.

strove to act as His agent. It was He who vouchsafed men the power to carry through their courses of action, and He who would remain the sole standard by which that action was to be judged, whatever pressures and suffering the world might impose. Although the early Friends strongly emphasized the direct, personal, inward revelation of God's way, it was also recognized that His presence might initially be manifested to men in outward experience as well; God might make any situation or event the medium of His revealing word, in order to call men to inward personal communication with Himself.[3] Thus, outward events, like inward experience, were to be considered with God as the primary referent. In sum, the presence of God as initiator, author, and judge completely pervaded the behavioral environment of the earliest Friends.[4]

The first generation of Quakers had all but died off by about 1700, and was supplanted by a generation which in some important respects was very different from its predecessors. Toleration had been granted to dissenters in 1689 and thus had freed Friends from a severe burden of persecution, thereby enabling them to exercise their well-recognized commercial and mercantile talents relatively unencumbered by outward constraints. The manifest result was a marked increase in worldly prosperity among Friends, accompanied by an equally marked decline in inward religious fervor and a corresponding increase in outward formalism. Of particular importance was the circumstance that the second generation of Quakers, unlike the first, contained many individuals whose ties to the church were by birth, and not necessarily by personal convincement. The presence of these offspring of convinced Quakers was formally acknowledged, and their place in the Society was secured by the Society-wide adoption, in 1737, of a policy of birthright membership, which differed from the Half-Way Covenant of the Puritans in that it granted full, unqualified membership to the children of acknowledged members of the Society of

[3] Margaret B. Hobling, *The Concrete and the Universal* (London, 1958), pp. 39–41.
[4] A. Irving Hallowell, *Culture and Experience* (Philadelphia, 1955), pp. 172–82.

Friends. This radical redefinition of the essential criterion for membership in the church did away with the requirement of first-hand inward experience of the Inner Light, and bypassed even the requirement of a formal profession of faith; the only requirement was a set of parents who were members in good standing of a Friends meeting.

These basic changes in the experience and recruitment of the second generation of Quakers were reflected in certain important cognitive reorientations which, after 1700, distinguished a major segment of the Society from its forebears. The Society was born in the midst of the political and religious turbulence of Cromwellian England, and the impulse of the First Professors to trust completely in the eternal God was well suited to a time when the affairs of men were so uncertain. Likewise, the strength derived from the Inner Light sustained the beleaguered Friends through the attendant trials of the period of persecution, when the hands of men were turned against them, and assured them of ultimate vindication. With the advent of toleration and the growth of prosperity, however, the Friends were less strongly in need of divine succor than formerly; moreover, those who achieved a degree of worldly success and public influence were thereby rendered more confident of their own human powers and less likely to maintain a constant dependence upon the Divine Arm. Nor was there any need to trust in eventual vindication when the way was cleared for immediate success.

In Pennsylvania especially, where Friends enjoyed a rapid growth of prosperity and witnessed the unhindered development of their own commonwealth under a government which they dominated, it was not until the 1750s that they were subjected to any real stress or adversity which might have made them doubt the sufficiency of their own human agency and seek the support of a higher power. Thus, although there is no question that their faith was still nominally in the power of God, many Quakers of the second generation, especially those of worldly substance and influence, tended to rely primarily upon worldly, human efforts and to consider the world around them in direct empirical terms, not first and foremost as a place subject to God's will, which it was man's duty to discover before acting. If they observed the code of simplicity in dress and demeanor at all, they did so in a formal manner, impelled more by tradition and public opinion than by sincere conviction based on spiritual experience.

All this is not to say that the spirit, outlook, and behavior of the First Publishers of Truth died out completely in the succeeding generation, but rather that, in addition, another and very different type of Quakerism came into being which, because it tended to characterize the wealthy, prominent, and influential among the Friends (though not them alone), strongly influenced the character of the Society as a whole. There still were members who remained attuned to the Inward Way, and who deplored the decline into worldliness and formalism, but their voice was muted during this second period, and their over-all contribution to the configuration of the Society was overshadowed by that of their more outward brethren. To the extent that Pennsylvania afforded more Quakers greater opportunities to achieve prosperity than were available in England, and a far greater degree of political control than that enjoyed by their disenfranchised English brethren, the tendencies discussed above were more marked in the colony than they were in the mother country.

Frederick Tolles, in his *Meeting House and Counting House*,[5] has documented with great insight the growth of, or rather the decline into, worldliness among the Pennsylvania Quakers during the first seventy-five years of the province's development. Unencumbered by religious persecution and political disability, and having first access to the best lands and mercantile opportunities the colony had to offer, the early settlers found the way to worldly wealth wide open to them, and many followed where it led. In the wake of the increase in worldly riches and political power there followed, almost inevitably, a decline from the early Quaker ideal

---

[5] 2nd ed. (New York, 1963).

of a meek, self-denying adherence to the principles of Truth and the attendance upon their Divine Author, who had chosen the Quakers to bear them to the world. Worldliness and compromise of the testimony were widespread and deep-reaching, and, though not confined solely to Quakers in Pennsylvania, took a special form there by virtue of the special position of the Friends in that province.

Samuel Fothergill, the indefatigable minister from England who figured so prominently in succeeding developments in Pennsylvania, provided an illuminating breakdown of the succession of generations in the Quaker colony in a letter to one of his correspondents at home.

> To begin with Pennsylvania, where I landed, There are a very great body of people who bear our name, and many who deserve to bear it. A noble seed, of several classes respecting age, though too few of the aged amongst them, who have kept their garments clean, and whose hands are strong. Their fathers came into the country in its infancy, and brought large tracts of land for a trifle; their sons found large estates come into their possession, and a profession of religion which was partly national, which descended like the patrimony from their fathers, and cost as little. They settled in ease and affluence, and whilst they made the barren wilderness as a fruitful field, suffered the plantation of God to be as a field uncultivated, and a desert. Thus, decay of discipline and other weakening things prevailed, to the eclipsing of Zion's beauty; yet was there a noble remnant, whose love was strong, and who remembered the Lord of the whole earth and his house, whilst they built their own.

This is the situation more or less as we have described it above, but Fothergill went on to offer an assessment of the prospects and potential of the emerging generation.

> A people who had thus beat their swords into ploughshares, with the bent of their spirits to this world, could not instruct their offspring in those statutes they had themselves forgotten. As every like begets its like, a generation was likely to succeed, formed upon

other maxims, if the everlasting Father had not mercifully extended a visitation, to supply the deficiency of their natural parents.

It consisted with his wisdom and mercy to reach forth a hand of love to many of them of the younger sort, and to subject their hearts to the work of his own power; and more especially of later time, he hath prevailed upon many in that province; brought some into the ministry, some fitting for it; and I trust for many, who are like the little sister, who hath no breasts to give to others the sincere milk of the word, he is building them up as a wall, upon which a palace of silver may be reared. I cannot but hope in that province, particularly in the city of Philadelphia, it may be said Truth prospers, and there is a prospect that the succeeding generation may excel the last.[6]

Fothergill's impression concerning the emergence of a new generation of spiritual leaders among the Pennsylvania Quakers during the early and mid-1750s was amply confirmed by numerous other observers, including James Pemberton, John Pemberton, Catherine Payton, Mary Peisley, John Churchman, and Anthony Benezet.[7]

One apparent contributing factor to the rising zeal of some of the younger Quakers was the atmosphere of heightened denominational self-consciousness generated by the Great Awakening. Although few Quakers fell directly under the influence of George Whitefield and his more immediate followers, the enthusiasm aroused in other denominations during the period of revival stimulated some Quaker leaders to bolster the sagging zeal of their own church in order to prevent any inroads among members of the faith.[8] John Churchman's heightened concern for the peace

---

[6] Samuel Fothergill to James Wilson, 9/xi/56, in George Crosfield, *Memoirs of the Life and Gospel Labours of Samuel Fothergill, with Selections from his Correspondence* (Liverpool, 1843), pp. 281–82 (hereafter cited as *Life of Fothergill*).

[7] James Pemberton to John Pemberton, 18/xi/52, PP, 8 : 92; John Pemberton to James Pemberton, 16/xii/52, PP, 8 : 108; Catherine Phillips, *Memoirs of the Life of Catherine Phillips* (Philadelphia, 1798), p. 138; Mary Neale, *Some Account of the Life and Religious Exercises of Mary Neale, formerly Mary Peisley* (Dublin, 1795), pp. 118–19; John Churchman to Samuel Fothergill, 15/x/57, in Crosfield, *Life of Fothergill*, p. 335; Anthony Benezet to Samuel Fothergill, 17/x/57, in George S. Brookes, *Friend Anthony Benezet* (Philadelphia, 1937), pp. 223–24.

[8] Sydney James, *A People Among Peoples* (Cambridge, Mass., 1963), p. 70.

testimony in 1748, followed very shortly by a behavioral transformation and the concomitant refusal of a political office that was not at the time implicated in any way in war measures, was an early manifestation of this spirit of reform taking root among American Quakers and paving the way for subsequent developments.

A far more important factor, however, was the impact of the political crisis of the mid-1750s, to which so much attention has been devoted in the foregoing pages. To a degree, the Great Awakening also helped to bring the crisis to a head, simply by making non-Quakers, especially the Presbyterians, more aware of themselves as a body and therefore more prepared to challenge the dominant, though numerically inferior, Quakers. But the crisis itself was more the consequence of a number of converging factors than the result of any single one. The changeover of generations, the growth of the reform spirit within the Society of Friends, a new awareness of the opposition, and the dynamics of European imperial politics all played a role, with the outbreak of the Indian wars providing the trigger which set off the ensuing train of explosive events.

When the Indians attacked the frontiers of Pennsylvania for the first time, the impact on the minds of Quakers in the province exceeded that of any other event in their history up to that time. Coming at a time when the spirit of reform was stirring within the Society of Friends, the wars took on an even greater significance than they might otherwise have had. Those who deplored the spiritual lassitude which had become widespread within the church proclaimed emphatically that the holocaust which threatened to engulf the colony was a visitation from God to arouse a backslidden and degenerate people. There is no doubt that the fears of the people gave considerable impetus to the campaign for reform. "Great is the perturbation of many," wrote Samuel Fothergill, "and plain the discovery now made of the unprofitable professions many have made of religion, in this time of clamour and rumour of war; few know where to have recourse for a rock of defence, and a safe hiding. Agitated with fear and horror, they feel their want of a good foundation in this time of need. I hope it may be profitable to many in the issue, though, for the present, it is painful to such as are concerned to labour amongst them."[9]

The reform movement derived additional impetus from the important circumstance that the moral consistency of the Quakers in government was central to the basic issues being contested in the public arena. While the Quakers were still a majority in the Assembly, the whole problem of defense hinged upon, or was believed to hinge upon, the degree to which they were committed to a strict upholding of the peace testimony, as discussed in an earlier chapter. The political sphere thus became a major area of concern to the reformers, and consequently to the Society at large, throughout the course of the Quaker revival. It remained so in large part because the political opponents of the Quaker party expressed much of their political enmity in attacks upon the Quakers as a body and upon their testimony. Although the reformers insisted that the worldly politicians were in fact acting counter to the testimony, it became clear to them that, besides satisfying their initial goal of redeeming the Friends from worldly corruption, a disengagement from partisan politics would improve the reputation of Truth as well.

As the pressures of the period increased, a number of forceful and energetic English ministers, of whom Samuel Fothergill was the most notable, together with Catherine Payton and Mary Peisley, felt the call to labor with and sustain their brethren in America through the difficult time. Their presence in Pennsylvania during the war years was a major factor in the progress of the reformation. As outsiders they were particularly well qualified to evaluate the spiritual state of the Society, and their judgments of those in office, as well as of the state of the church as a whole, were strong.[10] At the same time, however, they were actuated by

---

[9] Samuel Fothergill to Susanna Fothergill, 24/xi/55, in Crosfield, *Life of Fothergill*, pp. 226–27.
[10] Samuel Fothergill to Ann Fothergill, 3/x/55, in Crosfield, *Life of Fothergill*, p. 216; Phillips, *Memoirs*, pp. 129, 133, 138.

an earnest desire to renew and strengthen the spirits of their lapsed Friends, and numerous testimonies attest to the great support, comfort, and strength they afforded Friends in their time of need.[11]

Despite the accelerating emergence within the Society of the various opposing outlooks, value systems, and political orientations summarized above, dating from at least the late 1740s there was for a time no overt cleavage within the Philadelphia Yearly Meeting. It was the tax issue, arising in 1755, which brought the rifts within the Society to the surface. The question of acquiescence or refusal with regard to payment of the mixed taxes, one of the purposes of which was the funding of military ventures, was particularly significant at this time because it involved alternatives which other related issues did not. For example, if a member of the Society had decided to offer himself for direct military service, the Meeting's course would have been clear, because the bearing of arms was in open violation of the Discipline, the compendium of precedents and past decisions which was the formal basis for social guidance and control within the Society. In the case of mixed taxes, there were no rigid guidelines, but the weight of tradition was on the side of payment. Nevertheless, certain of the reformers, determined to resist every semblance of compromise, felt compelled by conscience to draw a halt to compliance. This decision will be discussed in more detail below.

The Yearly Meeting of 1755, held as usual at the end of September and the beginning of October, apparently triggered the open cleavage on the tax question and served as a rallying point for those who were conscientiously opposed to paying the taxes. At this gathering, the question was raised openly of the propriety of payment by Friends in view of the Society's principles against

---

[11] John Pemberton to Susanna Fothergill, 18/xi/55, in Crosfield, *Life of Fothergill*, p. 222; Ellen Evans to Ann Fothergill, vi/56, in Crosfield, *Life of Fothergill*, p. 259; Anthony Benezet to Jonah Thompson, 24/iv/56, in Brookes, *Friend Anthony Benezet*, pp. 220–21; John Pemberton to Samuel Fothergill, 15/ix/57, in Crosfield, *Life of Fothergill*, pp. 326–28.

war.[12] In answer to the reservations of the reformers, it was argued that the precedent in England and in the colonies was for compliance.[13] Some of those who were willing to pay the taxes were prepared to uphold the right of others to refuse, but were opposed to the Society's enforcing noncompliance. The upshot was that no decision was reached, and no one was satisfied.

The Meeting assigned a combined committee to consider the taxes, and it met in December, after the actual passage of a tax bill. The committee members could not achieve unity, however, and those whose minds were easy about paying eventually withdrew. Those who remained issued the Epistle of Tender Love and Caution.[14] It is essential to note, therefore, that the epistle did not represent the sense of any meeting on the issue. In fact, the failure of either the Yearly Meeting or the committee to achieve a unified position with regard to the taxes indicated deep disagreement, for unity within the Society was one of the highest of Quaker values and almost the *raison d'être* of the meeting system of church government. The earlier address to the Assembly by twenty-three Quakers had aroused strong reactions, but it represented only the personal statement of a small group of Friends.[15] The epistle, on the other hand, as the product of at least a segment of an officially appointed Quaker group, and advising all Friends in Pennsylvania not to comply with a law passed by an Assembly the majority of whose members were Quakers in good standing, was an extremely strong measure, and acted as a powerful stimulus to the polarization of opinion. As Samuel Fothergill wrote to John Churchman:

> Our Epistle from Philadelphia to the Monthly Meetings meets with a different reception as the people differ; the libertines, worldly-minded, and opposers of the reformation in themselves

[12] John Woolman, *The Journal and Essays of John Woolman*, ed. Amelia Mott Gummere (London, 1922), pp. 204–6; Israel Pemberton to John Fothergill, 27/xi/55, PP, 11 : 20; William Foster to John Smith, 14/x/55, Smith Corresp., p. 94.

[13] Israel Pemberton to John Fothergill, 27/xi/55, PP, 11 : 20.

[14] Woolman, *Journal and Essays*, p. 208; see above, pp. 30–32.

[15] See above, pp. 29–30.

and others, cavil and rage; but the seed is relieved, and the honest-hearted are strengthened. I see it will be a time of division between wheat and chaff, and that we shall find some amongst the latter we thought would have been more deeply weighty, and perhaps the contrary in some other instances. But the company, in which some who dissented from us find themselves left, will I believe, awaken some weak, honest hearts to ponder, whether divine wisdom hath changed the channel of instrumental insensible ministry, into the muddy pipes of the licentious.[16]

The closing months of 1755 thus were an important juncture in the history of Friends in Pennsylvania. The surfacing of the campaign for a new reformation within the Society opened up rifts and precipitated alignments among Friends which constituted a vital key to all the developments which followed.

[16] Samuel Fothergill to John Churchman, iii/56, in Crosfield, *Life of Fothergill*, p. 252.

IV

CLEAVAGE AND PATTERNS OF
POLITICAL BEHAVIOR

The year 1756, which began two weeks after the Epistle of Tender Love and Caution was issued, witnessed a sequence of events and developments which had vital long-term implications for the future of Quaker political behavior in Pennsylvania, including the unprecedented resignation of six Quakers from the Assembly and the end of the period of Quaker majority in the House. Underlying these developments and giving them direction, however, was a critical transformation in the alignment of politically relevant Quakers in the province.

Toward the end of Chapter I, in laying the groundwork for the analysis to follow, we attempted to delineate the emerging outlines of three different modes of political engagement which, toward the middle of the century, began to assume discernible form in the behavior of the Pennsylvania Quakers. These orientations were exemplified, respectively, in the behavior of Isaac Norris, Israel Pemberton, and John Churchman. In those early years, however, the political climate in Pennsylvania was such that the new patterns beginning to emerge had little effect upon the conduct of politics in the province. By the beginning of 1756, though, the explosive events of the preceding year had drastically altered both the political climate of the province and the apparent internal equilibrium of the Society of Friends. The crisis of the

Indian wars and the emergence of an overt reform movement within the Society drove wedges into the rifts which had already begun to open beneath the surface, and what had formerly involved the reorientation of a relatively small number of people and had been of no apparent practical consequence grew into an open cleavage within the Society. The result of these developments was the crystallization of three distinct political types among the politically relevant Quakers, each with its associated pattern of political behavior. It is the purpose of the present chapter to discuss these three types and the behavior patterns characteristic of each; this in turn will furnish a framework for the subsequent analysis of Quaker politics up to the time of the Revolution.

It must be noted at the outset that the three types as they are conceptualized here are not intended to constitute a formal typology of politically relevant Quakers. It might be more accurate to consider them as more or less discrete clusters of attitudes and attributes embodied in the identities and behavior of groups of real individuals. A series of capsule biographies of typical exemplars of the three behavioral types is presented in Appendix I as a supplement to the material outlined in the text. Of the three types, two were diametrically opposed to each other, and it was the tensions between them which set the boundaries within which all three interacted and which determined the over-all political complexion of the Society. The remaining type lay somewhere between the other two, and implicit in this third pattern of political behavior was an element of fluctuation, first toward one, then toward the other, of the two extremes. The two opposing types are relatively easy to distinguish—namely, the worldly, partisan, compromising faction, and the reformers. The third type will be less difficult to discern after we have discussed the first two.

The fundamental concern of the reformers, as noted earlier, was to uphold and defend the Quaker testimony in what they considered to be its pure form, and to re-extend its influence over their lapsed and worldly brethren. Their goal was to turn all their backslidden co-religionists away from their fixation on earthly things and to induce them to pursue the course of personal reformation by opening and submitting themselves to God's word. In other words, they wished to restore to importance within the Society what had been the essential criterion for membership at the time of the Society's emergence in the seventeenth century. Moreover, in keeping with this objective, the reformers were characterized by a cognitive orientation which was substantially similar to that of the early Quakers, as outlined in Chapter III. Nevertheless, their outlook is of crucial importance to the remainder of this study and should be elucidated in some detail within the context of the present discussion.

Calling for a return to the self-denying life of the First Publishers of Truth through a rejection of self-will and outward concerns and submission to God and His word, the reformers adopted as their text, "My kingdom is not of this world." Their guiding metaphor was crucifixion—the crucifixion of the self to the world —as the ultimate resignation of self-will. This is the notion of salvation through suffering, and the word "suffering" runs like a refrain through the writings of the period. Friends were constantly exhorted to suffer in God's cause rather than compromise the integrity of their consciences through conformity with the easy, and popularly accepted, ways of the world.[1]

The stress-absorbing potential of a group which subscribes to such a doctrine is self-evident: "We may be oppressed and despised, but he is able to turn our patient Sufferings into Profit to ourselves, and to the Advancement of his Work on Earth."[2] In effect, negative stress is neutralized and turned to the benefit of the sufferer, who is made willing to maintain the faith and endure his suffering, rather than bend to the pressure, under the assurance that it will conduce to the glory of God and his own salvation.

When pressed by the reformers, some of the worldly Quakers, possibly fearing the consequences to the Society of allowing others to gain control of government, fell back on the proposition that the concept of suffering was intended to apply only to the religious

[1] John Woolman, *The Journal and Essays of John Woolman*, ed. Amelia Mott Gummere (London, 1922), p. 385.
[2] *Ibid.*

49

sphere, not to the civil. The reformers, however, rejected this distinction and insisted that the same principles should govern all behavior, that in this sense no distinction should be made between the civil and the religious. Anthony Benezet, one of the most energetic of the reformers, wrote:

> I know some are for limiting this to suffering in what is generally called religious matters, but that's a device of the enemy. There is no distinction in Christianity between civil and religious matters. . . . The most sensible suffering is to give up our interest, and suffer matters to go contrary to our judgment, in common affairs. I know human nature will in this case make strong appeals to reason and vulgar opinion, in defence of its judgment and its interest, but it cannot judge in the present case, it has neither faculties, nor organs, to see into the deeply humbling mystery of Divine love; God becoming man, letting the whole power of hell spend its wrath upon him, and being finally made perfect through suffering, this being the means ordained by the wisdom of God, by which a deadly blow is struck to the very root and being of sin.[3]

Thus considering partisan politics to be a kind of pursuit of one's worldly interests, the reformers tended to turn their backs altogether on this realm of activity, in the manner of John Churchman. It is for this reason that they did not confine their reservations against officeholding solely to periods of war.

Although the First Professors subscribed to the doctrine of salvation through suffering, many of the later reformers held a view in this regard which was somewhat different stylistically from that of their predecessors. Because of the influence of quietism upon eighteenth-century Quakers, their orientation was more mystical and involuted—and placed greater emphasis upon the need to abase one's self—than that of the earlier Quakers. Rufus Jones, the twentieth-century Quaker theologian, has emphasized the influence of the doctrine of quietism on the thought of the eighteenth-

---

[3] Anthony Benezet to John Smith, 13/xii/57, in George S. Brookes, *Friend Anthony Benezet* (Philadelphia, 1937), pp. 224–25.

century reformers, and, indeed, the style and vocabulary of quiet-ism pervaded their writings and their behavior. Jones writes:

> The true and essential preparation for spiritual ministry, or for any action in the truth and life, seemed to the quietist to be the repose of all one's own powers, the absence of all efforts of self-direction, of all strain and striving, the annihilation of all con-fidence in one's own capacities, the complete quiet of the "crea-ture." Then out of this silence of all flesh, out of this calm of contemplation, in which the mind thinks and desires and wills nothing—this pure repose—divine movings will spontaneously come, the extraordinary grace of openings will be made, an inner burst of revelation will be granted, the sure direction of divine pointings will be given, a spiritual fecundity will be graciously vouchsafed.[4]

Recalling John Churchman's account of his experiences in 1748, one can see how closely they conform to the quietist pattern. Or an entry dating from 1757 in the journal of John Woolman (con-cerning his efforts against slavery and the slave trade) may be cited:

> The prospect of so weighty a work, and of being so distin-guished from many whom I esteemed before myself, brought me very low, and such were the conflicts of my soul that I had a near sympathy with the Prophet, in the time of weakness, when he said: "If thou deal thus with me, kill me, I pray thee, if I have found favor in thy sight." (Num. xi 15.) But I soon saw that this pro-ceeded from the want of a full resignation to the Divine will. Many were the afflictions which attended me, and in great abase-ment, with many tears, my cries were to the Almighty for his gracious and fatherly assistance, and after a time of deep trial I was favored to understand the state mentioned by the Psalmist more clearly than ever I had done before; to wit: "My soul is even as a weaned child." (Psalm cxxxi. 2.) Being thus helped to sink

---

[4] Rufus M. Jones, *The Later Periods of Quakerism*, 2 vols. (London, 1921), 1 : 36.

down into resignation, I felt a deliverance from that tempest in which I had been sorely exercised, and in calmness of mind went forward, trusting that the Lord Jesus Christ, as I faithfully attended to him, would be a counsellor to me in all difficulties.[5]

For the purposes of the present study, the importance of the reformers' complete submission of the self to God, or their constant striving to achieve this state, cannot be overemphasized. It meant, in analytical terms, that God constituted the dominant element in the reformers' behavioral environment, the source to which they owed their first allegiance, from which they took direction, and toward which they directed their behavior. Insofar as possible, they consciously and explicitly disregarded or refused to conform to the ways and standards of the world, of others, wherever these deviated from what they conceived to be the true religious way, as embodied in the Quaker testimony given by God to His chosen people. Where this entailed suffering, the suffering was to be rejoiced in and endured.

This is not to say that the reformers were unaware of or ignorant concerning worldly affairs, controversies, or external criticism. They recognized quite clearly that the crisis within the Society had been brought to a head by specific external events, that the clamor against the Quakers was in direct proportion to the pressure of Indian hostilities on the people.[6] God's will, after all, could be manifested in earthly events as well as communicated directly to the inner man. Moreover, like John Churchman in 1748, the reformers stood up before the authorities when moved to do so, and called them to account for their errors.[7] Even further, indi-

---

[5] John Woolman, *The Journal of John Woolman and a Plea for the Poor*, ed. John Greenleaf Whittier, paperback ed. (New York, 1961), p. 51.

[6] Samuel Fothergill to Susanna Fothergill, 17/xii/55 and 19/i/56, in George Crosfield, *Memoirs of the Life and Gospel Labours of Samuel Fothergill, with Selections from his Correspondence* (Liverpool, 1843), pp. 232 and 240 (hereafter cited as *Life of Fothergill*).

[7] John Pemberton *et al.* to Friends in Pennsylvania, MS 851, Quaker Collection, Haverford College Library, Haverford, Pa.; Samuel Fothergill, 9/iv/56, in Crosfield, *Life of Fothergill*, p. 261; James Pemberton to John Fothergill, 27/xi/55, PP, 11 : 20.

vidual reformers were not averse to *using* government, when necessary, to advance various causes of concern to them, such as the provision of relief for a party of Acadian neutralist refugees in 1755, or the imposition of prohibitive duties to discourage the slave trade. Rather, as it is the purpose of this discussion to clarify, the distinctiveness of the reformers' behavior lay in the way their actions were initiated, the methods they used, and the goals which motivated their behavior.

Coupled with an inward waiting upon God, the quietist reformers sought meaning and direction in a strongly apocalyptic reading of striking or extraordinary temporal events, which were interpreted as divinely caused and having particular reference to other earthly events, circumstances, or situations. John Woolman, for example, through a process of inference, saw the smallpox epidemic of 1759 as a further indication that Friends should stay out of the management of civil affairs.[8] When confronted by the strains, commotion, and dissension engendered by the political crisis of the mid-1750s, the reformers were not slow to attribute the calamities to divine judgment of the moral decline of the people. "The ingratitude of many to a merciful benefactor, their worldly-mindedness and forgetfullness of the Lord God of their fathers, is cause of awful alarm from him who justly challengeth the love and obedience of all flesh, and will get himself a name in the earth, in mercy or judgment, and be heard by all flesh. Oh that this people were wise and knew this."[9] Many prophetic warnings were issued of the sterner judgments which would be visited upon the people if they failed to heed those at hand, or attempted to circumvent them "by human worldly Wisdom."[10]

As with suffering in general, however, suffering under God's chastisement will, if it is borne patiently and is productive of

[8] Woolman, *Journal and Essays*, 227.
[9] Samuel Fothergill to Susanna Fothergill, 19/i/56, in Crosfield, *Life of Fothergill*, p. 240.
[10] Woolman, *Journal and Essays*, p. 229; Benjamin Lightfoot to Israel Pemberton, 1/vi/61, PP, 14 : 145; Anthony Benezet to Jonah Thompson, 24/iv/56, in Brookes, *Friend Anthony Benezet*, pp. 220–21; Samuel Fothergill to Susanna Fothergill, 6/xi/55, in Crosfield, *Life of Fothergill*, p. 219.

reformation, conduce to the good of those upon whom it is visited. God's punishment is imposed on a guilty people in order to bring them back to reliance upon Him and obedience to His word. John Woolman, whose sensitive soul suffered much distress during the war period, reflected, "This was such a time as I had not seen before, and yet I may say with thankfulness to the Lord, that I believe this tryal was intended for our good, and I was favoured with Resignation to him."[11] Herein lies another factor which bolstered the capacity of the reformers to absorb adversity: they had no doubt that God would eventually vindicate and reward their suffering. As the upholders of the true spirit of God, they were confident of participating in His ultimate victory and were prepared to suffer patiently in anticipation of that glorious day when "the Lamb and his followers will be finally victorious."[12]

Implicit in this conviction, of course, was the belief that human behavior influences God in His disposition of human events. In this light, the reformers saw themselves as intercedents on behalf of their brethren by virtue of their own upright religious behavior.[13] Carrying over into the political realm, this implied a special, indirect approach to earthly political situations which affected the Society—that is, doing one's religious duty as a Quaker, which, when perceived by God, would induce Him to turn the course of events in favor of the Friends. This is the mode of behavior urged upon Israel Pemberton in 1752 by the minister William Brown: "I am shure we can never work for a Beter master than we do, when we Labour to discharge our dutey, in his sight, this in thee my dear friend will not only procure Etarnell peace to thy one soul But be a blesen to ye societey in our Land a help in government & transmit Examples to other Nations & Loudly spake when thy soul is at Rest."[14]

The central importance of this political orientation will receive considerable amplification in the succeeding pages, but it is worthy

11 Woolman, *Journal and Essays*, p. 212.
12 Samuel Fothergill to John Pemberton, 2/xii/59, PP, 34 : 96.
13 Samuel Fothergill to Susanna Fothergill, 19/i/56, in Crosfield, *Life of Fothergill*, p. 240.
14 William Brown to Israel Pemberton, 29/iv/52, PP, 8 : 22.

of emphasis here that this type of behavior has not previously been recognized as fundamentally political in nature. The call for withdrawal from worldly politics issued by the Quaker ministers and their fellow reformers may have been negative with regard to partisan activity, but insofar as these men were concerned to influence the political behavior of their Quaker brethren, and actually did so in a great number of cases, they must be viewed as *political* leaders. This becomes still more apparent when the alternative behavior they fostered is viewed in its proper context.

The sure conviction on the part of the Quaker reformers that they were the bearers of God's word and the performers of His work carried with it the potential for conflict within the Society. Although all truth was considered by Friends to stem ultimately from the Divine Author, there was a variety of ways in which it could be perceived by men. On the one hand, it could be communicated directly and immediately to the individual through the agency of the Inner Light. On the other hand, because the divine calling had been experienced by generations of Quakers, past and present, and because corporate action by Quakers depended ideally upon the group's recognition of the rectitude of a position which might originally have been the inspiration of any one or a number of its members, as in the taking of the sense of the meeting, precedent also was heeded, principally as codified in the Discipline, but also in the shape of informal tradition. It was entirely possible, however, for present conviction and established tradition to be in conflict at times, as in the case of the small group of reformers who first refused to pay the mixed taxes. These reformers were very much aware that they were acting contrary to the precedent of three-quarters of a century, and those of their co-religionists who disagreed with their position lost no opportunity to remind them of this fact.[15]

[15] Woolman, *Journal and Essays*, pp. 204–6; Isaac Norris to John Fothergill, 25/v/55, INLB, 1 : 76–77; Isaac Norris to Robert Charles, 24/v/55 and 27/xi/55, *ibid.*, 1 : 76, 90–91.

Nevertheless, divergence of opinion which did not clearly violate basic Quaker tenets could have been accommodated within the Society; although unity was highly valued, freedom of conscience was no less so. For instance, John Woolman was one of the first to voice his scruples against the taxes and is believed to have been the principal, possibly the sole, author of the Epistle of Tender Love and Caution, yet he freely allowed that some of those who paid the taxes were upright men. For himself, he could not accept their example against the promptings of his own conscience.[16] In his relations with others, however, he was guided by the principle that "if such, who at times were suffering on Account of some scruples of Conscience, kept low & humble, and in their Conduct in life manifested a Spirit of true Charity it would be more likely to reach the witness in others and be of more Service in the Church, than if their Sufferings were attended with a Contrary Spirit and Conduct."[17] Too rigorous an insistence upon one's own views, after all, would leave one open to the suspicion of being motivated by self-interest.

There were those among the reformers, however, who were less able than Woolman to conform to the ideal of meekness and charity, and they assumed the role of the "rigidly righteous," zealously crying up the Discipline at every turn and at times seriously threatening the cohesion of the Society. This was probably more prevalent among the elders than among the ministers, because of the nature of their respective offices; the elders were generally more conservative than their ministerial brethren, laying greater emphasis upon the Discipline, while the latter tended to be more sensitively attuned to divine illumination. George Churchman, for example, felt it to be his "allotment, to be concern'd industriously (as far as the way opened) to use endeavours to stir up a care for proper attention to our Christian Discipline among my friends in this the land of my nativity."[18] Anthony Benezet noted the emergence of this contrary spirit, and warned against it.

[16] Woolman, *Journal and Essays*, pp. 208n, 204–5.
[17] *Ibid.*, p. 222.
[18] 23/ix/62, GCJ, 1 : 41–42.

I may with pleasure say, that there continues to be a great shaking amongst our dry bones, the Hearts of many amongst us, especially the Youth, are touched with love and Zeal for God. . . . The world & the Flesh allures on the one hand, and when that is in a measure overcome, another dangerous Snare presents from a kind of enthusiastick Spirit, which I apprehend very much prevails and often, too often presents itself amongst the Sons of God, even in otherwise honest hearted ones. A mixt fire in a great measure proceeding from the Passions of the Creature being warmed and raised by that which has the appearance of Zeal, and even in some I have feared from the melody of their own voice, which makes the Creature imagine it is as on the Mount, when its fruit, its Spirit and its Brethren's often, religious sense declares it is not. And this Spirit not being sufficiently leavened by that meekness, diffidence & doubt, which accompanies the true Gospel is impatient of contradiction and very apt to smite at the honest Fellow Servant, when put on reexamining their attainments, Prospects, & foundation.[19]

The English minister, Samuel Spavold, warned the Friends in Pennsylvania that they "were in great danger of splitting and suffering great hurt from an over zealous spirit which was for imposing its slight on others which was of a sour, bitter destroying nature, and if not prevented would cause division and bring great sufferings upon us."[20]

It should be made clear that the kind of division apprehended and deplored by Spavold was not the same as that which was welcomed by Samuel Fothergill.[21] Spavold was disturbed by the prospect of a breach between otherwise upright and honest-hearted men, precipitated by an excess of zeal on the part of one or both sides, whereas Fothergill hoped for "a division between wheat and chaff," employing the winnowing metaphor used so frequently by George Fox and the other early preachers of Quakerism to describe

---

[19] Anthony Benezet to Samuel Fothergill, 17/x/57, in Brookes, *Friend Anthony Benezet*, pp. 223–24.
[20] Anthony Benezet to John Smith, 1762, *ibid.*, p. 245.
[21] Samuel Fothergill to Susanna Fothergill, 19/i/56, in Crosfield, *Life of Fothergill*, p. 240; Samuel Fothergill to John Churchman, iii/56, *ibid.*, p. 252.

their labors to separate the truly godly from those weighted down with worldly corruption.

Regardless of the meekness or rigor of their dealings, however, all reformers were united in their opposition to the "worldly-minded, opposers of the reformation," "those whose building is upon the sand in the spirit and temper of an unstable world."[22] In the political realm, the backsliders were characterized by their primary commitment to partisan affairs, a striving for partisan advantage to the neglect—if not the compromise or violation—of Quaker religious principles.

In the manner of James Logan or Isaac Norris, men of this type manifested a tendency to view the Quakers as a political power group, almost a party in their own right, in opposition to, or alliance with, other religio-political groups such as the Presbyterians, Anglicans, Lutherans, and Moravians. Their attention was directed almost wholly toward secular issues, or secular aspects of issues which had religious implications, as discussed earlier in connection with the problem of military appropriations, mixed taxes, and the Quaker bloc in the Assembly. It will be recalled that the primary goal of the Norris faction was to protect and maximize the people's liberties and privileges, in the Whig tradition.

In contradistinction to that of the reformers, the political environment of the Quaker politicians was delimited solely by partisan and governmental boundaries, within the over-all context of Pennsylvania's status as a proprietary colony in the British Empire. The Proprietors, together with those who were friendly to their interests, constituted the opposition. Viewing the continued possession of political office as both desirable and necessary for the realization of their political goals, the adherents of the Quaker party accorded the desires of their immediate constituents high priority in the determination of their actions. In response to urgings that they resign, the reply of the Quakers who remained in the Assembly after 1756 was that "they should not think themselves excusable to

---

[22] Samuel Fothergill to John Churchman, iii/56, *ibid.*, p. 252; Samuel Fothergill to John Pemberton, 2/xii/56, PP, 34 : 96.

their *Constituents* if they should decline the Service."[23] The subordination of Society policy to partisan interest could not be more clearly expressed. John Pemberton, a minister and the younger brother of Israel and James, wrote of the worldly Quaker statesmen as those "that hearken to the clamours of the people and are dismayed with the world's dismay."[24]

There was, in fact, very little in the behavior of these worldly, partisan Quakers which was exempt from the criticism of their reformist brethren, from their admitted compromise of the peace testimony to their forsaking of the Heavenly Arm which had protected the province from attack since the time of its founding. But worst of all, in the view of the conscientious Friends, was the politicians' willingness to be accessory to the persecution of their more conscientious co-religionists for the sake of partisan advantage or the protection of their places in government.[25] Appealing to the constitutional guarantees of liberty of conscience, as well as to the Discipline, the tax-refusers and those who supported their position charged the assemblymen with having passed the tax law, which included penalties for noncompliance, in the full knowledge that some of the Friends would feel compelled to withhold payment and would therefore be subjected to persecution.[26] Quakers who held the office of county commissioner shared in this guilt, for they were the ones who actually enforced the penalties for non-payment.[27]

With the character of the reformers and the worldly politicians now before us, we are in a position to construct a portrait of the third of our political types. The pattern is far more difficult to distinguish than the others, because it shared elements of both, and

[23] PMS to LMS, 17/xii/56, italics added.
[24] John Pemberton to Susanna Fothergill, 18/xi/55, in Crosfield, *Life of Fothergill*, p. 222.
[25] Israel Pemberton to John Fothergill, 17/xii/55, EC, 2 : 8.
[26] *Ibid.*; John Pemberton to Samuel Fothergill, 6/iv/58, PP, 34 : 74.
[27] 1766, GCJ, 2 : 60–61.

the relative proportion of these elements fluctuated over time in the behavior of individuals. This probably accounts for the fact that this third type of behavior has not been clearly perceived, much less understood, by previous writers. A brief review of some of the events recounted earlier in the study may facilitate a clearer identification of the exemplars of the type of behavior we are trying to distinguish, and serve as groundwork for the closer examination of its characteristics.

Two of the most important figures among those falling within the middle group, to whom we shall apply the term "politiques,"[28] were Israel and James Pemberton. It will be recalled that our first mention of Israel Pemberton was made in connection with his attempt to promote within the Quaker party a rival slate of pacifist candidates for the Assembly in the election of 1744. In the ensuing years, he was noted as an active opponent of the various military measures called for by the Kinsey faction and its supporters.

James Pemberton has been discussed with reference to his reluctance to serve in the 1755–56 Assembly because of reservations about the conduct and policy of Isaac Norris and the prospect of an imminent war with France. He was a leader of the small dissenting faction in the Assembly which served, more or less, as the ally of the reformers within the House, voting against mixed taxes and the militia, and dissenting from the Assembly's condemnation of the address against taxes and the twenty-three Friends who subscribed to it. As a result of the governor's declaration of war against the Indians in April, 1756, James Pemberton and his colleagues found their positions in the House increasingly untenable, and two months later six of them resigned their seats for reasons of conscience. The following fall they were instrumental in bringing about a substantial withdrawal of Quakers from the Assembly, in large part on the grounds that service in the House

[28] The term "politiques" is borrowed from Sydney James, *A People Among Peoples* (Cambridge, Mass., 1963), p. 164, but the present referent is ours. The only parallel between the Quakers we have designated politiques and the original Politiques of the French religious wars is that both groups occupied an uneasy middle ground in a political field which involved mixed civil and religious issues. No other connection is intended.

during a time of war was incompatible with the peace testimony of the Quaker church.

With the above summary as background, we may turn to a consideration of the pattern underlying the behavior of the leaders we have discussed. Like the reformers, these men gave their fundamental allegiance to the Society of Friends, but not in the same way; their emphasis was less upon the religious testimony as such, and more upon the reputation of the Society in the world and the integrity of the Quakers as a special people. In contrast to the reformers, they were inclined to uphold and defend the Society by worldly political means, and with close reference to the partisan arena and to government.

This is not to say that they were not religious men, for some of them were deeply so, but a number of important characteristics set them apart from the reformers in this regard. Most obviously, they were not quietists; quietism involved a rejection of worldliness and self-will and called for a patient and humble submission to God. While a few individuals—such as John Pemberton, Samuel Emlen, Jr., and later, Nicholas Waln—who had access to considerable wealth and high social position and therefore to secular political power still chose the quietist way, they were exceptional in this respect. Most of those who turned their backs on earthly comforts and human power were on a lower socioeconomic level to begin with.[29] In a period when civic responsibility and political influence were considered the natural perquisites of wealth and high social rank, wealthy Quakers were susceptible, in varying degrees, to a dual pull. For some, whose commitment to Quakerism was only nominal, the impetus toward secular political activity was by far the stronger. These were the worldly, partisan leaders, little or none of whose political behavior derived primarily from their Quaker faith, men like Isaac Norris, Benjamin Shoemaker, John Mifflin, Joseph Fox, Thomas Wharton, and Samuel Rhoads. Others, however, like the Pembertons, *concentrated* on the Quaker aspects of issues that impinged upon the Society in any way. These were the men we have identified as the politiques.

[29] See Appendix II.

It is especially important to note that the education, administrative skills, leadership experience, and access to information of the wealthy Pennsylvania merchants, as well as the general deference paid to them by their brethren of lower social rank, gave them access to roles of authority within the administrative structure of the meeting as well as in the provincial government. George Churchman noted on one occasion, "I find it not an easy task for feeble country folk, to undertake to speak much among those who are wealthy, wise and Eloquent."[30] Whereas, from about the time of Kinsey's death (1750), leaders of the Norris type were not to be found among those active within the meeting structure, men like the Pembertons and their close associates shared the positions and tasks of responsibility with the more vigorous of the reformers.

The careers of the Pemberton brothers alone serve as models of this tendency. Israel Pemberton was clerk of the Yearly Meeting from 1750 to 1759. James was clerk of the Philadelphia Monthly Meeting from March, 1756, to October, 1777; of the Yearly Meeting from 1761 to 1766, 1768 to 1776, and 1778 to 1781; and of the Meeting for Sufferings from its inception, late in 1756, to February, 1762. John was clerk of the Philadelphia Quarterly Meeting from November, 1755, to November, 1777; of the Meeting for Sufferings from August, 1764, to late 1777; and of the Yearly Meeting of Ministers and Elders from 1766 to 1782. Outside the Society, Israel served in the Assembly during the session of 1750–51, but was vigorously active in the secular partisan political arena before and after this period, up to the Revolution. James also was energetic and indefatigable in extra-Societal politics. He was elected to the Assembly in 1755, resigned in 1756, then resumed his position in the House from the 1765–66 session through that of 1769–70. John was a minister, a reformer, and a quietist; he devoted himself wholly to the service of his religion.

Some of the correspondence between John Pemberton and his brothers points up quite clearly the contrarieties in their behavior. For example, on July 7, 1751, Israel wrote to John, who at that

[30] 25/ix/61, GCJ, 1 : 24.

time was in England: "I should be much pleas'd to have a good account to give thee of the State of the churches among us & of a prospect of a revival & reformation from that degeneracy & declension wch hath been Long spreading & I fear still increases—— Many Lamentable failures of various Kinds have happened, wch are cause of great affliction to the faithful & give the adversaries of Truth occasion to triumph."[31] But John, who was familiar with his brother's political activities, replied that Israel himself was too much involved in the world, and admonished him to turn away from it and manifest a more ready disposition to take up the cross in his own life.[32]

Later in the same year, James suggested in a letter to John that, "as we in this Province have been favd: above all the Families of the Earth the greater will our Condemnation be if we neglect answerg: the many calls afforded us, as God is Able of the Stones to raise Children unto Abraham."[33] As he did with Israel, in his reply John chided James to "endeavor to remove thyself farther from the World having dwelt long enough in the hurrys thereof. & Consider how Gracious & Good the Lord has been to thee . . . as thou says thou art at times comforted with a prospect of Zion again arising in her Antient beauty & the places of the Worthys whom the Lord has seen meet to remove from amongst us, filled up by a Succession of youth &c endeavor to put thy hand to the work to help forwd a Reformation."[34]

A number of additional statements by reformers concerning their more worldly associates' "endeavour to reconcile those two contrarities the World & Heaven" may be illuminating.[35] The following sympathetic passage, contained in a letter from Samuel Fothergill to Israel Pemberton, reveals the former's insight into the strain of his friend's situation.

---

[31] PP, 7 : 106.
[32] 27/i/52, *ibid.*, p. 159.
[33] 18/xi/52, *ibid.*, 8 : 92.
[34] 16/xii/52, *ibid.*, p. 108.
[35] Anthony Benezet to Jonah Thompson, 24/iv/56, in Brookes, *Friend Anthony Benezet*, p. 220.

I have seen thee, dear friend, in the hidden conflict, and the struggle between the two opposite powers, and have sympathized with and for thee, when thou has been bruised and hurt by the prevalence of that which stands as an armed man in thy way to rest. I am sensible of thy secret bemoaning at times, when loss hath been sustained, and the renewal of holy reaches for thy help and recovery; I earnestly wish for thee, as well as for myself, the thorough subjection of all within us to that abasing, humbling Hand, who prepares instruments for his service from the dust of Zion, and ordains praise out of the mouths of babes and sucklings.[36]

George Churchman's view was somewhat more strict. As he noted in his journal, "where Statesmen are Active in the Cause of Religion, & lean to their own Understanding, pure Wisdom doth not always bear Sway."[37] An entry made later that year is in a similar vein. "My simple Sentiment is, that where the minds of active members and others are involved in the pursuit of lower objects, & busied in the bustle of state affairs, there is but little ability for maintaining our discipline in the Wisdom that is only proper to qualify for that purpose."[38] For Churchman, as the latter statement makes clear, there was more at stake in the political conduct of Friends than the moral welfare of individuals. Rather, his concern was the connection between the political engagement of active Friends and the functioning of the very Society itself. The general position of the politiques within the meeting structure has been outlined, but the consequences of the alignments made within the meeting structure for the conduct of the Society's affairs require several chapters in their own right, in order to establish more concretely the sphere of operation of each of the three political types delineated in the preceding pages. This will provide a perspective from which to analyze the course of Quaker politics up to the time of the Revolution.

---

[36] 23/vi/55, in Crosfield, *Life of Fothergill*, p. 193.
[37] 16/iii/61, GCJ, 1 : 18.
[38] 1/ix/61, *ibid.*, pp. 23–24.

V

QUAKER POLITICAL TYPES
AND THE MEETING STRUCTURE

In the early years of the Society of Friends, when the meeting system first evolved, there was current among the Quakers a strain of antinomianism which had a lasting effect upon the organization of the Society. Although a formal hierarchy of meetings was found to be necessary for the survival and development of the church, the freedom of every acknowledged member of the Society to attend meetings at any level of the hierarchy was self-consciously preserved.

This egalitarianism notwithstanding, it was inevitable that individual differences of personality and experience should manifest themselves in differential degrees of participation in meeting activities. The practice developed of designating representatives from among those most active in the meeting as official delegates to the meeting at the next highest level, although all members of the Society remained free to attend as well, and being an official delegate was not a necessary qualification for appointment to any of the committees set up at the Quarterly and Yearly Meetings.

In reality, however, the Yearly Meeting came to be constituted by a relatively small group of activists, and was controlled by a group that was smaller still. Analysis of the rosters of delegates recorded in the minutes of each Yearly Meeting at Philadelphia reveals that at no time during the period under study did the number of representatives at this highest level exceed roughly 1.5

percent of the total membership of the Society; much of the time it was well below 1.0 percent. The average length of service of all the representatives from the Quarterly Meetings, comprised wholly or in part of monthly meetings located in Pennsylvania, was approximately 3.35 Yearly Meetings, with about 70 percent of the total number of representatives falling below the average, and a mere 6 percent (about sixty-five to seventy men over the entire fifty-year span) serving ten or more years. These figures are approximate, but they do give some indication of the fact that, at the highest level, the affairs of the Society were in the hands of a relative few. Moreover, those who participated actively in the Yearly Meeting acquired thereby a higher degree of influence at the subordinate levels, for they were the ones who transmitted Yearly Meeting directives and who served on certain committees appointed by the Yearly Meeting to carry out particular services within the Society. One such committee will be discussed presently in more detail.

As was noted in Chapter I, once the secular government of Pennsylvania diverged from the religious organization of the Society, the meetings were very little occupied with external political matters as long as the Quakers continued to predominate in the elective offices of the province and their position was not seriously threatened. Even after the challenge of the Proprietary party began to increase in intensity (around 1740), the Quakers in government were able to retain the upper hand without difficulty.

By the mid-fifties, however, the situation had altered significantly. As a result of the crisis precipitated by the Indian wars, the threat to the Quaker hegemony was very real and immediate. Although concerns of this magnitude, affecting the reputation of the entire Society and the rights of all its members, were the province of the Yearly Meeting, this body lacked the flexibility to deal with fast-changing events, for it was convened only once a year, at a set time. As a result, other means for coping with the ongoing crisis had to be developed.

In May, 1755, for example, the campaign to exclude Quakers from the Assembly was gaining momentum on one side, while the virulence of the attacks mounted by the Norris faction against the Proprietors was increasing on the other. The pressure of events was such that certain Quakers felt impelled to take measures to alleviate the situation. The first of these took the form of an epistle from the Philadelphia Quarterly Meeting to the London Meeting for Sufferings, dated May 5. Let us defer, for a moment, a discussion of the letter's contents, and take note of some of the more important circumstances involved in its composition and transmittal.

The Quarterly Meeting clearly was better able to deal with situations as they arose than was the Yearly Meeting, by virtue of its more frequent meeting schedule. The London Meeting for Sufferings was the appropriate body to address because any measures depriving the Pennsylvania Quakers of their political rights would have to be taken by the Home Government. Also, the London Meeting for Sufferings, besides being on the scene and having as one of its functions the protection of the rights of Friends, met throughout the year, and had among its members a number of highly influential men with direct access to the high levels of government and to Thomas Penn.

The fact that the epistle was sent by the Philadelphia Quarterly Meeting in particular is itself worthy of consideration. One important factor contributing to this was the fact that Philadelphia was the seat of government in the province, and its residents were consequently better informed, by and large, concerning provincial politics. Furthermore, Philadelphia was the center of mercantile activity and the home of the wealthy and influential men we have identified as politiques. These men constituted a strong, often dominant, force in the Philadelphia Quarterly Meeting and in the Yearly Meeting as well. The epistle of May 5 was prepared by a committee of eight members, all but one or two of whom were active in Yearly Meeting affairs, most notably Israel Pemberton, then clerk of the Yearly Meeting, and John Reynell, a wealthy merchant who will figure prominently in the ensuing discussion. These leaders were accustomed to speaking for the Society, and no doubt did so through the Quarterly Meeting without reservation.

The mixed orientation of the politiques is quite evident in the document which the committee produced. Note the following excerpt, which is at once an apology for compromise on the part of Quaker officeholders, a voicing of approbation for those who found officeholding incompatible with their religious principles, an expression of the desirability of Friends' being relieved from government service, and a statement of the necessity that they continue to serve nevertheless.

Those who are conversant in the management of Publick Affairs must know, that where many of various dispositions and sentiments are concerned, it is not easy, scarce possible, to conduct every design and carry it into execution in the most unexceptionable way. Some allowance must therefore be made for human imperfections, and we hope it may with truth and justice be said small allowances are requisite to reconcile the conduct of the people of this Province so far as they have been concerned in the Legislature to these Christian principles of fearing God, honouring the King, and promoting peace and good will among men, and we hope the desire of pursuing measures consistent with these principles will still animate the sensible and judicious of our Society, and that they will freely resign the right we have in the government, whenever it may appear impracticable for us to preserve it and those principles.

We have the more just grounds for this hope, as it is well known that many have voluntarily declined acting in the executive powers of government, and some in the Legislature, as they found themselves incapable of preserving the peace and tranquility of their own minds and steadily maintaining our Christian testimony in all its branches. And were there a sufficient number of men of understanding, probity and moderate principles proposed for our Representatives in whose resolution we could confide to preserve our liberties inviolate, we should be well satisfied to have the members of our Society relieved from the disagreeable contests and controversies to which we are now subjected, but while arbitrary and oppressive measures are publickly avowed by those who desire to rule over us, and our country so heartily and unanimously calls upon us to maintain the trust committed to us, we cannot after the most deliberate consideration judge we should be faithful to them, to ourselves, or to our posterity, to desert our stations and relinquish the share we have in the legislation.[1]

With political tensions in the province growing ever more critical, and with them the need for Quaker vigilance, a special standing committee was appointed at the ensuing Yearly Meeting for the purpose of guarding the Quakers' interests more efficiently. This would be accomplished by standing ready to take action in any situation wherein the privileges of Friends might be affected and by corresponding when necessary with the London Yearly Meeting and the London Meeting for Sufferings. Most of the men appointed to the committee had signed an endorsement of the Quarterly Meeting epistle of May 5, expressing their approbation of its contents; their assigned task now was to perform the same sort of function as their colleagues in the Quarterly Meeting, but on a standing basis. The Yearly Meeting specified that the group's sessions were to be meetings of record, and thus accorded it a status unique among all the committees of the Yearly Meeting. We will return to the activities of this committee shortly, but one particular aspect of its early history requires brief elaboration.

In addition to its primary functions, the Yearly Meeting assigned the Correspondence Committee, in combination with another group, the task of deliberating the issue of mixed taxes; this was discussed earlier. The other half of the joint body consisted of a committee made up largely of ministers, whose primary function was to visit the quarterly and monthly meetings and assist them in upholding and maintaining the faith and the Discipline. When the composite group convened in December, 1755, after the passage and signing of the tax bill, it was unable to achieve unity on the central problem of whether payment of the levy would be consistent with Quaker principles. Some were prepared to uphold the freedom of others to withhold payment, but were opposed to making refusal the official policy of the Society, to be enforced by the Discipline, as some of the zealots demanded. Those who felt free to pay the taxes eventually withdrew from the Meeting, while the

[1] PQM to LMS, 5/v/55.

69

members whose qualms persisted remained behind and framed the Epistle of Tender Love and Caution. A draft copy of the epistle has been found among John Woolman's papers, and thus suggests that he took a leading role in its composition. Certainly the contents, which are very strongly representative of the reformers' position on the issue, were approved by him, for his name appears among the signatories to the document.

It is highly significant in this connection that, of the twenty subscribers to the epistle, fourteen were members of the visiting committee, while only one belonged to the Committee of Correspondence. The remaining five had not been appointed to either body, but participated in the proceedings out of personal concern. The absence of a member's name from the epistle does not necessarily mean that he dissented from its contents; it may indicate merely that he was not present at the deliberations in the first place. On the other hand, the fact that fourteen of the signers were members of a committee composed mostly of ministers and assigned an essentially reformist task, while only one represented the committee comprised largely of politiques, whose function was directly related to worldly politics, gives a rather clear indication that, in fact, differences in outlook among the meeting elite were of sufficient magnitude to prevent the attainment of unity on certain issues. Another attempt was made to deal with the tax issue in the Yearly Meeting of 1757, but the cleavage persisted and once again stymied the Meeting's efforts.

Because the reaching of a unified sense of the meeting was almost the *raison d'être* of the Quaker meeting system, and because this unity was among the paramount values of the Society, no failure to attain it should be dismissed easily, as has been done by those analysts of Quaker political behavior who view the meeting elite as a unitary group, usually said to be dominated by Israel Pemberton, in opposition to the worldly politicians, led by Isaac Norris, who did not participate in Society affairs.[2] In large part,

[2] Dietmar Rothermund, *The Layman's Progress* (Philadelphia, 1961), p. 85; Sydney James, *A People Among Peoples* (Cambridge, Mass., 1963), pp. 158–59; William S. Hanna, *Benjamin Franklin and Pennsylvania Politics* (Stanford, Calif., 1964), p. 99.

this view is an outgrowth of the a priori exclusion of the reformers from considerations of Quaker political behavior because they did not take an active, positive part in the partisan arena. The present study represents a departure from this perspective in that it considers the negative efforts of the reformers, aimed at promoting as complete a withdrawal from worldly politics as possible, to be as fully political as the behavior of the reformers' more outward brethren.

Once one is attuned to the differences in political behavior patterns which are revealed in the personal documents, the different strains in the meeting records often become distinguishable, as in the contrast between the strongly reformist epistle from the Yearly Meeting of 1754 to the London Yearly Meeting, and the characteristically politique statement of the epistle sent by the Committee of Correspondence to the same body roughly a year and a half later.[3] Unfortunately, in most cases it is difficult or impossible to go beyond this kind of extrapolation of behavioral patterns characteristic of individuals onto the actions of the Yearly Meeting and its subordinate structures. Although we can identify specific individuals of known political type attending particular meetings or appointed to particular committees, it is usually impossible to know exactly which of them drafted the epistle or report issued in the name of the mixed group; the data upon which the above discussion of the tax issue is based are exceptional in this respect. The fact that a committee may deliberate an issue, achieve a degree of unity thereon, and approve a report on the matter, does not imply that each individual member would have written the report in the same way. The Yearly Meeting minutes record only the committee members' names and their final written report.

Some questions may arise as to why the potential cleavage between the reformers and the politiques did not surface in the meetings more frequently. The answer lies to a great degree in the high value placed upon unity within the Society. The Book of Discipline exhorts Friends to "avoid all Tokens of open Division

[3] PYM to LYM, 1754; PMS to LYM, 21/v/56, in the Preface to the ongoing minutes of PMS.

amongst us," and urges, "let us unite and be strong in the Lord, against all our Adversaries and their Attempts to divide us both within and without."[4] In order to achieve this goal of unity, the Friends cultivated the ability to find a commonly acceptable ground among the views put forward in the course of deliberating an issue if there were differences of opinion among the members. This ability was the prerequisite for leadership within the meetings and was highly developed within the Society, to the extent that it was often exercised almost unconsciously. To cite one appropriate example, although the reformers desired the withdrawal of Quakers from political office because of the worldliness and compromise attendant thereon, while the politiques initially urged withdrawal only during times of war, the immediate practical objective was the same. The reformers could freely support the politiques' position, for to this extent it coincided with their own and seemed right for the Society at that particular time. In a great many cases, Friends viewed it as perfectly consistent to assent to decisions which they considered to be expedient for the Society at a particular time, although they supported a different policy for the long run.

The standing Committee of Correspondence appointed at the Yearly Meeting of 1755 was maintained in that form for only one year. During that time, the need for such a body became even more evident than it had been when the committee was established; the sense of political crisis at the time of the Yearly Meeting of 1756 was intense. The Yearly Meeting, it will be recalled, was convened at the end of September and lasted through the first few days of October, adjourning immediately before election time. In 1756, in addition to bearing political pressures, the Quakers, in common with all Pennsylvanians, were oppressed by the fear of Indian attacks and the widening war.

Given these circumstances, the Meeting took the logical step of replacing the fifteen-member Correspondence Committee with a

---

[4] "Charity and Unity," Philadelphia Yearly Meeting Book of Discipline (1762 version), Quaker Collection, Haverford College Library, Haverford, Pa.

larger and more organized agency, granting it a wider sphere of operations and constituting it as the Philadelphia Meeting for Sufferings, on the model of the London body.

The London Meeting for Sufferings had been established in 1675 for the purpose of legal defense, to keep Friends from suffering persecution when the law owed them protection. Its aim was to inform Quakers of the legal limits of the powers of law officers and to point out the avenues of legal redress for unjust persecution. In time, the body assumed the more general executive function of representing the Society in all matters in which the interest or reputation of the church was implicated, and it came to exercise considerable power and influence in Society affairs.

In Pennsylvania, the Meeting for Sufferings was assigned a series of functions which roughly paralleled those of the London body:

> To hear and Consider the Cases of any Friends under Sufferings, especially such as suffer from the Indians or other Enemies and to administer such relief as they find necessary, or to apply to the Government or Persons in power on their behalf. To Correspond with the Meeting of Sufferings or the Yearly Meeting of London and to represent the State of the Affairs of Friends here and in general to represent this Meeting and appear in all Cases, where the Reputation & Interest of Truth and our Religious Society are concerned; provided that they do not meddle with Matters of Faith or Discipline not already determined in the Yearly Meeting, and that at least Twelve should Concur on all Occasions, and in matters of great Importance that notice be given or sent to all the Members of the Committee.[5]

Although the wording of the first section emphasized the current apprehension of suffering from Indian attacks, this danger was temporary and intermittent. The Meeting did in fact deal with sufferings brought about by the Indian trouble, but in the long run its energies were occupied to a far greater degree by sufferings of a legal nature, both actual and potential. For exam-

'5 PYM, 1756.

ple, one of the principal problems faced by the Meeting during its early years was the persecution of Friends in Delaware (most of whom were under the jurisdiction of the Philadelphia Yearly Meeting) under various militia laws which did not provide for exemption from service on conscientious grounds. The Meeting's labors took the form both of appealing to the government on their behalf and of endeavoring to prevent the passage of other potentially oppressive laws as they were proposed. In time, this type of preventive lobbying became one of the routine functions of the Meeting.

Carrying out the generally worded functions outlined in the second section involved a variety of activities and tasks. The most important of these was the publication of memorials or epistles for the vindication and defense of Friends in the face of external pressure provoked by the faithful exercise of their religious duties. A typical instance was the publication of extracts from the writings of ancient Friends which vindicated the Quakers' non-participation in public fasts when a fast day was proclaimed in Philadelphia in 1757. With increasing frequency, the Meeting's action took the form of a public dissociation of the Society from the acts of worldly Quakers in the Assembly, and often outside it as well, when these acts deviated from Quaker principles or adversely affected the reputation of the Society. It was the performance of this task which most often required correspondence with London, for that was the seat of colonial policy-making. Throughout the colonial period, a steady stream of political information ran in both directions across the Atlantic, with the English Friends assuming the role of advocates for their distant brethren.

On a lower level, the Philadelphia Meeting for Sufferings performed a number of other services for the Society, such as serving as an agency for gathering information, diffusing the Quaker testimony through the publication, translation, and distribution of doctrinal literature, and conducting certain types of public relations activities, such as waiting upon a newly appointed governor to convey the Society's respects.

Because the need for an agency of the Society which could act quickly in emergencies was one of the principal reasons for establishing the Philadelphia Meeting for Sufferings, it was necessary to ensure that a sufficient number of members could be assembled on short notice. Philadelphia was the center of information for the province, but travel conditions made it difficult for city Friends to communicate rapidly with those in the country, or for country Friends to come often to the city; the problem was solved by providing for a membership from the city large enough to transact the business of the Meeting, while preserving a voice for Friends who lived farther afield. Four representatives from each Quarterly Meeting joined twelve members appointed by the Yearly Meeting. In addition to their more general qualifications, the latter were selected on the basis of living in or near Philadelphia, "for the convenience of their getting soon together." It was decided that meetings would be held at least once a month, with more frequent sessions being called as circumstances demanded.

In discussing the establishment of the London Meeting for Sufferings, Arnold Lloyd makes the highly suggestive point that the founders and moving spirits of the organization were mainly recent converts to Quakerism, such as William Penn, William Meade, and Thomas Ellwood, men who were familiar with the ways of worldly government and believed in using law to defeat illegality, unlike many of their more innocent brethren.[6] In Pennsylvania, where Friends had free access to the franchise and to positions in government, knowledge of worldly politics was not limited to recent converts, but neither was it evenly diffused throughout the Society. Because the work of the Meeting for Sufferings was tied directly to the external political situation and demanded of its members attention to worldly politics, the politiques were better equipped, and generally more willing, to undertake the service than were the more quietistic reformers. The predominance of Philadelphians among the membership of the Meeting also tended to increase the role of the politiques in its activities. This is not to say that no reformers were well suited for

[6] Arnold Lloyd, *Quaker Social History* (New York, 1950), p. 85.

75

membership, for based on the number of committees on which they served until the Revolution, Anthony Benezet, William Brown, Samuel Emlen, Jr., John Pemberton, and Mordecai Yarnall all were active figures in the Meeting. Judging by the same criterion, however, their position in the Meeting was far overshadowed by that of the politiques. Of those who served on ten or more committees (the average of all members was four committees), four out of five were politiques—namely, James Pemberton, (twenty, also clerk), Israel Pemberton (thirteen), John Reynell (twelve), and Isaac Zane (ten). Anthony Benezet (fifteen) was the lone reformer. Once we see the political complexion of the Meeting for Sufferings in these terms, we have an important key to understanding its conduct of those crucial public affairs in which it was embroiled from the very moment of its establishment.

We have described the politiques at work in the Yearly Meeting and in control of the Meeting for Sufferings as well. Now we must go outside the meeting structure to examine their role in the most problematic of all Quaker political agencies, the Friendly Association for Regaining and Preserving Peace with the Indians by Pacific Measures.

VI

THE QUAKER POLITIQUES
AND THE CAREER OF
THE FRIENDLY ASSOCIATION

Of all the early concerns of the Philadelphia Meeting for Sufferings, one in particular affords an especially clear insight into the configuration of Quaker political behavior which emerged from the crisis of 1755–56. This is the Meeting's relationship with and defense of the Friendly Association for Regaining and Preserving Peace with the Indians by Pacific Measures.

The background of the Friendly Association may be traced to the action of a number of pacifist Quakers in the Assembly during the fall of 1755. Gravely disturbed by the mounting agitation over war preparations, these men sought an alternative approach to the Indian problem which would be more consistent both with the history of the Quaker colony and with their own religious principles. They maintained that the proper approach to the situation called not for military operations but for an inquiry into the grievances which had driven the Indians to attack, and for the just and equitable settlement of those grievances once they were determined. Investigation led them to the conclusion that the source of the trouble lay in the Indians' dissatisfaction with certain land transactions, but before they could pursue the issue the Assembly's attention was drawn to the disputes surrounding the taxation of Proprietary estates, and the proposed pacific program was pushed aside.[1]

---

[1] James Pemberton to Jonah Thompson, 25/iv/56, MS 325, Quaker Collection, Haverford College Library, Haverford, Pa.

The following spring, however, the issue was revived, as a result of Governor Morris' declaration of war against the Indians and the receipt of the first reports from England concerning the desperate efforts of Friends there to preserve the civil liberties of Quakers in Pennsylvania. A private group of Friends addressed the governor, urging him to reconsider the declaration of war and to institute an inquiry into the alienation of the Indians. The group further suggested that a lack of integrity in dealing with the natives lay at the root of their disaffection. The subscribers to this address also announced their willingness to do everything in their power to help secure peace, even to the extent of contributing more money to the peace effort than they would have been obliged to pay in taxes. As early as November, 1755, Samuel Smith had inquired of John Smith by "wht method the Frds who waited on the Assembly propos'd to show their benevolence &c in Lieu of that propos'd by the Ass.y," and the later offer to the governor was intended "to demonstrate [that] their refusal [to pay the taxes] does not proceed from a penurious disposition."[2]

During the month of April, the group made its first approaches to the Indians themselves and found them receptive to peace overtures. The Friends derived additional encouragement from the assurances of Conrad Weiser, an interpreter and Indian agent, that the Indians were in fact aggrieved because of unscrupulous land dealings, and that the only way to save Pennsylvania from ruin was to endeavor to promote peace with them, using peaceful, not military, means. These events convinced the Quakers that they had indeed hit upon the right course for vindicating the reputation of the Society.[3]

Accordingly, they informed Morris of the Indians' disposition and of the suggestion made by one of the natives that peace messengers be sent out to the hostile tribes. To back up its report, the group offered a loan of five thousand pounds to the provincial treasury, then badly depleted, for use in financing the negotiations

[2] 9/xi/55, Smith Corresp.; James Pemberton to Jonah Thompson, 25/iv/56, MS 325, Quaker Collection, Haverford College Library.
[3] John Reynell to Elias Bland, 20/iv/56, JRLB, 1754–56.

which they hoped would ensue. Their hopes were soon rewarded, for by June a cessation of hostilities was effected on the frontier.[4] Within a short time, arrangements were made for a treaty with the Wyoming Delawares, who had gathered at Easton and, to the gratification of the Quakers, had expressed a particular desire for the participation of Friends in the proceedings.

To follow up these developments, several Philadelphia Friends came together on July 20, 1756, and issued a proposal that a subscription be raised among Friends "to promote the interest, welfare, and peace of our country, by contributing toward the expenses of treaties with the Indians, in such a manner as may tend to improve the confidence the Indians have repeatedly, and especially of late, expressed in men of our peaceable principles."[5] The subscription was drawn up on July 22, and three days later more than twenty Quakers were on their way to Easton, well provided with gifts for the Indians.

Nothing conclusive was achieved at the treaty, but arrangements were made for a second conference to be held the following fall. The new talks were to include the representatives of the Six Nations Iroquois, who claimed political suzerainty over the Delawares. The Quakers would have preferred that a separate and immediate peace be negotiated with the Delawares, but the first treaty had at least enabled them to ingratiate themselves further with the Indians, and they believed on the whole that "the time we have been long waiting for, seems now to come in wch we may do ourselves & the Truth we profess the Justice due."[6]

As the time approached for the second treaty, a number of Philadelphia subscribers to the general fund called a meeting for November 2 at the Great Meeting House, the purpose of which was to formulate proposals concerning the Indians for submission to Governor William Denny, who had replaced Morris the previ-

---

[4] Samuel Hazard, ed., *Register of Pennsylvania*, 16 vols. (Philadelphia, 1828–36), 5 : 360.
[5] Samuel Parrish, *Some Chapters in the History of the Friendly Association for Regaining and Preserving Peace with the Indians by Pacific Measures* (Philadelphia, 1877), p. 17 (hereafter cited as *History of the Friendly Association*).
[6] Israel Pemberton to John Fothergill, 2/viii/57, EC, 2 : 26.

ous August. At this meeting, attended by eighty-three Friends (four from Chester County, three from Bucks County, three from Philadelphia County, and the remainder from the city), the Friendly Association was organized, although it did not receive its permanent name until later. A committee was appointed to formulate bylaws for the organization, and these were presented at a general meeting on December 1, after the proceedings at Easton.[7]

At the December meeting also, a slate of officers was elected, the composition of which reflected the overwhelming predominance of city Friends in the Association. Thirteen of the sixteen-member Board of Trustees were from Philadelphia, as were the clerk and the treasurer. The three remaining trustees were from Berks, Philadelphia, and Chester counties. Eligibility for the office of trustee was confined to members of the Society of Friends in good standing who had contributed to the common fund of the Association at least ten pounds, a substantial sum at that time. In 1758, the only year for which published figures are available, at least nine of the trustees chosen in 1756, plus the treasurer, donated between twenty and one hundred pounds to the Association, and it is likely that the initial contributions of most of them were larger.[8] The eleven Association officers were Abel James, John Reynell, William Callender, Jonathan Mifflin, Joseph Morris, James Pemberton, Israel Pemberton, Joseph Richardson, Jeremiah Warder, Richard Wistar, and Isaac Zane. The trustees were empowered to conduct most of the business of the Association and to call general meetings of the larger membership. Ten of their number constituted a quorum.

As is apparent from the foregoing account of the Friendly Association's development, the organization was an agency of the politiques. Of the officers mentioned above, William Callender, James Pemberton, Israel Pemberton, Isaac Zane, Abel James, and John Reynell were prominent exemplars of the type, as were Owen Jones and Peter Worral, who served as trustees in subsequent

[7] Theodore Thayer, *Israel Pemberton: King of the Quakers* (Philadelphia, 1943), p. 124.
[8] Parrish, *History of the Friendly Association*, pp. 99–101.

years. Abel James, in addition to his position as trustee, was chosen clerk of the Association, and John Reynell was its treasurer. Israel Pemberton was the sustaining spirit of the organization, and its dominant figure. Although Quakers of all types, as well as some non-Quakers (chiefly German pietists), contributed to the Friendly Association and occasionally participated in its activities, the dominance of the politiques is unquestionable.

Other aspects of the Association, however, give rise to questions, chief among them the problem of the group's relationship to the Society and the meeting structure. With its leadership limited to acknowledged members of the Society, its leaders all active in Society affairs, and its stated aim to promote peace by pacific measures consistent with the Quaker testimony in order to vindicate the reputation of the Society and the testimony, why was the Friendly Association a private undertaking, and not directly sponsored by the Yearly Meeting?

At one point, apparently, the possibility of the Society's sponsoring the peace program was in fact raised. As stated in the first epistle of the Philadelphia Meeting for Sufferings to its London counterpart, written in mid-December of 1756, "Our Yearly Meeting was briefly informed of the Conduct & Proceedings of those Friends principally concerned in promoting these Measures, but tho the Assistance of Friends in general is desired therein, yet divers Considerations & partly that of their Business being of a civil Nature induced them to decline to have this Affair come under the immediate Direction of the Yearly Meeting that it was thought sufficient there to express an Approbation of the Design & to recommend it to Friends in general to encourage the carrying it on in the same Manner it was begun." Thus, the organization of the Friendly Association as an undertaking of "some of us in our private Stations" was an attempt to achieve a situational and organizational separation of "civil" and "religious" activity, the implication being that certain kinds of behavior were inappropriate within the organization of the Society, but acceptable, even laudable, outside it.

The Friendly Association program, it will be remembered, grew out of the position of the small group of pacifist Quaker assembly-men who wanted the government to undertake an investigation of Indian grievances. The group which addressed the governor the following spring also held, quite reasonably, that the inquiry should have been made by the administration. The involved Quakers contended, therefore, that their continued activity was made necessary by the governor's unwillingness to pursue the course best calculated to bring peace to the province.[9]

On the other hand, the Society had been heavily criticized from the very beginning of the crisis because of its alleged connection with the Assembly Quakers, who were charged by the Proprietary propagandists with having failed to provide adequately for the defense of the colony. The Society was therefore anxious to avoid furnishing the opposition with grounds for the charge that the Quakers as a body were attempting to usurp the functions of government, although the opposition made the charge anyway. It was probably this, more than anything, which led the Yearly Meeting to decline sponsorship of the Indian program that was emerging. While the success of the program would redound to the credit of the Society and enhance the reputation of the Quaker testimony, the Society could dissociate itself from those aspects which came under criticism.

It was in fact inevitable that the Friendly Association would come under attack by outsiders, for, despite the protestations of its leaders to the contrary, the Association's program carried it right into the midst of the partisan melee. To review for a moment, we recall that one of the earliest objectives of the men who later founded the Friendly Association was to vindicate the position of the pacifist Quakers in the Assembly who deplored the willingness of their colleagues to abandon the peaceful heritage of the colony, and who wished instead to restore peace with the Indians by peaceful means. Especially after the pressures of conscience compelled them to resign their seats, these men and their supporters felt the need to prove that such measures would prevail where

9 Hazard, *Register*, 5 : 359.

force of arms could not, and thereby to discredit the military policies of the defense-oriented Quakers and the Proprietary supporters while elevating the reputation of Truth. Their program hinged upon the contention that land frauds had provoked the disaffection of the Indians and that the way to peace lay in a just settlement of their grievances.

Significantly, the politiques claimed to be motivated by still another concern. Although their basic loyalty was to the Quaker party as against the Proprietary party, they were perturbed by the amount of bitterness and rancor which had entered the disputes between the governor and the Assembly. To a degree, they saw themselves as being in a position to moderate between the two hostile camps. For instance, the following paragraph refers to events that occurred after the Quakers' initial contact with the Indians, through which they confirmed the natives' willingness to participate in peace negotiations.

> Gov. Morris was immediately informed of what had passed; and as there appeared some prospect of improving this disposition of the Indians to the public benefit, he was assured if he would advise and direct the manner of proceeding, nothing more was desired by us than under his direction to proceed therein, in such manner as would be most agreeable to him, most effectually answer the purpose intended, and demonstrate that we did not act from views of private advantage thereby.—And least the differences then subsisting between him and the Assembly about the raising money for public services . . . should discourage or retard his proceeding therein, he was told that whatever sum of money should be wanting, even to the amount of £2000, he should be immediately supplied with, and by every part of our conduct should find our hearty concern for the public welfare, to be our principal motives.[10]

Other offers of financial assistance were couched in similar terms.[11]

This moderating role was prompted partly by the apprehension that the violent state of provincial politics would add fuel to the

[10] *Ibid.*, p. 360.
[11] Parrish, *History of the Friendly Association*, p. 57.

arguments then beginning to be voiced (by Benjamin Franklin and others) for a takeover of the Pennsylvania government by the crown. Many Quakers feared that such an eventuality would endanger the rights enjoyed by Friends under the existing charter.[12] This became an issue of considerable importance a few years later and will be discussed in more detail in Chapter VII.

The flaw in the Quaker program, however, was a very basic one. To begin with, their strategy rested on the premise of land fraud; because only the Proprietors or their representatives were empowered to purchase land from the Indians, any claims of fraud which might have been established would have reflected discredit upon the Proprietary interest. Furthermore, any success achieved by the Quakers would in itself have constituted a negative reflection upon the administration's lack of initiative at a time when the Proprietor and the governor were very much on the defensive and jealous of those prerogatives which remained to them. If the Quakers could have effected a peace by peaceable means, the contention that the troubles of the province were caused by the Friends' unwillingness to prepare the colony militarily would have lost much of its force, and the blame for the crisis would have fallen back on the Proprietors.

In marked contrast to the Proprietors, the worldly Quakers had absolutely nothing to lose from whatever successes the Friendly Association might achieve. Although willing to provide for military defense, they desired peace as earnestly as did the pacifists, and as Quakers they would certainly have had no objections to achieving it by peaceful means. What is more, in view of their attitude toward the Proprietor and his henchman, any embarrassment suffered by the Proprietary party would have been welcome.

As for the attempt of the politiques to segregate the civil realm from the religious, it too was doomed to failure. The leaders of the Friendly Association all were prominent men, men well known for their influence within the Society. The overlap in personnel between the meetings and the Association was obvious to out-

---

[12] Thayer, *Israel Pemberton*, pp. 134–35.

siders, and the anti-Quaker forces had long based their harangues against Quaker domination of the province on evidence of civil-religious connections which was far less clear. Just as important, however, was the fact that the politiques themselves were unable to maintain the separation at all times; their failure to do so is the key to the subsequent history of the Friendly Association and of the Society itself.

Cracks began to appear in the façade of restrained and deferential relations between the governor and the Friendly Association at the first treaty of Easton, in the summer of 1756. Morris was piqued by the Quakers' successful endeavors to ingratiate themselves with the Delaware leader, Teedyuscung, and informed them that he would view as enemies of the crown any Quakers or others who treated with the Indians on matters relative to government. The incident was smoothed over, but it is apparent that, as the conference progressed, it was accompanied by considerable political fencing and maneuvering between the Quakers and the governor's party. The Quakers reported that they could gain entrance to the conference only by presenting themselves at the door and "crowding ourselves in." Once inside, they openly criticized Morris' conduct of the proceedings, and at the close of the treaty they engaged in pettish jockeying with him over whether their gifts would be presented separately or mixed together with the province's meager offering.[13]

Morris left his post after the conference, and was succeeded by William Denny. The new governor readily assented to the Association's request to participate in the second set of talks, in November, not having been a party to any of the previous disagreements between the Quakers and the administration.

The second treaty opened auspiciously for the Quakers. On the day before the start of the proceedings, which coincided with the usual time of the weekly meeting in Philadelphia, they met

[13] Parrish, *History of the Friendly Association*, p. 21; Thayer, *Israel Pemberton*, p. 109.

together at their quarters "and were favored with a satisfactory evidence of the renewings of Divine regard towards us, uniting us to each other, and encourging us in the prosecution of our business."[14] Thus assured of divine regard, they were further pleased when the inexperienced Denny opened the conference by asking Teedyuscung whether the government of Pennsylvania had wronged the Indians in any way to cause them to go to war. Here was the opening the Quakers had been waiting for. At the first treaty, Teedyuscung had merely requested assurance that the white men would not seek any more Indian land, but now, as Wallace describes it, he burned the bridges behind him by charging that the deeds on which the Proprietors based their claims in the Walking Purchase of 1737 were fraudulent; he further alleged that the Six Nations Iroquois had had no right to sell the Delaware lands included in the Purchase of 1749, and consequently that the Proprietors had had no right to buy them.[15]

Not surprisingly, these charges provoked an outraged reaction on the part of the Proprietors' supporters. Richard Peters, the Proprietary secretary in Pennsylvania, angrily confronted a group of Quakers and charged them with "putting things into the Indians' heads." The allegation that the Proprietors were greedy in buying land and had purchased from those who had no right to sell "was Mr. Franklin's interpretation, to blacken the Proprietors and support a party."[16] Once again, with characteristic Quaker coolness and tact, the Friends were able to calm the situation, but privately they recorded their conviction that the secretary had the "fixed purpose . . . to confuse, misrepresent, and obstruct an honest, fair inquiry, in order to [word missing—prevent?] an amicable adjustment of the difficulties."[17] Thus, only a few days after piously welcoming indications of Divine approbation of their activities, the Quakers were embroiled in bitter partisan wrangling.

[14] Parrish, *History of the Friendly Association*, p. 32.
[15] Anthony F. C. Wallace, *King of the Delawares: Teedyuscung* (Philadelphia, 1949), p. 133; Thayer, *Israel Pemberton*, p. 128.
[16] Parrish, *History of the Friendly Association*, pp. 35–36.
[17] *Ibid.*, p. 37.

When asked what would be necessary to give the Indians satisfaction for their grievances, Teedyuscung replied that compensation with interest must be given for the land, but that there were many others not in attendance at Easton who also were concerned in the matter and who therefore must be party to a general settlement at a subsequent treaty, whereupon, the conference closed, leaving the Quakers highly satisfied with the outcome. The naïve Governor Denny was now convinced that Proprietary injustice had precipitated the alienation of the Delawares, and he expressed gratitude for the Quakers' presence at the treaty. Richard Peters and Conrad Weiser were cordial and deferential in taking their leave of the Quakers, and Teedyuscung was so moved at parting from his friends that "it appeared to be the effect of a Divine visitation to a savage barbarian."[18]

Moreover, the Friendly Association gained ground among the Quakers as well. During the course of the treaty, some Friends came to Easton from different parts of the province and were invited to a special meeting of the Association. The minutes of the previous three days' conferences were read, and some time was spent in correcting "misapprehensions" concerning the conduct and view of the members and the importance of Friends being united in the prosecution of their work. Thus, some Friends "who had hitherto been backward" decided to subscribe to the Association.[19]

After the return from Easton, certain circumstances continued to favor the Association, enabling it to win the good regard of several important public officials. More important, though, were other less favorable developments which occurred during the same period. One of these involved the decision, made shortly after the treaty, to obtain copies of all the deeds on record for purchases of Indian land in Pennsylvania. In January, 1757, the Association applied to Richard Peters for access to the minutes of the Provincial Council, wherein these transactions were recorded. Peters' reply was curt.

18 *Ibid.*, pp. 39–40.
19 *Ibid.*, p. 38.

Gentlemen:—I laid your application with regard to the inspection of the council books, before his honor, the Governor, and in answer thereto, I am commanded to acquaint you, that as these books contain the most important affairs of government, many of which require the greatest secrecy, he cannot allow the perusal of them, to any but those concerned in the administration; and further, that he looks upon the transacting of business with the Indians in this Province, to be a matter so entirely pertaining to himself, that he cannot permit any but such as are immediately empowered by the King's authority, or by his own, to treat with or intermeddle in the affairs of that people. Nevertheless, if it be conceived that anything is contained in the minutes of Council, that does or may concern the right, or property of any person whatsoever, such person, by a proper application, and by particularly pointing it out, may be furnished with a copy of it. I am, gentlemen, your most humble servant,

Richard Peters.[20]

Peters was by now convinced that the work of the Friendly Association represented a threat to the interest of the Proprietors. Having seen the group in action during the first two conferences, he did not look forward to a Quaker presence at the prospective conference the following summer. He warned his employers that

Israel Pemberton and the Association will mold, fashion, turn, twist, and manage matters at the ensuing treaty as they please. When they have made the Proprs as black as the enemy of mankind, then they will officiously come with towels to wipe off the dirt they have thrown on them, then they will offer cash in aid of the poor Proprs and publish to the world the innocense and righteousness of their proceedings, their love of justice and their great regard for the Proprietaries.[21]

It was not surprising, then, that the Friendly Association encountered strong resistance from the governor in July, when a committee sought his approval to attend the proceedings at Easton later

[20] *Ibid.*, p. 58.
[21] Thayer, *Israel Pemberton*, 134.

in the month. Denny replied that he had received a communication from the Proprietors informing him of the extreme disapproval expressed by officials of the Home Government concerning the Quakers' presumption, as private citizens, in treating with "Foreign Princes." Not only was this an outrageous invasion of His Majesty's royal prerogative, but it was productive of divisions and partisan contention among the people. Therefore, Denny concluded, the Proprietors had directed him not to suffer the Quakers or any other body or society in Pennsylvania to concern themselves in any treaty with the Indians, or to give presents to the Indians at such treaties, much less to have their presents joined with the public ones. As he put it, "it would be prudent in you to decline going in a body, your attendance at treaties as a distinct Society, having given great offence to the ministry."[22]

The leaders of the Friendly Association responded to the governor's message with a forceful and strongly worded address, insisting, in quasi-legalistic terms, on their right to attend the treaty, and asserting their intention of doing so despite his advice to the contrary. The following tendentious statement is indicative of the tone of the message.

> ... And if the complaints of the Indians appear to be just, and the proprietaries and their agents should refuse to make them such satisfaction, as in justice they ought to have, rather than the lives of our distressed fellow subjects should be sacrificed, their properties destroyed, and so large a part of the King's dominions be laid waste, they [other religious societies] will freely join with us in contributing towards the satisfying such just claims of the Indians, or at least to pacify them, till the immediate authority of the King (of whose justice and paternal care we have not the least doubt) can be interposed, and justice, equity and mercy, be again restored and maintained among us.[23]

In view of the fact that many of the Quakers feared a change to royal government almost as much as the Proprietors did, it is diffi-

[22] Parrish, *History of the Friendly Association*, 69.
[23] Hazard, *Register*, 5 : 361.

cult to resist the conclusion that the above harangue was intended solely to irk and provoke the opponents of the Association's policy.

Nor did the leaders of the Association stop there. They directed a committee to visit the governor and ask his consent to publish his message together with their address, in order to remove "the prejudices and false reports" against the organization. If his consent was withheld, the Association's address would be published by itself.

With the scheduled treaty only days away, the Quakers' threat of publication had a telling effect. Fearing that their allegations would jeopardize his position with the Indians, and perhaps also recognizing that the Indians would resent his attempt to keep the trusted and generous Quakers away from the Treaty, Denny could only reply weakly that the Association's address misrepresented certain transactions and cast reflections on the Proprietors' conduct which were without foundation; he suggested that publication would be unseasonable and improper because it might inflame the minds of the Indians and obstruct the treaty. His implicit concession of the Quakers' upper hand deprived his repeated advice against their attendance of any effect it might otherwise have had. The Quakers clinched their victory by agreeing to suspend publication of their address "for a few days," to show that their regard for the public interest was greater than their concern for their private characters. With the governor's resistance thus neutralized, the Quakers proceeded to attend the conference.

Still anxious to establish land fraud on the part of the Proprietors, the Friends continued to push for copies of the deeds to purchased lands by having Teedyuscung make the demand at the conference. Reluctant to arouse the Indian leader's resentment, the Proprietary representatives agreed, after some diplomatic fencing, to accede to his demands for the documents and for royal adjudication of the land claims, on the condition that in the meantime he join in the conclusion of a formal peace. The Quakers were all for resisting this compromise and for pressing for the deeds and royal review prior to the concluding of a formal peace, but at this point Teedyuscung's own followers, who had become as anxious for peace as the Proprietors, and who were unconcerned about the Quakers' political affairs, threatened to revolt against their leader's authority if he did not accept the peace offer. Indeed they reminded him, the conclusion of a peace, and not the adjudication of land claims, had been the first and main objective of their negotiations with the province. Teedyuscung had lost sight of this, and so, to an extent, had the Quakers. Their position at the first treaty had been to press for a quick and separate peace with the Delawares, but now their primary commitment was evidently to discredit the Proprietary party. Teedyuscung had no choice but to submit to the pressures of his followers, and the peace belts were at last exchanged.

When the Quakers received the deeds, they realized that most of them were too vaguely framed, and their exact meaning too heavily obscured by antiquity, to provide the strong evidence of Proprietary wrongdoing which they had anticipated, so they fell back on their intensive search for conclusive proof of fraud in the Walking Purchase of 1737. This also proved fruitless in the end, but it occupied the efforts of the Association for four more years.

The treaty of July, 1757, marked a kind of turning point in the fortunes of the Friendly Association. True, the organization achieved a few of its tactical objectives, such as getting hold of the land-purchase documents, but the small victories were more than offset by the resultant increase in anti-Quaker feeling and the alienation of some formerly sympathetic public figures. In fact, by its manner of proceeding, the Association had succeeded in bringing about the very end which the group had been organized to prevent, the identification of the Society with the Assembly Quakers and with the Friendly Association itself. As William Penn wrote to Richard Peters, "What you say is too true that you were holding a treaty with the Quakers and the Assembly, not . . . the Indians."[24]

As if to add substance to the identification of the Friendly Association with the Society, the Meeting for Sufferings chose at this time to come to the defense of the Association.

[24] Thayer, *Israel Pemberton*, p. 148.

It being remarked to this Meeting that by various Letters which have been received from England, as also from what has been observed by the Friends who attended the late Treaty at Easton that many gross Misrepresentations of the Conduct of Friends at the several late Indian Treaties have been industriously propagated here, & transmitted to London in Order to calumniate Friends as a Society & to bring a Reproach on the Cause of Truth; on Consideration whereof it becomes the Concern of this Meeting in Order to obviate the Prejudices of our Adversaries against us that an impartial Account should be collected of the Part which Friends have taken in Contributing their Endeavours towards restoring Peace with the Indians & of the Motives which appear first to have induced them thereto. . . .[25]

The compilation of the "impartial account" was entrusted to an eight-member committee, six of whom were officers of the Friendly Association—namely, Israel Pemberton, Isaac Zane, John Reynell, William Callender, Owen Jones, and James Pemberton.[26] All remaining doubts concerning the direct connection between the Friendly Association and the Society as a corporate group were erased when the committee concluded that its purpose would best be served by publishing the minutes of the Friendly Association and related documents.[27] Still, public opinion continued to run against the Association, at home and in England. Almost the only encouragement came from the English Friends, who continued to work on their co-religionists' behalf.[28]

Significantly, Friends in Pennsylvania also began to voice their doubts and their criticism of the Friendly Association.[29] John Churchman, for example, discerned "the workings of the dark revengeful spirit, which opposed the measures of peace," among the Friends at the July treaty, and he warned them that this was one of the causes of their distress.[30] Perhaps the most telling

[25] PMS, 10/viii/57.
[26] *Ibid.*, 10/viii/57 and 13/x/57.
[27] *Ibid.*, 5/xii/57.
[28] John Fothergill to Israel Pemberton, 12/vi/58, EC, 2 : 32.
[29] John Pemberton to Samuel Fothergill, 6/iv/58, PP, 34 : 74.
[30] John Churchman, *An Account of the Gospel Labours and Christian Experiences of . . . John Churchman*, The Friends' Library, vol. 6 (Philadelphia, 1842), pp. 241–42.

statement was made by Churchman's fellow reformer, Anthony Benezet, who was a member of the above-mentioned committee of the Meeting for Sufferings and thus had an opportunity to observe the behavior of the Friendly Association's leaders during the closing months of 1757. His judgment was voiced in a letter to John Smith dated December 13, 1757.

One would think, by the general conduct of even the better sort of Friends, in matters of *property*, that some of our Saviour's positive injunctions to his followers had no meaning, even where some of these injunctions or precepts are as positive as that which says Swear not at all. I mean when he sets his meek, self-denying suffering doctrine in opposition to the natural one, which required an eye for an eye, and a tooth for a tooth. But I say unto you, I who am the Lamb, who was neither to strive, nor cry, whose voice was not to be heard, who was not to open his mouth even when led to the slaughter; I who am meek and lowly in heart, and have pronounced such a heart blessed, as being the only way to true rest and peace, I say unto you, *that ye resist not evil*, but rather suffer wrong and thus overcome evil with good. But say some, if we should suffer such a spirit to prevail, we shall often become a prey. I grant that it will be so in great measure, but that this is no cause of grief our Saviour has himself declared when he tells his followers not only to rejoice thereat, but even to shout for joy. I know some are for limiting this to suffering in what is generally called religious matters, but that's a device of the enemy. There is no distinction in Christianity between civil and religious matters; we are to be pure, holy, undefiled in all manner of conversation; since the time which we laid claim to Christ, we are no more our own, but are to live wholly unto him that died for us. The most sensible suffering is to give up our interest, and suffer matters to go contrary to our judgment, in common affairs. I know human nature will in this case make strong appeals to reason and vulgar opinion, in defence of its judgment and its interest, but it cannot judge in the present case, it has neither faculties, nor organs, to see into the deeply humbling mystery of Divine love; God becoming man, letting the whole power of hell spend its wrath upon him, and being finally made perfect through suffering, this being the means

93

ordained by the wisdom of God, by which a deadly blow is struck to the very root and being of sin.[31]

The strong insistence in this letter that "there is no distinction in Christianity between civil and religious matters," that "we are to be pure, holy, undefiled in all manner of conversation," brings to mind the original grounds on which the Yearly Meeting declined to sponsor the Friendly Association, that is, the inappropriateness of the church's involving itself directly in civil affairs. Although Quakers believed that in the ideal society to come there would in fact be no distinction between the civil and the religious, this is not what Benezet was referring to. He did not mean to deny that a distinction existed between the two realms in mid-eighteenth-century Pennsylvania. Rather, he was asserting the conviction that engagement in common affairs—worldly politics—in defense of one's interests, or even of the Society's interests, was incompatible with true Quaker principles; the true Quaker does not limit his meekness and suffering to personal spiritual matters while self-assertively contending with others outside the Society. Christ's precept must be the sole standard: "resist not evil, but rather suffer wrong and thus overcome evil with good." If the defense of the Society in the civil sphere requires deviation from this standard, then this defense must be foresworn. Patient endurance of the suffering which may ensue then becomes a means to salvation.

These views, as expressed by Benezet, are not in themselves unique; we have in fact defined them as characteristics of a general type of individual within the Society at the time. The important factor is the context in which the letter was written, the fact that it refers to the behavior of the politiques as exhibited in the activities of the Friendly Association. It would be of still greater interest to find a recognition of these same views on the part of the politiques themselves, but for this we must carry the account of the Friendly Association somewhat further.

[31] In George S. Brookes, *Friend Anthony Benezet* (Philadelphia, 1937), pp. 224–25.

After the summer of 1757, the next Indian treaty was held in the fall of 1758, and it was at this conference that the ultimate failure of the Friendly Association was sealed. The treaty was arranged at the behest of Sir William Johnson, royal agent for Indian affairs of the northern district. The Board of Trade in London had reviewed Teedyuscung's charges and passed the matter on to Johnson, with the recommendation that he settle the issue. This in itself boded ill for the Friendly Association, for Johnson was a known opponent of the organization's extragovernmental attempts to infringe upon the government's prerogatives. In addition, Johnson was closely connected with the Iroquois, who had been implicated in Teedyuscung's charges and wished now to be heard and to take a hand in the settlement of the issue.

It is essential to note here that the Delawares were, by virtue of conquest, a subject tribe of the Iroquois. Teedyuscung's charges against his overlords and his attempt to stand as the leader of an independent power vis-à-vis the Pennsylvania government were extremely presumptuous in the eyes of the Iroquois, and they provoked strong resentment. It was the Iroquois' presence at the treaty which led to Teedyuscung's loss of status and triggered the collapse of the Quaker design.

The Iroquois were prepared to be conciliatory toward the Delaware leader and to support him in some of his claims, in return for his acknowledgment of their suzerainty. Instead, he refused to submit, and engaged in various forms of outrageous behavior which provoked the Six Nations' representatives to humiliate him publicly and to strip him of his authority by denying that he had ever held it. Deprived of the sanction of the Iroquois, Teedyuscung faced the immediate prospect of desertion by his followers, and so had no choice but to submit. In order to regain his position, he was compelled to go to the governor and withdraw his claims to the lands which he had accused the Iroquois of selling without proper authority.[32] Thus, at a stroke, one of the two main pillars of the Quakers' case against the Proprietors was removed. After dealing with Teedyuscung, the Iroquois turned the proceed-

[32] Wallace, *King of the Delawares*, pp. 192–94.

ings to concerns of their own, and, upon settlement of these, the conference was closed, leaving only the Delaware claims concerning the Walking Purchase unresolved.

The Quakers tried for several more years to secure absolute proof of Proprietary fraud in the transaction of the Walking Purchase, but never succeeded in doing so. In 1762, a much humbled Teedyuscung, his leverage upon the governor further weakened by the conclusion of the war, was finally persuaded by Johnson to withdraw the last of the charges. The Indians still claimed that the boundary established in 1737 by the Walking Purchase was not the one they had intended, but they absolved the Proprietors of willful fraud and accepted a settlement of twelve hundred pounds.

Back in Philadelphia in November, 1757, with the reverses suffered at Easton still fresh in their minds, the leaders of the Friendly Association faced yet another crisis. Some time during that month, Israel Pemberton received a letter from Dr. John Fothergill in London, warning that the Quakers would probably be blamed for the "late Indian ravages," as well as for Teedyuscung's complaints against the Proprietors, on the basis of their purported role in the treaty of July, 1757. Fothergill quoted from a London newspaper a passage which had been taken from the report of a committee of the Provincial Council of Pennsylvania to the governor.

> We cannot but impute the said Teedyuscungs making that base charge of forgery against the proprietors to the malicious suggestions and management of some wicked people, enemies of the proprietaries—and perhaps it would not be unjust in us, if we were to impute it to some of those busy, forward people, who in disregard of the express injunctions of his Majestys *ministers* against it, and your Honours repeated Notices thereof served on them, would nevertheless appear in such crowds at all the late Indian treaties, and there shew themselves so busy and active in the management and support of the Indians in these complaints against the proprietarys.[33]

[33] 25/ix/58, EC, 2 : 33.

Dr. Fothergill's information was placed before the Meeting for Sufferings, which once again rose to the defense of the Friendly Association. After several futile attempts to obtain the full text of the report from Governor Denny, the Meeting for Sufferings decided to lay its defense directly before the Proprietor, with a profession of the Quakers' continued high regard for him, which rang somewhat hollow in the light of the tactics of the Friendly Association.[34] Accordingly, materials to establish the Meeting's case in favor of the Friendly Association were sent to Friends in London. One passage in the accompanying epistle to the London Meeting for Sufferings makes the Society's dilemma with regard to the Friendly Association strikingly clear.

> . . . Altho' our Situation makes it difficult to express our Minds so fully as we could desire, being unwilling to interfere in any Matters but what are immediately relative to us as a Religious society, yet, some affairs which appear to be principally of a Civil Nature are so connected with the Reputation & Honour of the Cause of Truth & the Advancement of that holy Principle of Peace which we profess to the World, that we are not easy longer to omitt giving you some account thereof.[35]

The difficulty would have been obviated, of course, by the disengagement of Friends from extra-Societal worldly affairs of a civil nature; the reputation of Truth and the well-being of the Society were not enhanced by their involvement, but were rendered more susceptible to attack. While this expedient would have been consistent with the quietistic views of the reformers, the politiques were still a long way from taking this step. The subsequent history of the Friendly Association, until its demise in about 1764, was marked by same sort of partisan wrangling and manipulation as characterized its earlier years, although progressively less was at stake for the province.

To leave the analysis of this point, however, would be to disregard certain crucial evidence of the emergence of a behavior

[34] PMS, 5/xii/57 *et seq.*
[35] *Ibid.*, 1/ii/59.

pattern that must be understood if the political behavior of the Pennsylvania Quakers during the next forty years is to be put in proper perspective. The signs are found in a letter written by Israel Pemberton in response to the disturbing information sent him by Dr. Fothergill.

> The intelligence thou has communicated affords me occasion of divers necessary & I hope they will be profitable reflections, the difficulties we meet with both there & here daily appearing to me more evidently to be little more than a prelude to what still seem to await us: and tho' we must as Members of Society steadily Endeavor to fulfill the duties or our Stations in the Concerns both of this & our future Life, almost every Event of our Endeavor determines with me in this conclusion that Infinite Wisdom is directing us to a more inward Self denying Path than we of most of our immediate Predecessors have trod in—it seems at times as if our Enemies were employ'd to instruct us in this lesson, at least their unjust Treatment should serve to impress it on our Minds, & tend to alienate us from the desire of seeking the Friendships or honour of Men, since the most sincere & disinterested Concern for their real good renders us the more imediate objects of their ill will: to bear this injustice with patience & prudence human reason & resolution is not sufficient to qualify us, & to obtain Superior aid requires an abstraction & devotion of heart, which I have hitherto rather seen than attain'd, yet cannot but seriously desire, with so much earnestness, as to lament the seeming necessity of our late and present Circumstances, by which I have heretofore thought myself debarr'd of it, but am thankful that I find Aspirations Still renewed & a will rais'd to prefer the obtaining it to every other Consideration.[36]

Let us summarize the essential points in this passage, to bring them more clearly into view. Pemberton was expressing the conviction that every station in society—that is, civil society, society at large—carried with it certain obligations or duties with regard to the earthly and the future life of man. Presumably Pemberton saw

[36] 22/xi/58, EC, 2 : 34.

it as the duty of wealthy, upper-class Quakers, in a province founded by and for Quakers, to take a leading part in the determination of that province's civic affairs. In his own case and that of his contemporaries, however, endeavors to fulfill that duty by promoting peace with the Indians, or by moderating between the administration and the Assembly, only served to provoke the hostility of the very people who would have been the beneficiaries of these efforts. To bear this injustice with the patience and prudence befitting a Friend would have required a degree of spiritual fortitude, but to qualify for the support of Superior Powers demanded an abstraction and a devotion of heart of a kind which would direct one inward, away from the worldly commotion of public affairs. The ill-will of others thus seemed calculated by Providence to turn Friends away from the pursuit of honor in worldly affairs and to lead them to a more inward, self-denying dependence upon Infinite Wisdom.

The chief significance of Pemberton's reflections lies in the fact that his statement was the expression of a Quaker politique who had been made to realize, under pressure from political adversaries outside the Society, that engagement in worldly political affairs was incompatible with adherence to Quaker standards for a pure life. The solution which suggested itself to Pemberton called, in essence, for an environmental reorientation and a concurrent change in behavior. The hostile attacks of outsiders could be prevented, or at least disregarded, through a withdrawal from worldly politics and a turning inward to God, whose protection is vouchsafed to all who put their trust in Him and follow His way, as embodied in the testimony.

Quite clearly, the reaction experienced by Israel Pemberton was of a kind most likely to affect the politiques. The reformers had disengaged themselves from worldly affairs to begin with, while the worldly politicians were so loosely tied to the testimony and the Discipline that they did not feel their pull. It is important to stress, however, that no claim is made for the universal occurrence of role strain among the politiques, at this or any other time in the period. Nor do we intend to convey the notion that, once the realization of behavioral inconsistency was achieved by an individual, an immediate and permanent changing of ways resulted. Rather, what appears to have occurred is that conflict was experienced with increasing frequency and strength of conviction among the politiques as they experienced the cumulative stresses of a succession of crises beginning in the mid-1750s and leading up to the Revolution. These men were strongly habituated to their pattern of leadership, however, and tended to lapse quickly back into their old ways as the pressures of particular crises waned; recognition of the necessity of submitting to the Divine Arm, when it occurred, was apparently confined to those times when the force of outward circumstances made it especially clear that all other efforts had failed. It was only in such situations that the religious strategies of resignation, stillness, and reliance upon God's direction seemed to constitute a more viable alternative than the worldly political strategies to which they were accustomed. In other words, the politiques were inclined to give up their worldly political efforts only after they had failed or gotten into strong difficulty, but not when there still seemed to be a reasonable chance of success. How different this was from Anthony Benezet's insistence that "the most sensible suffering is to give up our interest, and suffer matters to go contrary to our judgment in common affairs,"[37] or from John Woolman's observation:

> It requires great self-denial and Resignation of ourselves to attain that state wherein we can freely cease from fighting when wrongfully Invaded, if by our Fighting there were a probability of overcoming the invaders. Whoever rightly attains to it, does in some degree feel that Spirit in which our Redeemer gave his life for us, and, through Divine goodness many of our predecessors, and many now living, have learned this blessed lesson, but many others having their Religion chiefly by Education, & not being enough acquainted with that Cross which crucifies to the world, do manifest a Temper distinguishable from that of an Entire trust in God.[38]

[37] Brookes, *Friend Anthony Benezet*, pp. 224–25.
[38] *The Journal and Essays of John Woolman*, ed. Amelia Mott Gummere (London, 1922), p. 207.

44895

The politiques had been brought to a recognition of the need for an entire trust in God, but they could not yet bring themselves to the state of resignation which such a trust demanded. We have seen, however, that the potential for a conscious recognition of conflict was present among the politiques and could be activated by the adverse pressure of external events. The stresses surrounding the Friendly Association may have eased after 1757, but the potential for role strain remained, and, what is more important, political conditions in Pennsylvania became increasingly more likely to activate this potential in the years which followed the Friendly Association's demise.

VII

THE CRISIS OF THE EARLY 1760s

Despite the ambiguity of status which resulted from the civil nature of its activities, the Friendly Association was accorded the support of the Meeting for Sufferings when it came to the test. When the Society itself was implicated in the attacks on the Friendly Association for matters from which the corporate body had desired to remain aloof, the overlapping personnel of the meetings and the Association, and the Quaker-oriented goals of the latter, brought the Meeting for Sufferings to the Association's aid. When the Society was linked with the civil activities of certain other Quakers, however, no such factors were operative, and the Meeting for Sufferings acted as forcefully to dissociate the Society of Friends from these affairs as it had to espouse the cause of the Friendly Association. Those who were repudiated were, of course, the worldly Quaker politicians, whose activities continued to be a source of embarrassment to reformers and politiques alike.

The withdrawal of Friends from the Assembly in 1756, we recall, was viewed by many—probably most—Quakers as a temporary expedient undertaken to avert the threat of political disablement at that particular time. As early as mid-1757, John Pemberton noted that country Friends seemed already to regret the absence of Friends from the Assembly, and expressed the conviction that, if precautions were not taken by members of the

Society who desired to keep Friends out of office, it would be next to impossible to prevent a Quaker majority from being chosen in the ensuing elections.[1]

There was in fact no real change in the number of Quaker representatives elected in 1757, but those who were chosen continued to be a source of distress to the Society. The problem was raised during the Yearly Meeting of 1758 in the report of a committee which had been appointed to inquire into the involvement of Friends in furnishing wagons to Colonel Bouquet for the conveyance of military stores during the campaign against Fort Duquesne. In confirming that this constituted a military service and therefore violated the peace testimony, the committee noted that "many Friends were persuaded or drawn aside in this matter by the Examples and Injunctions of some members of our Society who are employed in offices and Stations in Civil Government." Because these offices required of the incumbents certain duties, activities, and measures which brought added burdens to their brethren and promised to produce still more difficulties, the committee recommended that the Yearly Meeting advise and caution all Friends against accepting or continuing in such offices, and that it direct the lower meetings how far to proceed against those who failed to heed the advice.

The Yearly Meeting approved the report and issued the following advice; it was the Society's first formal attempt during the period to redefine the pattern of Quaker political behavior in Pennsylvania and to provide grounds on which unregenerate officeholders could be excluded from the organization (although in practice these proved to be ineffectual).

And as the maintaining inviolate that Liberty of Conscience which is essential to our Union and welbeing as a religious Society evidently appears to be our indispensible Duty This Meeting doth with fervent and sincere desire for the present and future Prosperity of Truth among us and the Preservation of Individuals on the true Foundation of our Christian Friends to beware of accept-

[1] John Pemberton to Samuel Fothergill, 4/vii/57, PP, 34 : 57.

ing of or continuing in the Exercise of any office or Station in Civil Society or Government by which they may in any respect be engaged in or think themselves subjected to the necessity of enjoining or enforcing the Compliance of their Brethren or others with any Act which they conscientiously scruple to perform and if any professing with us should after the Advice and loving Admonitions of their Brethren persist in Conduct so repugnant to that Sincerity Uprightness & self denial incumbent on us, it is the Sense and Judgment of this Meeting that such persons should not be allowed to sit in our Meetings for discipline nor be employed in the Affairs of Truth until They are brought to a sense and acknowledgement of their Error.[2]

Violation of the cherished liberty of conscience and the fostering of deviant behavior among Friends were in themselves serious transgressions, but the Quaker assemblymen were a source of discomfort to the leaders of the Society on other grounds as well. Even after acknowledged Quakers ceased to constitute a majority in the House, the party which continued to oppose the Proprietary interests retained the label Quaker party, and prominent Quakers, such as Isaac Norris, remained among its leaders. Popular suspicion of the Quakers, aroused by William Smith's *Brief State* and *Brief View*, was widespread in Pennsylvania and in England, and it fostered the belief that the Friends were still in control of the province's public affairs, a notion which derived additional support from the extragovernmental manipulations of the Friendly Association.[3]

Smith had continued to be a thorn in the side of the Quaker party, and in 1758, when he and another Proprietary politician were imprisoned by the Assembly for allegedly committing libel against the House, the case became the partisan *cause célèbre* of of the year. To the dismay of its leaders, the Society was widely assumed to have been implicated in the proceedings against Smith

---

[2] PYM, 1758.
[3] John Fothergill to Israel Pemberton, 12/vi/58, EC, 2 : 32; William Smith, *A Brief State of the Province of Pennsylvania* (1755; reprint ed., London, 1865); *idem*, *A Brief View of the Conduct of Pennsylvania for the Year 1755* (London, 1756).

because of its purported connection with the Quaker officeholders and the indiscreet remarks made by other Friends in approval of the Assembly's action.[4] Consequently, the Meeting for Sufferings felt called upon to disclaim any responsibility for the actions of Friends in the House and to express its disapproval thereof on behalf of the Society. In an epistle to the London Meeting for Sufferings, the Philadelphia Meeting for Sufferings upheld its position by pointing out that, far from being dominated by the Society, the Quaker assemblymen and other officeholders had in fact concurred in measures which had produced sufferings for conscientious Friends.

Early in 1760, the Meeting for Sufferings appointed a committee to attack the problem at its source by treating directly with the officeholders themselves and suggesting that withdrawal from the Assembly would be most conducive to their own peace of mind as Quakers and to the honor of the testimony. The committee met with all the Quaker representatives who were in town except Norris, and was received in a uniformly friendly manner, but on the whole did it not consider the service to have been very successful. Accordingly, the committee was continued at intervals throughout the year, but to no apparent avail,[5] for the Meeting was compelled to report the following year that the number of Quaker officeholders in the province had actually increased.[6] This disturbing trend continued through the election of 1761, as a result of which, according to James Pemberton, acknowledged Quakers constituted nearly half of the 1761–62 Assembly, and there was "a large majority of such who do not qualify by the oath."[7] The Meeting for Sufferings reacted to the situation by appointing a new and greatly enlarged committee to treat with Friends in the Assembly, but, notwithstanding its occasionally optimistic reports, this group also failed in its efforts. The worldly politicians continued to undermine the Discipline, and the election

---

[4] PMS to LMS, 1/ii/59.
[5] PMS, 25/iii/60 *et seq.*
[6] PMS to LMS, 24/iii/61.
[7] James Pemberton to John Fothergill, 10/xii/62, PP, 34 : 121.

of 1762 had substantially the same results as that of the preceding year, despite the advice of the Yearly Meeting, just before the election, against Friends being accessory to the promotion or choice of others of their number for any office which might subject them to the temptation of deviating from their Christian testimony.[8] James Pemberton commented apprehensively that "in case of any dispute our opponents may have an oppo[rtunity]: of misrepresenting us."[9] The dispute he anticipated was not long in coming, and it proved to be the most explosive ever witnessed in Pennsylvania.

After Sir William Johnson's settlement of the Walking Purchase claim in June, 1762, Pennsylvania enjoyed a welcome interlude of political calm for the first time in many years. The lull proved to be a short one, however, for twelve months later the province was again subjected to the horrors of Indian attack, in the uprising known as Pontiac's War.[10] The Assembly responded to the first reports of hostilities by providing for a militia of seven hundred men to be raised among the back inhabitants; it then adjourned for the customary summer recess, while fear and agitation mounted on the frontier. By September, when the House reconvened, the Indian depredations had become more severe, and General Amherst had called upon Pennsylvania to contribute to the general defense effort. The House answered his call by sending a supply bill to Governor Hamilton, which he declined to accept because it contained a paper-money provision, thus raising once again the issue which had plagued the defense efforts of the mid-1750s. The bill was sent up and refused a total of four times, whereupon the House adjourned for the annual elections in mid-October.

[8] 5/iii/63 and 8/viii/63, GCJ, 1 : 57, 62–63; PYM, 1762.
[9] James Pemberton to John Fothergill, 10/xii/62, PP, 34 : 121.
[10] In the account which follows, I have drawn upon John R. Dunbar, *The Paxton Papers* (The Hague, 1957); Theodore Thayer, "The Quaker Party of Pennsylvania, 1755–1765," *Pennsylvania Magazine of History and Biography*, 71 (1947) : 19–43; and Theodore Thayer, *Pennsylvania Politics and the Growth of Democracy* (Philadelphia, 1953).

When the new Assembly convened a short time after the election, the frontier situation had become so pressing that the members capitulated to the governor and passed a bill which lacked the controversial paper-money provision. Military demands continued to increase at a rapid rate, however, and in November Amherst issued a call for more men and supplies. After some indecision concerning what form the bill should take (although none at all about whether one should be passed), the Assembly once again seized the initiative by passing a supply bill which would be funded by a tax on all property, including Proprietary holdings. The bill reached Governor John Penn (who had replaced Hamilton) on February 25, 1764, and, to no one's great surprise, it was refused.

The executive and legislative branches continued to dispute until May, when the House reconvened after an adjournment during which the Proprietor had succumbed to public pressure by signifying his willingness to submit to the taxation of Proprietary estates. The Assembly had already agreed to meet his other objections, so the supply bill was finally accepted. The two sides could not agree on a militia bill, however, and none was ever passed.

Although Hamilton and Penn probably were more responsible than the Assembly for delays in providing for defense, the frontiersmen lay the blame for their troubles at the doors of the House and the Society of Friends, as they had done in the previous Indian war. From the first outbreak of renewed hostilities, the frontiersmen believed themselves threatened by a double enemy, within and without, and they struck back at both.

The backwoodsmen never were too kindly disposed toward the Indians, even under normal circumstances, but, as their fear and danger increased, so did their hatred of the red men. Heightened by the violence of the war, this hatred fell upon several small groups of semicivilized Indians who lived among the whites—a mixed group of Christianized Delawares, remnant Mahicans, and Wampanoags, who sheltered in the Moravian settlement at Bethlehem, and a small group of twenty Susquehannocks, living at Conestoga, near Lancaster. These Indians had connections among the hostile tribes and were immediately suspected of giving aid to the enemy, if not actually slipping out to join in their raids. The Moravian Indians were moved to safety from the retributions of the frontiersmen through the intervention of the governor, but the Conestogas were not so fortunate. On December 14, 1764, a group of more than fifty frontiersmen, predominantly Scotch-Irish from Lancaster County, descended upon the Indian settlement and murdered the six natives who had the misfortune to be there at the time. Two weeks later, they rode into Lancaster, where the remaining fourteen had been quartered, ostensibly for their protection, and in one quick stroke killed them all—men, women, and children.

While a law-abiding element in Lancaster deplored the massacre of the Indians, public sympathy was so overwhelmingly in favor of the men who perpetrated it that they went unpunished. The authorities and substantial citizens of Philadelphia, however, were plainly horrified—by the deed itself, by the failure of the authorities in Lancaster to afford the Indians protection, and by the apparent immunity of the attackers from prosecution. They read the situation, and rightly so, as an indication that law and order had broken down on the frontier, and they viewed with alarm the spread of sympathy for the back inhabitants to the city itself, among the frontiersmen's Presbyterian co-religionists.

The fears of the Philadelphians increased still more a month after the Conestoga massacre, when reports began to reach the city that preparations were being made on the frontier for a march on Philadelphia to exterminate the Moravian Indians and to deal harshly with their protectors as well. Israel Pemberton was among those singled out for special attention, for his leading role in the Friendly Association and other Quaker political endeavors had made him a symbol of all that the westerners identified as hostile to their interests: the wealthy, pacifist, Quaker, Indian-loving, eastern ruling class. For a little more than a week, Philadelphia was in turmoil as rumors proliferated and spread, and as preparations were made to defend the city; the latter included the building of fortifications, the mustering of men, and the passage of "An

Act for preventing Tumults and Riotous Assemblies and for the more speedy and effectual Punishing the Rioters."[11] Significantly, a considerable number of Scotch-Irish and Germans in Philadelphia declined to participate in the defense preparations, or joined with reluctance, for they were more inclined to support their brethren from the frontier than to side with the ruling class in the city.[12]

The alarms reached their height between February 5 and 7, as the Paxton Boys, so called after the frontier town from which many of them came, approached the outskirts of the city. To the great surprise of many of the citizens, large numbers of Quakers, mostly young men, shouldered arms and joined the defenders. Estimates of their number vary between one hundred forty and two hundred men.[13] What is more, the Germantown Meeting House was used as a sheltering place for the armed defenders during a heavy rainstorm on the seventh.[14] Although attempts were made to excuse the participation of Quakers on the grounds that the affair was a civil action, or that defensive warfare was justifiable, the bearing of arms was nevertheless contrary to the peace testimony, and was deplored by those who were concerned for the reputation of Truth. Some of the Quaker defenders acknowledged their error before the Philadelphia Monthly Meeting, but many did not, and, although the Meeting continued to deal with them until well into 1767, none was ever disowned.[15]

Happily, the Paxton affair never came to violence, for Benjamin Franklin and Joseph Galloway of the Assembly, together with Benjamin Chew and Thomas Willing for the Provincial Council, persuaded the marchers to disperse and return home. On behalf of the House and the governor, this committee-of-four agreed to give the westerners' grievances prompt attention if presented in the

[11] Dunbar, *Paxton Papers*, pp. 38–39.
[12] William S. Hanna, *Benjamin Franklin and Pennsylvania Politics* (Stanford, Calif., 1964), p. 153.
[13] James Pemberton to Samuel Fothergill, 13/vi/64 and 7/iii/64, PP, 34 : 130–31, 125.
[14] James Pemberton to Samuel Fothergill, 7/iii/64, *ibid.*, p. 125.
[15] PYM, 1765, 1766, and 1767.

proper manner. This satisfied the groups' spokesmen, and within a few days the marchers departed.

On February 14 the leaders of the Paxton Boys sent the Assembly a two-part statement of their grievances and demands, as agreed at Germantown. The document was subsequently published in Philadelphia and took its place in a growing flood of pamphlets, eventually numbering in the sixties, in which the various parties and factions in the province harangued and contended with each other and the public in the ensuing months. The demands made in the Declaration and Remonstrance of the Paxton Men were for more equal legislative representation, guarantees against being removed to eastern Pennsylvania for trial in cases involving murdered Indians, banishment of the Moravian Indians from the province, exclusion of all Indians from "inhabited" areas in time of war, provision of care for those wounded in defense of the province, restoration of the bounty on Indian scalps, and prohibition of any dealings by private citizens (read, Quakers) with the Indians.[16] As it happened, only the demand for the scalp bounty was acceded to. Nevertheless, the ensuing pamphlet war had far greater and more long-term effects on the province than this would indicate, and not least upon the Quakers.

Criticism fell heavily upon Friends for several reasons. First, the party in control of the Assembly was still known as the Quaker party, and the majority of its members were of Quaker extraction, although slightly less than half were acknowledged members of the Society.[17] The aggrieved westerners and their sympathizers, however, were resentful of the slowness of the government in furnishing military and financial aid to the beleaguered frontier; mindful of the situation eight years earlier, when acknowledged Quakers did constitute a majority in the House, they were not inclined to make the above distinction, thus confirming Pemberton's fear that, "in case of any dispute our opponents may have an oppo[rtunity]: of misrepresenting us." One anti-Quaker pam-

---

[16] Dunbar, *Paxton Papers*, pp. 99–110.
[17] James Pemberton to John Fothergill, 7/iii/64, PP, 34 : 125; PMS to LMS, 3/ix/64.

phlet, for instance, alleged that Quakers held twenty-two of the thirty-six seats in the House.[18] To other opponents of the Quakers, numbers were beside the point.

> But it may be ask'd, why all this Clamour against Quakers? Surely they don't solely govern. True. Thank God they do not: But if a few artful bad Men in the Administration may be very detrimental, what may we apprehend where so many Quakers are entrusted, who have lately prov'd their very Religion to be a political Engine, to which they themselves pay no conscientious Regard, but as it suits their crafty Purposes.[19]

Moreover, because of the activities of the Friendly Association, the Quakers were identified with the hated policy of conciliating the Indians and lavishing gifts upon them, which, the critics contended, made them hold the whites in less regard and despise them for their weakness. The Quakers' generosity toward the Indians was contrasted with their apparent lack of concern for the sufferings of the frontiersmen, who were protecting the sheltered easterners from the savages' depredations.

The pamphleteers seized triumphantly upon the action of the Friends who had borne arms in defense of the city, as evidence that the peace testimony was based not on principle, but on policy; they castigated the Quakers for their apparent willingness to take up arms to protect a group of murdering Indians while pleading principle as grounds for withholding this protection from the back inhabitants. Here again, to the distress of the Yearly Meeting, they would not recognize the distinction between actions sanctioned by the Society as such, and actions performed by Quakers in violation of Quaker principles. The fact that none of the arms-bearers was disowned, and that the Germantown Meeting House was opened to the defenders, seemed to confirm their allegations.

The pro-Indian, anti-Presbyterian frontier policy attributed to the Quakers was thought by their opponents to stem from a dual

[18] Hugh Williamson, *The Plain Dealer: Or, a Few Remarks upon Quaker Politics* (Philadelphia, 1764), p. 6.
[19] David Dove, *The Quaker Unmask'd* (Philadelphia, 1764), p. 11.

desire to reap the riches of the Indian trade and to preserve their political hegemony. Clearly, it was charged, the Indians represented no challenge to Quaker political power, while the Presbyterians did; the destruction of the back inhabitants would serve to lessen the growing influence of the Quakers' political opponents, making their own places even more secure. In a similar vein, what measures the Assembly did provide for the aid of the frontier were dismissed as the Quakers' concession to political expediency, granted grudgingly when their seats could not be retained in any other way.

The penmen of the Quaker party answered the attacks of the opposition with numerous pamphlets of their own, but the Society as a body issued only a single rejoinder, in answer to the Declaration and Remonstrance of the Paxton Men. The statement took the form of an address to Governor Penn, and was written by a Meeting for Sufferings committee composed of James and Israel Pemberton, Abel James, John Reynell, and Owen Jones. Appealing to the historical position of Quakers in the colony, the authors noted that, from the beginning until a few years past, the government of the province had been entrusted chiefly to Quakers. During that time, peace with the Indians had prevailed, and citizens had been granted the full enjoyment of their religious and civil liberties. But in the last few years, they lamented, the situation had altered, and the province had become the victim of war from without and strife within, a circumstance which the Quakers had observed with grief and sorrow. They continued:

> We have as a Religious Society ever carefully avoided admitting Matters immediately relating to civil Government into our Deliberations, farther than to excite and engage each other to demean ourselves as dutiful Subjects to the King, with our Respect to those in Authority under him, and to live agreeable to the Religious Principles we profess, and to the uniform Example of our Ancestors. . . .
>
> Yet as Members of Civil Society, Services sometimes occur, which we do not judge expedient to become the Subject of the Consideration of our Religious Meetings, and of this Nature is the

[Friendly] Association formed by a number of Persons in religious Profession with us. . . .

The invidious Reflection against a Sect "that have got the Political Reins in their Hands, and tamely tyrannize over the good People of this Province," tho' evidently levelled against us, manifests the Authors of these Papers are egregiously ignorant of our Conduct, or wilfully bent on misrepresenting us; it being known, that as a Religious Body, we have by public Advices and private Admonitions, labour'd with, and earnestly desired our Brethren who have been elected or appointed to public Offices in the Government for some years past, to decline taking upon them a Task become so arduous, under our late and present Circumstances; and that many have concurred with us in this Resolution is evident by divers having voluntarily resigned their Seats in the House of Assembly, and by others having by public Advertisements signified their declining the Service, and requesting their Countrymen to choose others in their Places, and that many have refused to accept of places in the executive Part of the Government. We are not conscious that as Englishmen and dutiful Subjects we have ever forfeited our Right of Electing or being Elected; but because we could serve no longer in those Stations with Satisfaction to ourselves, many of us have chosen to forbear the Exercise of these Rights, and wish a Disposition of a contrary Nature was not so manifest in our Adversaries.[20]

For reasons discussed above, the dissidents were not inclined to accept the Quakers' disclaimers, and, needless to say, the address changed the views of no one. Nor did the succeeding months furnish any tangible evidence that the Quakers at large were disinclined toward involvement in partisan issues. Quite the reverse appeared to be the case, for reasons hinted at in the last line quoted—that is, the growing political activity and power of the Presbyterians.

It must be remembered that the Quakers' fear and distrust of the Presbyterians was deep-seated and of long duration. One of the pamphlets written in defense of the Quakers who took up arms

[20] PMS, 25/ii/64.

against the Paxton Boys expressed the sentiment of many Friends, although it was written by a non-Quaker.

> . . . In Boston Government, where the Quakers were used in the most cruel Manner, that the Serpentine Nature in Man could invent, they bore cruel Whippings, cutting off their Ears, and several were murdered, and for no other reason, then for their faithful obedience to CHRIST: And this was all acted by . . . Envious Malicious, Hard-hearted Presbyterians. I don't remember ever reading, or hearing tell, that any one Quaker was ever put to Death, for his Religious Principles, but in Boston Government out of the Hands of Presbyterians; for I believe they never had it, but that one Time, since the building of Babel; and I pray, they never may have it more, until Time is swallowed up in Eternity.[21]

The Great Awakening had split the Presbyterians into factions whose mutual antagonism was open and frequently bitter, but in 1758 these factions were reunited, and the energies of their members were freed to turn against a common adversary. The new-found strength of the Presbyterians was brought home to the Quakers by the events of 1764, in a manner which gave the Friends abundant cause for alarm. The influential Quaker councilor William Logan was moved to write to his cousin John Smith: "Our Town seems to be Getting into Ferments of which thou wilt hear more soon than I think proper to relate. The Devil is got loose to a very Great Degree."[22] John Reynell believed the situation to be equally ominous.

> Peace is a blessing I hope we shall be long favored with, tho' we can hardly say it quite restored to our Borders[,] Owing as I apprehend to the imprudent Conduct of a Sett of Men who are very violent in their measures & want to get into the Seat of Government, tho not fit to be trusted with it[. A] Presbyterian Government will if possible be intruded upon us, but hope we shall be

[21] *The Quakers Assisting to Preserve the Lives of the Indians in the Barracks Vindicated*, no. 2, quoted in Dunbar, *Paxton Papers*, p. 392.
[22] Smith Corresp., 1764, p. 197.

preserved from it[;] they are grown numberous[,] have joined in with the proprietary party to strengthen themselves[,] have been continually abusing & calumniating the Quakers in Order to weaken their Interest here with the People and represent them odious to the Government at home[;] no lies for that purpose have been omitted[. A]t the same time some of them have been guilty of such atrocious Crimes as in most other Governments they would stand fair for the Gallows. They have insulted the Government[,] committed divers Riots & murdered the Indians under the protection of the Government & are still going on in acts inconsistent with all good Government[;] yet these are the People that want to govern us, but I hope we shall never come under their power[. I]f we should they would serve us perhaps in the same manner they did some of our Brethren in New England.[23]

The Quakers noted that the Presbyterians had already gained control of the executive branch of government in some counties through Proprietary patronage, and they feared that by mobbing and violence, and increased numbers, they would gain control of the legislative branch as well.[24] Goaded by their apprehensions of a Presbyterian takeover, many Quakers abandoned their pose of detachment from partisan affairs and sought avenues by which to block this eventuality. The most efficacious way of checking the Presbyterians, as well as of ending the disputes between the Assembly and the governor, seemed to be to join in the burgeoning movement, led by Benjamin Franklin, to bring Pennsylvania under royal government, which thereby would end Proprietary patronage and hopefully would restore law and order to the province. The backers of the movement hoped that one of the effects of the change would be to give those who had promoted it first access to the appointive offices which would be created under the royal charter.

Franklin had long advocated a change in government as a means of ridding the colony of the recalcitrant Proprietors. It will

---

[23] John Reynell to James Shirley, 14/v/65, JRLB, 1762–67.
[24] James Pemberton to Samuel Fothergill, 13/vi/64, PP, 34 : 130–31; Thomas Wharton to Benjamin Franklin, in Thayer, *Pennsylvania Politics*, p. 104.

be recalled that this was an active issue as early as 1757. After John Penn refused the Assembly's tax bill in February, 1764, the movement gathered steam, and when the House adjourned in March it issued a statement of its case against the Proprietors. Despite Penn's acceptance of a later bill, in May the Assembly adopted a petition written by Franklin, which solicited the crown to take over the government of the colony. The petition had been circulating throughout the province in the intervening months; it had aroused an extremely high degree of political interest and had accumulated more than fifteen hundred signatures.[25]

As in 1757, however, some apprehension concerning a change in government was prompted by the Quakers' concern for the liberties and privileges guaranteed to Friends under the charter, including freedom from an established Episcopal church, access to the franchise, and eligibility for public office.[26] This concern was expressed in part by a separate petition, signed by Quakers, supporting the change of government, but asking that the rights and privileges granted by the charter be preserved.[27] For others, however, including Israel Pemberton, the possible threat to Friends' rights and privileges outweighed the admittedly strong arguments for change, and they refused to support the movement at all.[28]

Nevertheless, the connection of the movement with the Quaker party, the participation of a number of prominent politiques—including Henry Drinker, James Pemberton, and William Logan—plus the signatures of many Friends on the two petitions led to the identification of the Society with the campaign for a change in government. By the time of the Yearly Meeting, it was becoming evident that the public was not to be swayed by disclaimers from the Society concerning its putative connection with the Assembly

---

[25] Henry Drinker to Pigou and Robinson, 30/iv/64, HDLB, pp. 13–14; *Votes and Proceedings of the House of Representatives of the Province of Pennsylvania* (Harrisburg: Pennsylvania Archives, 8th ser., 1931–35), 7 : 5604 (hereafter cited as *Votes*).

[26] PMS, 21/vi/64.

[27] *Votes*, 7 : 5605–6.

[28] Israel Pemberton to David Barclay, 6/xi/64, PP, 17 : 103; John Reynell to Mildred and Roberts, 17/vi/65, JRLB, 1762–67.

Quakers, and that the latter were not inclined to submit to persuasion by the meetings to give up their seats. Consequently, the Yearly Meeting shifted its strategy with regard to the officeholders and began to concentrate on avoiding any occasion "of ministering grounds to our adversaries to charge us as a Body with a Connection with them." Of course, the issuance of statements dissociating the Society from the actions of the Assembly did no harm in this respect, and were continued, but the Meeting began also to counsel Friends more closely on the type of behavior best calculated to preserve the testimony inviolate while upholding the reputation of the Society.

The deviation of those Quakers who participated in the defense against the Paxton Boys was one of the principal concerns of the Yearly Meeting of 1764, in part because the bearing of arms was in violation of the peace testimony, but also because the action afforded "the adversaries of Truth" a stick with which to belabor the Quaker body. The committee which was appointed to consider the problem saw it as being bound up with the question of officeholding, for participation in government had led some Quakers to promote military service and even to countenance offensive war. Accordingly, the necessity was suggested of taking up the latter issue before the Paxton affair could be dealt with effectively. After due deliberation, the Meeting finally issued the following advice:

> It is earnestly & affectionately recommended to the Quarterly & Monthly meetings, and to Friends individually to bear in mind the Spirituality of our Profession that by living near the Divine Principle of Truth our Testimony thereto may be preferred to every temporal Consideration, and the Profits and Honours of the World neither sought after, nor too readily accepted by any of us and as the Execution of Offices of Trust, and the acting in Stations in Civil Government hath been for sometime past, and continues to be attended with great difficulties under the Circumstances of public affairs, Friends in their several Quarterly & Monthly meetings are desired to excite each other to care & Circumspection & timely to caution their Members against accepting of Offices in Legislation, or the Executive part of Government. . . . and the former advice of

this Meeting in the Year 1710 on this subject is particularly recommended to the Observation of Friends with this further admonition to be careful that we be not accessary in promoting or electing any of our Brethren to such Offices which may immediately lead them into the danger of deviating from the attentive Care incumbent on all of maintaining true Gospel Unity & Fellowship in the Church & with each other, and that the same way be manifested through the whole tenor of our Conduct and Conversation.[29]

The committee which issued the above advice was, as we have come to expect, a mixed one, including among its members such reformers as Anthony Benezet, John Churchman, John Woolman, and Isaac Child, and politiques like Israel Pemberton, Owen Jones, John Reynell, Aaron Ashbridge, and Peter Worrall. The reformers, of course, were very much dismayed by the turbulence which prevailed during 1764 and by the related attacks upon the Society of Friends and the reputation of Truth. Predictably, their action was to reaffirm their faith in the Divine Arm and to double their calls upon fellow Quakers to turn away from the snares of worldly pursuits and do likewise, more or less in the vein of the above statement.

John Churchman, for instance, wrote to James Pemberton:

> Time only can Make Manifest whether Friends have been right who have Joyn'd in applying to the King, to take the Government of this Province into his own Hand. For my own part it always has & Still remains to be Distressing to me, My Heart within me Seem'd Sensible, that a Patient Resignation to ye working of the Hand of Providence was our Safest Situation, as Professed followers of Him who Said my Kingdom is not of this world, Oh! may the Lord by the Power of his own Kingdom turn & over turn Untill he Come whose right it is to rule & Reign Even him whose Throne is forever & Ever the Scepter of whose Kingdom is a right Scepter for he Loveth Righteousness & therefore will be Exalted above all Men Forever.[30]

[29] PYM, 1764.
[30] vi/64, PP, 17 : 68.

Samuel Emlen counseled Friends to take up "a steady Course of weldoing to put to Silence the Ignorance of foolish Men, inasmuch as there is great Reason to believe that if when we do well we suffer & take it patiently this is acceptable with God & a Disposition he notices with Pleasure, resolving in his own Time not only to mitigate these afflictions but gloriously reward them."[31]

In much stronger terms, George Churchman castigated his fellow Quakers for having failed to heed the judgments of the past years by reforming their conduct and promoting the reformation to which God had called them.

> Hath an Ensign been held up to the Nations consistent with our principles on behalf of the peaceable kingdom of Jesus? Or rather, Hath not the Conduct of too many, instead of exalting his Standard, in the late troublesom times, had a different Effect? And have not visible marks of a greater declension in some instances, & with some professors rather increased from year to year, By mixing with the world, in the noises, Tumults, Parties and Confusions, that have appear'd, instead of dwelling alone, and preferring the Peace & Welfare of New Jerusalem to their chiefest Joy?[32]

An epistle from the Meeting for Sufferings hints at an implicit realization that Friends were more visible in times of crisis, their behavior subjected to greater public scrutiny, and that it was therefore more important for them to adhere closely to Quaker standards, in order to discredit the allegations of their adversaries.

> In this time of great Probation & public distress the minds of many are mercifully preserved in calmness & Composure, with desires for its more general prevalence, that we may manifest to the World our Relyance to be principally fixed in humble Resignation to the allwise disposer, whose Divine protection on many occasions has been eminently extended for our help and deliverance, having an assured hope whatever through the Course of his

---

[31] Samuel Emlen to Henry Drinker, 24/ix/64, Manuscript Letterbook RS 181, Philadelphia Yearly Meeting, Department of Records, Philadelphia, Pa., p. 13.
[32] 1764, GCJ, 2 : 51.

Providence is permitted to attend "that all things will work together for good, to them who dwell in his holy Fear."[33]

But what of the politiques? We know that as committee members and correspondents numbers of them were at least exposed to, and aware of, the sentiment for withdrawal from worldly politics and reliance upon Divine support which was so frequently expressed during the months of stress following the Paxton affair. The extent to which their behavior followed a course consistent with the tenor of the above-quoted statements will be discussed in some detail later. But, whether or not the instruction was followed, there is evidence that a lesson was in fact drawn from these events by the politiques, just as Israel Pemberton drew a lesson from the disappointments of 1758.

We know, first of all, that some of the politiques participated in the corporate expression of the sentiment we are concerned with. To take an immediate example, Abel James, Owen Jones, Isaac Zane, and James Pemberton all were members of the committee which issued the above-quoted epistle. There is also a record of an individual politique experiencing the same reaction, which bolsters the argument still further. Writing in June, 1765, before the events initiated early in 1764 had run their course, the active and influential Quaker leader John Reynell was moved to reflect: "We are now in a miserable Condition, but I hope the good hand & Arm that hath hitherto been with and preserved a Remnant, will still be with us & Support us through all our Difficulties. & I have no Doubt of it, if we closely attend to him & come up in our respective Places & Services, but we are got too much into the world & into the Spirit of it which hath brought a dimness on our Sion."[34] Here is another clear instance of a politique reacting to the strain of political crisis by condemning the worldly entanglements which rendered the Quakers susceptible to the stress imposed by adverse circumstances, and turning his view toward Divine Providence for direction and a way out of the difficulties which beset the Society.

[33] PMS to LMS, 3/ix/64.
[34] John Reynell to Mildred and Roberts, 17/vi/55, JRLB, 1762–67.

A striking introduction to events immediately following the Yearly Meeting of 1764 is contained in a journal entry made by George Churchman on his way home from Philadelphia.

On the way met Numbers of People going to the Election for Chester County. Thus we see many fellow men anxious for the management of State-Affairs according to their several Conceptions of rectitude in those Matters; whilst others believe they find sufficient to occupy their time in securing an Inheritance in that Kingdom which is not of this World, by walking in watchful humility before the Heavenly Father, who is the Great Controuler of Human Events; and who, because of the great backsliding of the Children of his People from the ways of Purity & peace, hath permitted Changes in the State of outward affairs in a once peaceful Land; whereby difficulties occur to minds possessed of tender Scruples, and doubts, concerning the Propriety of their mixing with others in anxiety about Political matters; lest through any polluting fellowship with Works of Darkness, their Interest with, & near access unto him who is the Author of Light, King of Kings, & Prince of Peace, should become lessen'd, when closer Trials, and further overturnings take Place, if that should be ever permitted.[35]

The election of 1764 aroused an extremely high degree of interest in Pennsylvania, for important issues were at stake. The Quaker, or Old Ticket, party stood on its advocacy of a changeover to royal government, while the Proprietary, or New Ticket, party, its ranks bolstered by aroused anti-Quakers and opponents of the change in government, at least saw a chance to make inroads into the solidly entrenched Quaker party majority in the Assembly. Because of their strong feelings on the change-of-government issue and a deep apprehension concerning the prospect of Presbyterian gains, Quaker politiques could not remain aloof from the election, and a number were prominently involved. James Pemberton and William Logan were active on behalf of the Old Ticket party; Israel Pemberton, often a maverick, feared that a change of

[35] 1/x/64, GCJ, 1 : 79–80.

government would threaten Quaker rights and privileges under the charter, and therefore he supported the New Ticket.

Although the sanguine expectations of the Proprietary partisans were not fully realized, the election did result in a gain of seats for their party, a gain made more dramatic by the fact that two of the places were won by the defeat, in Philadelphia City, of Benjamin Franklin and Joseph Galloway, the two most prominent leaders of the Quaker party after the retirement of Isaac Norris. The Old Ticket retained a substantial majority, however, and carried its campaign for royal government forward by sending Franklin to England to lobby before the Home Government.

Proprietary gains in 1764 frightened some of those who had deserted the Quaker party back into the ranks, as their fears of a Presbyterian takeover were played upon during the course of the year. A measure of the seriousness with which the New Ticket threat was regarded is the fact that James Pemberton himself stood for the Assembly during the election of 1765, tying George Bryan (later a prominent figure in the Revolution) in the balloting, and then defeating him in the runoff. In addition to his Proprietary opponent, James had to contend with his brother, Israel, who stood at the Court House on the day of the election and urged Friends not to vote. Upon hearing of his brother's activity, James went out and persuaded Israel to return home.[36]

James Pemberton explained his resumption of office in a letter to Dr. Fothergill and Hinton Brown, two of his London correspondents. There is no need to question the sincerity of the reluctance he expressed—his reasons for standing again, and the factors which influenced his decision, are clear enough.

> Thou wilt probably hear that my fellow citizens have again called me to the Arduous task of being one of their representatives. with reluctance I consented to their makg use of my name at the late Election from Experience of the difficulties of that Station, but thro the solicitation of ffrds & others in order to preserve unanimity to keep out an Envious Pre———n & to contribute as far as I might

[36] William Logan to John Smith, 1765, Smith Corresp., p. 209.

FOR THE REPUTATION OF TRUTH

be enabled to the preservation of our rights & Liberties as they had fixed upon me as a Candidate I was prevailed upon to decline persisting in a refusal;—I hope my passive complyance will not interfere with the agreement of our worthy ffrds. in London on our behalf. as the house is at present constituted, it has been with the approbation of Friends here, Should ffrds in London conclude it unadvised I shall be more uneasy. for wch reason I mention it & I shall be glad to have freely thy Sentiments hereon which will be of use to determine my resolutions next year if there Should be occasion—I can assure thee it will be with great diffidence I shall assume a seat in that house under the present circumstances of Public Affairs tho: ye Interest of our Society has Suffered in Some cases either through inattention or thro absence of members acquainted w. our circumstances.[37]

The basic objective professed by Pemberton and his backers was the protection of the interests of the Society and the rights and privileges of Friends. This goal was in fact the same as that pursued by Israel Pemberton, although the brothers apparently disagreed on the immediate means to be applied in the pursuit; Israel believed that a change of government, promoted by the Quaker party, represented the major threat, and he was willing to risk an increase in the power of the Presbyterians to prevent it, while James believed the opposite to be the case, and so pursued a different course. The essential point is that both men acted on their beliefs in the partisan arena.

James's letter makes explicit an essential point of contrast between his behavior and that of the reformers. In allowing himself to be persuaded to run, he succumbed to the worldly reasoning of others, where a Churchman or a Woolman would have heeded the reservations of conscience which Pemberton professed to have felt. The Friends who approved his candidacy could not have been those who subscribed to the beliefs expressed by George Churchman and quoted above. For them, the following statement would have represented a contradiction in terms, both in itself and in the

[37] James Pemberton to John Fothergill and Hinton Brown, 17/xii/65, PP, 34 : 137.

light of James's rejection of intimations from a higher intelligence when he chose to stand for election: "I avoid mixing with the Multitude in ye discussion of political points, thinking it safest to remain unbyass'd in my judgment, & Endeavourg to pursue what I apprehend will promote the Genl Good as far as I am capable to determine, & may be assisted by Wisdom Superior to my own, wch I find as necessary to be attended to in that Station, as in Business which may be look't upon of a more Religious nature."[38]

Nevertheless, it is of the highest significance that Pemberton should have felt the need to qualify his behavior so strongly to his correspondents, to profess to be attendant upon Superior Wisdom in the conduct of his office, and perhaps to attempt to be so. The critical stress of political events in the mid-1760s may have impelled him back into office because office afforded the kind of power he knew best how to employ, but it also made him more than ever acutely aware that the best hope for the Quakers lay in a power which came from a higher source. This awareness appears to have been obscured somewhat in 1767, when he relinquished the clerkship of the Yearly Meeting to George Churchman because of the press of his Assembly duties, but events were in motion which would bring it once again into relief.

---

[38] James Pemberton to John Fothergill, 14/i/66, *ibid.*, p. 147.

VIII

THE STAMP ACT, NON-IMPORTATION,
AND THE PRE-REVOLUTIONARY PERIOD

Although the inertia generated by the events of the preceding year-and-a-half continued to influence the political behavior of Quakers well past the middle of 1765, the external pressures upon the Society had diminished substantially by that time. The fervor aroused by the Paxton affair had waned, and the political situation in England made it inexpedient for Franklin to press his party's case for a change of government. The minutes of the Meeting for Sufferings, generally a good index to the externally imposed difficulties of the Society, show little or no business transacted from June through the remainder of the year. This is not to say that Pennsylvania as a whole was quiet during these months, but only that the predominant issues did not involve the Quakers as a body. There was, in fact, considerable political commotion in the province—as there was throughout the colonies—resulting from the controversial Stamp Act.

In itself, the Stamp Act was religiously neutral. Those who felt they were being oppressed by it, and who therefore resented and opposed it, did so as colonists and Englishmen. Thus John Reynell, who in June had reacted to the possibility of a change of government as a threat to the rights and privileges of Quakers, in November was found denouncing the Stamp Act as a deprivation of "our Rights & Priviledges as English Men, of being taxed only by our Representatives."[1] His approach, however, bore the Quaker stamp, for he suggested that it would be "best to stand still, & be quiet," while awaiting further developments.[2]

Apparently, the advent of a major political issue involving no direct threat to the Quakers as such, and on which both major parties were in agreement, enabled the Quakers to maintain a degree of moderation and reserve which was considerably closer to the standard urged by the Yearly Meeting than had theretofore been achieved. Upwards of eighty Friends signed the Non-Importation agreement, including eight who were members of the Meeting for Sufferings, but, as Sharpless points out, this kind of peaceful resistance accorded fairly well with the Quaker tradition.[3] Although exercised here within a worldly context, it was passive, quiet, and carried no incentive to officeholding. The moderation of Quaker merchants—meeting activists and worldly traders alike— helped to suppress any tendency toward violence on the part of the more "mad headed People" in the province while the law was in effect, and to prevent "immoderate rejoicing" on the occasion of its repeal.[4]

After the difficult times just past, the Meeting for Sufferings found in these developments grounds for self-congratulation.

Under the Violent ferment reigning at this time in the Colonies, the Observation that the People of Pensilvania & New Jersey have hitherto kept more free from Tumults & Riots than their Neighbours, gives us cause to believe that the Conduct & Conversation of Friends hath in some measure tended to promote this good effect. The divers occasions we have had to revive our Testimony against every breach of the Public Peace, have probably ministered instruction & reflection to many, & we often fervently desire that the difficulties we have been & are subject to, may still more evidently excite us to such an improvement of them as you justly Recom-

---

[1] John Reynell to John Southall, 23/xi/65, JRLB, 1762–67.

[2] John Reynell to Mildred and Roberts, 8/xi/65, *ibid.*

[3] Isaac Sharpless, *A Quaker Experiment in Government*, 2 vols. (Philadelphia, 1898), 2 : 77.

[4] John Reynell to Mildred and Roberts, 30/iv/66, JRLB, 1762–67; James Pemberton to John Fothergill, 7/vi/66, PP, 34 : 143.

mended to. Thus we should manifest that we not only remember the Faithfulness of our ancestors, & their Patience under suffering, but that we are sincerely Concerned to follow their Examples.[5]

Just the same, the Meeting took the added precaution of issuing a letter of advice to Friends, cautioning and exhorting them to stick close to their peaceable profession, and recalling the words of George Fox in 1685: "Whatever Bustlings & Troubles, or Tumults, or outrages should rise or be in the World, keep out of them, but keep in the Lords Power, & peaceable Truth that is over all, in which power you seek the Peace & Good of all Men, & live in the Love which God hath shed abroad in your hearts through Jesus Christ, in which Love no thing is able to separate you from God & Christ."[6]

The role of the Quakers in setting and maintaining a tone of moderation earned the Society the approbation of English Friends and the Home Government.[7] Here was one case in which the leaders of the Society were well pleased when a dominant role was attributed to Quakers.[8] As the Revolutionary movement progressed, this kind of positive reinforcement from England served to alienate the Quakers from their fellow Pennsylvanians—indeed, it already had begun to do so—but for the time being it was very welcome, after more than a decade of misrepresentation and criticism.[9]

Even the reformers saw cause for a measure of optimism in the way events had turned in 1766. The annual epistle from the Philadelphia Yearly Meeting to the Yearly Meeting of London was written by John Woolman, John Churchman, and Joseph White, a minister from Bucks County. Averring that "it is cause of rejoicing, when we can feel the circulation of Life to move in the various Branches from the fulness of the True Vine," the authors went on to express in interesting metaphorical terms an anxious

[5] PMS to LMS, 20/ii/66.
[6] PMS, 20/ii/66.
[7] *Ibid.*, 20/xi/66.
[8] Samuel Emlen to John Pemberton, 20/iii/66, PP, 18 : 108.
[9] Henry Drinker to Samuel Emlen, 20/ix/66, HDLB, pp. 18–19.

hope for the continuance of true Quaker behavior, invoking God's "government" to contrast implicitly with the world, and stressing the need for attentiveness to direction from the divine realm.

And dear Friends, may a Godly Jealousy more & more prevail among the Members of our Society every Where, that we may come to a true Examination by the Light of Christ, whether in singleness and fear we steadily under the power of his Cross, and faithfully labour for the increase of that Government and Peace which was foretold by the Prophet should never have an End, the which our Predecessors bore Testimony to, & in times of Trouble from without, witnessed it to be begun in them, and blessed be the Lord we trust there is a Remnant this day not only believe but can from Experience declare that the Kingdom of Christ is not of this world. May we therefore faithfully labour for the increase of this Righteous Kingdom & Government, under the immediate Instruction of Christ, who in every age, hath pointed out to his People the Business peculiar to them.

Should any of us now, whom he hath called to his Work suffer our Minds to be so taken up with the things of this World, & the unsettled state thereof, as not to attend humbly & singly to the leadings of Truth, we may ignorantly fail in the Performance of our duty, Labour and entangle ourselves in the Dark, & draw off from that holy habitation where the increase of this Government is Experienced.[10]

After the repeal of the Stamp Act, political calm prevailed in Pennsylvania, and the Society was able to turn its attention to routine internal matters. The major problem confronting the Meeting for Sufferings until approximately the middle of 1769 involved repairs to the meeting house in distant Charleston, South Carolina, which had come under the care of the Philadelphia Yearly Meeting after the local meeting there dwindled away.

These days of calm were numbered, however, by the passage of the Townshend Acts late in 1767. Opposition to these measures mounted steadily through 1768, and by mid-summer of the following year the Meeting for Sufferings lamented that, "the enemy of

[10] PYM to LYM, 1766.

our peace [has] so far prevailed as to interrupt the quiet which had subsisted."[11]

In contrast to New England, Philadelphia's initial reaction to the trade acts was marked by restraint. The merchants agreed that the measures were unwarranted and oppressive, but declined at first to endorse the Boston Resolves, for fear of the heavy losses a cessation of all trade with the mother country would engender. Boston, however, had made implementation of the Resolves conditional upon their acceptance by New York and Philadelphia, so the program of non-importation was forestalled by the Pennsylvanians' stance.[12] Philadelphia's position was in no small part determined by that of the Quaker merchants, who still dominated the city's trade, and they in turn were encouraged in their moderation by Friends in England. Both groups were influenced in a negative way by the Bostonians, whose radical spokesmen and propensity for mob action were viewed with distrust by the more temperate Quakers.[13] Dr. Fothergill had written earlier to James Pemberton: "By what means can the increase of P.b.t.n. [Presbyterian] power in America be most effectually checked consistently with liberty of conscience and the genius of British freedom? I see that sometime America will be P.b.t.n. a persuasion altogether intolerant, and I could wish to retard it, as long as possible."[14] This purpose, shared by most Pennsylvania Quakers, would not be served by succumbing to the pressure of the local Presbyterians to join in measures promoted by New England Presbyterians.

Still, there were other avenues by which opposition could be expressed, for unquestionably opposition to the Townshend Acts existed among Quaker merchants—not as Quakers, but as "Free born Englishmen."[15] In November, ten Philadelphia traders (four of them Friends) addressed a memorial to British merchants and

[11] PMS to LMS, 5/viii/69.
[12] Arthur J. Mekeel, "The Quakers in the American Revolution" (Ph.D. diss., Harvard University, 1939), p. 142.
[13] James Pemberton to John Fothergill, 20/x/68, PP, 34 : 154; John Fothergill to Israel Pemberton, 5/vii/68, EC, 2 : 58.
[14] 10/v/66, EC, 2 : 54.
[15] John Reynell to Henry Groth, 2/ii/69, JRLB, 1767–69.

manufacturers, enlisting their aid in pressing for repeal of the Townshend Acts. John Reynell, one of the four Friends, expressed great pride at having been the first to sign the epistle.[16]

By the summer of 1769, when it became apparent that no relief was forthcoming from Great Britain, the sentiment in favor of non-importation finally prevailed, and an agreement was signed by most of the merchants in the city. The Non-Importation Association appointed a committee to carry out the provisions of the agreement, and to correspond with merchant groups in other colonies. Eight Quakers were named to this committee, including its chairman, John Reynell.[17]

Shortly after its inception, the Non-Importation Association experienced its first test, when a cargo of malt consigned to the Quaker brewer Amos Strettel arrived. Strettel applied to the committee for permission to land the cargo, and the committee convened a general meeting of the inhabitants of the city to decide the matter. The city's brewers, including three Quakers, settled the issue by declaring that they would not use the malt; permission was denied, and the ship sailed for Ireland.

This action by the Association marked a visible turning point in the position of the Society with regard to the Revolutionary movement in Pennsylvania. The coercive and extralegal action of the Association deeply disturbed most of the leaders of the Society, who were concerned that Friends stay clear of such measures. Israel Pemberton in particular was zealous in his opposition to the methods used.[18]

Of particular concern within the Society was the impropriety of Quakers allowing their actions to be directed by decisions of the mob in a public meeting. On the one hand, such gatherings were not imbued with the selflessness, peaceable spirit, and attendance upon divine direction which were supposed to characterize Quaker decision-making by groups as well as by individuals.[19] On the

---

[16] John Reynell to Henry Reynell, 15/v/69, *ibid.*, 1769–70.
[17] Mekeel, "The Quakers in the American Revolution," p. 35.
[18] William Logan to John Smith, vii/69, Smith Corresp., p. 272.
[19] PMS, 1/ix/69 (Epistle of Advice and Caution).

other hand, and more important in terms of the history of the American Revolution, the Quaker meeting leadership lacked confidence in the peoples' ability to decide wisely in matters of such importance.[20] The politiques in particular believed that the public influence of the Quaker elite was being eroded by the leaders of the lower-class mobs, and were disturbed by their own waning influence in public affairs. Israel Pemberton, for example, described the calling together of the inhabitants as "wild" in deploring their actions to his brother, John.[21] The Philadelphia Monthly Meeting advised its members "wholly to withdraw from and keep [out?] of" the further measures of the committee,[22] and the Yearly Meeting expressed the fervent hope that "the Remembrance of that Purity of life we profess, be so impress'd upon our minds, that our inward breathings may be to him who alone can preserve us in safety from the subtle wiles and allurements of the adversary, who is Endeavouring to rend and divide, by drawing the unwary into practices inconsistent with our holy profession, by joining with the Spirit of the world, in which is noise & Tumult, the instructive language of the spirit of Truth is disregarded, and the Beauty and Excellency thereof hid, to the great loss of such."[23]

It is illuminating to note the implicit assumption in this passage and elsewhere[24] that Friends needed to be "drawn into a conduct inconsistent with our religious principles." Phrasing the problem in this way drew attention to the dangers of involvement with outsiders, excluded the possibility that sincere Friends would engage in such conduct of their own accord, and suggested the necessity of building up a resistance to outside influence.

The Society's spokesmen suggested two additional reasons for Quakers to remain aloof from the measures employed by the Non-Importation Association.

---

[20] PMS to LMS, 5/viii/69.
[21] Theodore Thayer, *Israel Pemberton: King of the Quakers* (Philadelphia, 1943), p. 206.
[22] PMS to LMS, 5/vii/69.
[23] PYM to LYM, 1769.
[24] PMS, 29/vii/69.

We therefore seriously exhort all carefully to guard against being drawn into measures which may minister occasion for any to represent us as a people departing from the principles we profess, and that such who have been so incautious as to enter into engagements, the terms and tendency of which they had not fully considered, may avoid doing any thing inconsistent with our principles, ever bearing in mind the deep obligation we are and have been under to the King and his loyal Ancestors for the indulgence and lenity granted to our predecessors and continued to us.[25]

This was a caution learned from the bitter experience of the Paxton confrontation and the pamphlet war of 1765, as well as from the campaign for a change of government, but with one new aspect. Continuation under the Proprietary charter was preferable to coming under direct control of the crown, but it was the crown, after all, which had granted the charter for the Quaker colony, and which could revoke it if the colony grew too rebellious. If it came to a showdown between the liberties the Quakers already enjoyed and the ones for which the radicals were contending, those concerned for the welfare of the Society would be compelled to preserve the former.

The combined fear of misrepresentation and a sense that initiative and influence had been lost to other elements in society had extremely important consequences for the future of Quaker political behavior in Pennsylvania. Some of the Friends who joined in the non-importation program initially did so ostensibly because their former weight in provincial affairs had led to their being solicited by others to take part, and because they hoped to exercise a moderating influence on the situation as they had done at the time of the Stamp Act. When it became apparent, however, that they could not moderate the program of the Association, or keep its activities within the bounds set by Quaker principles, a number of the politiques, prompted by advice from the meetings, curtailed or ceased their participation. Henry Drinker, for example, withdrew from the Philadelphia Merchants' Committee and announced

[25] *Ibid.*, 1/ix/69 (Epistle of Advice and Caution).

his determination to refuse nomination for public positions thereafter.[26]

The political atmosphere was such that even James Pemberton
advertised his intention not to stand again for the Assembly. Much
to the disgust of his brother John, however, he allowed himself to
be persuaded to alter this decision; and he was re-elected for one
last term, after which he did decline to run.[27] By 1771, this most
political of politiques was a leading spokesman for Quaker withdrawal from civil affairs, although he occasionally found it difficult to adhere to this position himself.[28]

The Yearly Meeting of 1770 continued the process of institu-
tionalizing the dissociation of Friends from the Revolutionary
movement by reinforcing the barriers against "mixing with those
who are not convinced of our Religious principles, in their human
policy and contrivance," and urging its members to "seek after
Quietude and stilness of Mind, in order that under the direction
of true Wisdom, we may be Enabled to administer advice to any
of our Brethren, who may be inadvertently drawn aside to join
with or countenance . . . the Commotions prevailing." Above all,
"The cause and Reputation of Truth" was emphasized as the
paramount consideration.

Apparently, the efforts of the Society's leaders to draw Friends
inward were proving successful to a degree, for the Yearly Meeting was "thought to be the largest ever, presided over by love and
harmony."[29] This is confirmed by Joseph Oxley, an English minister, who was in attendance at the gathering.[30] James Pemberton
wrote to Dr. Fothergill that numbers of Friends were uniting in
an engagement and concern for the preservation of others, thus
indicating a heightened and active desire for internal stability,[31]

---

[26] Henry Drinker to Abel James, 16/v/70, cited in Mekeel, "The Quakers in the
American Revolution," p. 44.

[27] John Pemberton to James Pemberton, 2/x/69, PP, 21 : 75.

[28] James Pemberton to John Fothergill, 3/v/71, *ibid.*, 34 : 159.

[29] PMS to LMS, 21/ii/71.

[30] *A Journal of the Life and Gospel Labours of Joseph Oxley* (London, 1837),
pp. 317–18.

[31] 3/v/71, PP, 34 : 159.

and the Yearly Meeting of 1771 took comfort from the progress being made in the separation of Friends from "all unnecessary concerns."

From the very beginning of the second Non-Importation campaign, the leaders of the Society recognized and conceded the grievances of the people, and even reluctantly granted the expedience of the Non-Importation measures themselves. But as commotion and disorder began to trouble the colony, the more committed Friends were driven to place ever more emphasis upon the need for divine direction and to search the environment for the cause of the spreading lawlessness which seemed to presage heavier trials to come. Once again they found the explanation in the idea of divine retribution for the degeneracy of a backslidden people, but this time the blame was placed not upon their own Society, but on the people at large, and on the government for failing to check their decline into immorality.

The Quakers, of course, shared the general Puritan abhorrence of profane amusements, such as gaming, stage plays, horse racing, and lotteries, as well as of the moral abuses of drunkenness, swearing, and profanation of the Sabbath. From time to time in earlier years, the Society had assumed the role of moral guardian to the province by petitioning for administrative or judicial measures against one or another of these abuses.[32] Now, in 1770, the appeals took on another dimension.

During the course of 1769, first the Philadelphia Monthly Meeting and then the Philadelphia Quarterly Meeting had addressed memorials to Governor Penn condemning the stage plays and horse races which were being held on the outskirts of the city. When their efforts proved unavailing, the problem devolved upon the Meeting for Sufferings, which was to petition the governor "on behalf of Friends in General in these Provinces."[33]

---

[32] PMS, 22/v/59; *Votes and Proceedings of the House of Representatives of the Province of Pennsylvania* (Harrisburg: Pennsylvania Archives, 8th ser., 1931–35), 6 : 5288; PQM, 4/v/67; Thomas J. Wertenbaker, *The Golden Age of Colonial Culture*, 2nd ed. (Ithaca, N.Y., 1959), pp. 79–80.

[33] PMS, 21/xii/69.

The authors of the Meeting's address reminded the governor that it lay within the province of the administration to do away with corrupt amusements, and that the good order of government itself depended upon the care taken in removing these causes of evil. Neglect thereof would not only diminish the government's authority over the people, but bring down the wrath of God upon the guilty land for the "wildness and looseness" of its inhabitants. Although the governor gave no expectation of discouraging either the plays or the races, the Meeting's representatives expressed satisfaction at having done their moral duty.[34] This was an important manifestation of a nascent tendency, on the part of the Meeting for Sufferings at least, to adopt the posture of the reformers in doing right, resigning itself to God for vindication, and refusing to countenance the rebuffs bestowed by the outside world. The address also represented the first major statement of what was to become the orthodox Quaker theory of the cause of the Revolutionary War.

John Penn relinquished his office for two years in 1771, and was replaced during the interim by his kinsman Richard Penn. The task of paying the Society's respects to the new governor fell, as usual, to the Meeting for Sufferings, which appointed a committee to prepare and deliver an appropriate address. Taking advantage of the opportunity, the committee devoted a major portion of the address to impressing upon the governor the need "to suppress vice & immorality, and to promote Piety & virtue, the practice of which Essentially concerns the happiness of the People, whose Civil & religious rights, & Liberties being maintained by thy Care, may tend to unite all Ranks in the same Noble purposes."[35] In effect, these suggestions represented a bipartite program by which the government could counteract the rising tide of revolutionary agitation: first, by suppressing vice and immorality, which fostered violence and dissidence; and second, by protecting the rights and liberties which were the cause of popular concern. Unfortunately,

34 *Ibid.*, 18/i/70.
35 *Ibid.*, 22/xi/71.

as the Revolutionary movement grew steadily more violent, the leaders of the Society became preoccupied with the first factor and lost sight of the second, thereby alienating many of their fellow citizens and large numbers of their co-religionists as well. Moreover, the commitment to the moral interpretation of the Revolution was self-perpetuating, for, once having chosen to ignore the social and economic factors involved, the Quaker leaders were unable to gain an understanding of them thereafter, and so relied to an ever-increasing extent upon a view which ordered things in a way they believed they could deal with.

Much earlier in this work, the point was emphasized that activity of a negative kind, aimed at effecting a disengagement from the common political arena, must nevertheless be viewed as political activity in its own right. This perspective is particularly important in connection with the behavior of the Quakers during the years immediately preceding the Revolution. We are by now accustomed to viewing the reformers in this light, but during the early and mid-1770s the behavior of the politiques underwent a reorientation which demands certain discriminations we have not hitherto been required to make, or at least to emphasize, in connection with that group. As the politiques came to urge their fellow Quakers more and more frequently not to join with others in "contending for liberty," and to rely upon divine guidance alone, it is tempting to conclude that they were withdrawing from the outside political activity which they had for so long been attempting to reconcile with their role within the Society. To the extent that they did in fact curtail their political cooperation with others, this conclusion would be valid, but on the whole it represents an oversimplification of their behavior, as the ensuing discussion will attempt to show.

An incident which occurred in Philadelphia in June, 1773, is of interest as an indication of the nature of the political involvement of the Society at that point. One of the major targets of popular resentment in the city was the privileged, firmly entrenched, self-coopting city corporation, whose wealthy members were responsible to no one but themselves. In mid-1773, this body made the highly unpopular decision to erect a shambles in Market Street, and resolved to carry it through despite the widespread opposition the measure aroused on the part of the inhabitants. The affair quickly advanced to a general disputation of the powers and privileges of the corporation itself, and violent measures were threatened by the aroused citizenry. Fearing that Friends might "be unwarily drawn in, to countenance acts of Violence," some of the leaders of the Society felt impelled to intervene. One committee was appointed to go among the members of the Society and "excite them to stillness & peace," and another, including James Pemberton, was sent to wait on the mayor and aldermen, "to persuade them to exert their Influence with the Corporation to reconsider their Resolution, & agree to have the matter put in a way to be Judically determined & in the mean time to desist from further progress in building."[36]

It is apparent from James Pemberton's account of the affair that he and his colleagues were still disposed to take a hand in external political matters; they did not confine themselves to influencing Quakers alone, but went out to effect a settlement between the dissident elements and the city officials to whom they still had access. They aimed at keeping Friends out of un-Quakerly activity, but were themselves fully involved in the issue; there was no suggestion of merely sitting still and trusting to God. More severe trials were to be faced before a real disengagement could be effected.

[36] James Pemberton to Phineas Pemberton, 26/vi/73, PP, 25 : 39.

IX

ON THE VERGE OF THE REVOLUTION

While the Revolutionary movement was giving rise to new political forces in Pennsylvania, the Quakers continued to be viewed by the populace as a political factor to be reckoned with. After General Gage landed in Boston, in May, 1774, to enforce the Boston Port Act, Paul Revere journeyed to Philadelphia to mobilize support for the New Englanders and to promote a united opposition to British oppression. Revere met with some of the more radical of the local leaders, and the meeting ultimately resulted in the appointment of a committee of twenty prominent citizens charged with requesting the governor to convene the Assembly in order to consider the emergency, and with summoning a general meeting of the Philadelphia inhabitants if circumstances required. Six of the twenty were members of the Society of Friends, but none were active in Society affairs.[1]

The committee of twenty invited representatives from each of the city's religious groups to participate in planning the general meeting, which would be held at the State House. Although the leaders of the Society of Friends were known to be opposed to the radicals and to the holding of mass meetings, their participation

---

[1] Theodore Thayer, *Pennsylvania Politics and the Growth of Democracy* (Philadelphia, 1953), pp. 155–58.

was desired in order at least to prevent their blocking the measures which the meeting was likely to adopt. Six Quakers were invited, of whom Owen Jones, James Pemberton, George Roberts, and Thomas Wharton attended. The following is Pemberton's account.

> Some Friends were fix'd upon, and particularly solicited to attend the proposed Conference, the Propriety of which being doubtful, they communicated their Sentiments to some of the most Judicious of their Brethren, by whose Advice, and the Consideration of the Possibility of their having some Influence to Correct if not Prevent, ill-timed and rash Proceedings, they were prevail'd upon to comply with the solicitations to give their attendance, but on hearing the Debates & Proposals made at the Conference, the impropriety of any Members of our Society meeting in such a Mixture to Confer on Affairs of this Kind, became still more Evident, so that after giving our Opinion and Advice as it appeared necessary, and finding they were much divided in Sentiment, we forbore further attendance. . . .[2]

The above probably refers only to Owen Jones and James Pemberton; Wharton and Roberts both accepted appointment to the Committee of Correspondence set up at the State House meeting, as did nine other Quakers, many of whom were later disowned for their Revolutionary activities. It is a measure of James Pemberton's political prominence that he too was appointed to the Committee of Correspondence, although he did not attend and was known to be opposed to the proceedings. He immediately declared his unwillingness to take part, and prevented publication of his appointment in the newspapers.[3] The others all agreed to serve, and persisted in their decision when visited by a committee of the Meeting for Sufferings, which urged their resignation.[4]

Apparently as a result of Pemberton's and Jones's experience, the Meeting for Sufferings came to an important realization con-

---

[2] James Pemberton to several Friends in London, 1/vi/74, MS 325, Quaker Collection, Haverford College Library, Haverford, Pa.

[3] *Ibid.*

[4] Arthur J. Mekeel, "The Quakers in the American Revolution" (Ph.D. diss., Harvard University, 1939), p. 61.

cerning the Society's position vis-à-vis the Revolutionary movement.

> A Considerable time was spent in this meeting in a weighty Consideration of the fluctuating State of People's minds under the situation of Public affairs[;] it appeared to be the sense of this meeting that it would be safest, & most Consistent for us as a Religious society to keep as much as possible from mixing with the people in their human policy & Contrivance & to forbear meeting in their Public Consultations, as snares, & danger may arise from meetings of that kind, however well-disposed particulars may be to mitigate, & soften the violent disposition too prevalent.[5]

This amounted to nothing less than an official foreclosure of the moderating approach the Quaker politiques had cherished since the days of the Friendly Association. According to the Meeting for Sufferings minute, the decision was based on the realization that, regardless of worthwhile motives, engagement in public affairs entailed the risk of being drawn into spiritually dangerous activities. This, of course, was hardly a new theme within the Society. James Pemberton's statement, however, suggests another factor growing out of the current situation, one far more significant in immediate terms. The events surrounding the State House meeting represented the first time that the Quaker politiques, although willing and prepared to participate in external political matters, were forced to concede from the outset that they could not hope to influence the course of events in the direction they wished them to take. The Revolutionary movement was the most important domestic issue of the day, and circumstances were such that all the initiative and influence belonged to others, either non-Quakers or Quakers upon whom the Society exercised only a weak, tenuous hold.

It is true that the revolutionaries themselves viewed the politiques as powerful, a political force to be reckoned with, but the crucial point is that it was the new leaders who held the initiative

---

[5] PMS, 16/vi/74.

and set the terms on which the Quakers were free to participate. The succession of crises beginning in the 1750s, together with the reformist movement within the Society, had brought the politiques to the point where they were particularly sensitive to the dangers of spiritual contamination inherent in worldly politics; attempts to moderate the Revolutionary movement from within the Society were out of the question. The Society had already attempted to purify the political atmosphere by treating the manifestations of public discontent as a moral problem, but the approach was indirect, and not even the instrumental ends (such as suppressing stage plays or horse races) were achieved. In mid-June, 1774, Society leaders found themselves in a position which allowed them *no alternative approach* to the current situation other than to remain as spectators, though not unaffected ones, and attempt to preserve the Discipline within the Society.

To this end, a large committee was appointed by the Yearly Meeting to prepare an epistle to all Friends, urging them under the present trying circumstances to put their trust in God alone and conduct themselves in accordance with their principles. In the communication, the committee drew a strong parallel between the unsettled conditions which then prevailed and the situation which had existed in England at the time of the church's founding: both were periods of spiritual and moral decline, commotion, and war; yet, despite the evil and oppressive treatment inflicted upon them, the First Publishers of Truth had been able to "put to Silence the Ignorance of foolish men" and to effect the religious reformation which gave birth to the Society of Friends. The first generation of Friends had remonstrated against the deprivation of their rights, and their appeals had gained strength from the fact that they showed themselves to be a people who, despite their grievances and sufferings, would not become involved in plots, insurrections, or conspiracies against the government which oppressed them, but rather stood as models of morality to the world. Ultimately, through God's grace, they had won the full enjoyment of their civil and religious liberties in the charter granted to Pennsylvania. The lesson to Friends in 1774 was quite clear: do not contend for

144

your rights in non-Quaker ways, but follow the example of your ancestors. Moreover, the epistle continued, the king had granted the colony to William Penn, and thus Friends owed a debt of gratitude to the crown. It was therefore incumbent upon members of the Society to discourage disrespect or expressions of disfavor to the king, to manifest dislike for writings which expressed such sentiments, and to remain clear of attempts to defraud the king of his dues, whether or not the exactions appeared to be just.

Their solicitude for their own rights and privileges apparently blinded the authors to the inconsistency of refusing to pay provincial taxes, which might be used for objectionable ends—namely, defense—and enjoining the payment of duties which were believed to be unjust in their own right, in addition to being levied for the same purpose as the mixed taxes—that is, for the funding of the colonial defense effort. The times were not conducive to consistency, however, and the duties were not considered by anyone to be in violation of basic Quaker principles. Besides, the grievances stemming from the British colonial policy were viewed as merely the immediate and outward cause of the prevailing turmoil; the real causes of the animosity and discord were "Vice & immorality & temptations to promote them in various appearances [which] have of late years much increased, & [are] too little discountenanced by those who are in authority."[6]

The Society's leaders received and continued to seek the approval of their English brethren for their detachment from the Revolutionary ferment surrounding them.[7] Daniel Mildred even noted with satisfaction that the Home Government itself would undoubtedly see the Quakers' behavior as redounding to the great credit of the Society. Unfortunately, this same behavior provoked quite different reactions from the Friends' fellow Pennsylvanians.

The epistle, in fact, kept the Society very much in the public eye. Quakers still had an important place in Philadelphia society, and their annual meeting was an important event. Consequently, the

---

[6] PMS to LMS, 21/vii/74.
[7] Ibid.; Daniel Mildred to John Pemberton, 26/vii/74, PP, 26 : 128; James Pemberton to Daniel Mildred, 6/xii/74, PP, 27 : 30.

general epistles issued by the Yearly Meeting assumed the status of public documents, and circulated beyond the limits of the Society. Christopher Marshall, a disowned Quaker and one of the leading patriots in the city, made the following entry in his diary on September 24, 1774: "This same day began the Quakers' Yearly Meeting ... from which meeting, they sent forth an epistle that has given great offence to the friends of freedom and liberty in America."[8]

The antagonism of the patriots toward the leaders of the Society was further aggravated by the activities of the group of nominal Quakers who were vigorous participants in the Revolutionary movement. These men—Thomas Mifflin, Clement and Owen Biddle, Timothy Matlack, and others—were visible, active, and widely known to the Quakers. For example, Anthony Benezet recorded the reaction of Patrick Henry, who was in Philadelphia for the first Continental Congress in September, 1774, to an explanation of Quaker pacifism.

> To this, with seriousness, he replied, that it was strange to him, to find some of the Quakers manifesting a disposition so different from that I had described.
> I reminded him, that many of them had no other claim to our principles, than as they were children or grandchildren of those who professed those principles. I suppose his remark principally arose from the violent spirit which some under our profession are apt to show, more particularly in the congress, amongst whom I understand one of the deputies from your city [Burlington], and one from ours, appear as principles for promoting such means.[9]

When the Pennsylvania Assembly voted unanimous approval of the proceedings of the Congress, some observers were led to believe that Friends as a body were swinging over to the colonial side, for the House contained eleven Quaker members. The fact

[8] *Extracts from the Diary of Christopher Marshall*, ed. William Duane (Albany, N.Y., 1877), p. 10 (hereafter cited as *Diary*).
[9] Anthony Benezet to Samuel Allinson, 23/x/74, in George S. Brookes, *Friend Anthony Benezet* (Philadelphia, 1937) p. 322.

that these Quakers found it possible to give their active support to the colonial cause made the continued aloofness or opposition manifested by the others still more irksome to the anti-British activists. It was the same old situation of the Society's being judged by the worldly political behavior of nominal members, although this time the pressure stemmed from the political allies of the deviant Quakers, not their enemies.

The Society responded, as it had many times in the past, by appointing a committee of the Meeting for Sufferings to treat with the Quakers in the Assembly and urged them to alter their behavior.[10] Not surprisingly, the mission was unsuccessful, and the Meeting next resorted to another general epistle to Friends, urging them to "consider the End & purpose of every measure to which they are desired to become parties, & with great Circumspection & Care . . . guard against joining in any for the asserting & maintaining our Rights & Liberties which on mature Deliberation appear not to be dictated by that 'Wisdom which is from above which is pure peaceable gentle & full of Mercy & good Fruits.' "[11] The Meeting warned that anyone who manifested a disposition to contend for liberty in any manner contrary to the peaceful profession of Friends would be dealt with according to the Discipline of the Society.

The epistle was accompanied by a covering letter in which the activities of the Continental Congress and the Non-Importation Association were condemned as being "in their Nature & Tendency . . . manifestly repugnant to the peaceable Principles of our Christian Profession, & subversive of the Laws & order of the Government under which we live."[12] The letter went on to reaffirm the 1710 minute of the Yearly Meeting warning against participation in government, and to enjoin the elders, overseers, and other guardians of Truth to treat with those implicated in the Revolutionary measures either through first promoting them, consenting to them, or acting as committeemen to execute them.

[10] PMS, 15/xii/74.
[11] *Ibid.*, 5/i/75.
[12] *Ibid.*, 19/i/75.

Five days later, the Meeting for Sufferings issued yet another statement of opposition to the Revolutionary movement. This testimony was the most tendentious, defiant, and provocative in the series issued in rapid succession by the Meeting. The following excerpt gives some idea of its content:

> The Divine Principle of Grace & Truth which we profess, leads all who attend to its dictates to demean themselves as peaceable Subjects and to discountenance, and avoid every measure tending to excite disaffection to the King as Supreme Majistrate or to the legal Authority of his Government, to which purpose many of the late political Writings & Addresses to the People appearing to be calculated, we are led by a sense of Duty to declare our entire Disapprobation of them, their Spirit, & Temper, being not only contrary to the Nature & Precepts of the Gospel, but destructive of the Peace & Harmony of Civil Society, disqualify Man in these Times of Difficulty, for the wise & judicious Consideration & promoting of such measures as would be most effectual for reconciling Differences or obtaining the Redress of Grievances. . . .
>
> We are . . . incited by a sincere Concern for the Peace & Welfare of our Country publickly to declare against every Usurpation of Power & Authority, in Opposition to the Laws & Government, & against all Combinations Insurrections Conspiracies & illegal Assemblies, & as we are restrained from them by the conscientious Discharge of our Duty to Almighty God, by whom Kings Reign & Princes decree Justice, we hope through his Assistance & favour, to be enabled to maintain our Testimony against any Requisitions which may be made of us, inconsistent with our religious principles, & the Fidelity we owe to the King & his Government as by Law established. . . .[13]

The testimony naturally infuriated the patriots, and provoked considerable ill-feeling against the Society among those who favored the Revolution and supported the Continental Congress.[14] By way of perspective, it may be noted that the testimony was

---

[13] *Ibid.*, 24/i/75.
[14] Marshall, *Diary*, p. 13; Mekeel, "The Quakers in the American Revolution," p. 77.

approved and commended by Governor Murray of Virginia, one of the most bitterly hated opponents of the colonial cause.[15] Two days after the testimony was issued, a letter containing the following passage was received from Dr. Fothergill in England; it was written, of course, with reference to earlier events, but, by virtue of the time of its arrival, it would have served to reinforce the position taken in the testimony.

> We may safely we think inform thee that the conduct of Friends in general on your side the water has been prudent—nay more, praiseworthy;—to keep in any degree of order, so many young fiery, unexperienced persons, as must be growing up among you, is indeed an arduous task, and in which you have been enabled to succeed, we doubt not, beyond your own expectations. Government is well informed of your sentiments and conduct—they coincided so much with their wishes, that you may be assured they are pleased with your conduct. They wish that all America was like minded. Indeed our principles lead to this patient acquiescence. We have actively no share in legislation. We must therefore submit to the powers that are.[16]

The difficulty was, what constituted "the powers that are"? Nominally, the colony was still subject to the Home Government and the crown. In addition, there was still considerable pro-British sentiment in the colony, so the Quaker position was not without the support of other "considerate People," as the Meeting for Sufferings preferred to think of them.[17] On the other hand, political initiative and control were rapidly passing to the revolutionaries, in whose eyes the Quakers were showing themselves more and more to be enemies of the patriots' cause. A closer consideration of the strength of popular feeling would have spared the Society considerable suffering in the difficult years which followed.

Nor would a less vocal, less denunciatory stance necessarily have required a compromise of Quaker principle. On the contrary,

[15] Edward Stabler to James Pemberton, 16/v/75, PP, 27 : 144.
[16] John Fothergill to James Pemberton, 26/i/75, *ibid.*, 34 : 171.
[17] PMS to LMS, 25/iii/75.

viable alternatives were advanced within the Society by members of unquestionable religious integrity, who were nevertheless made uneasy by the vigorously censorious statements issued in the name of the church. For instance, Samuel Sansom, four times a representative of the Philadelphia Quarterly Meeting at the Yearly Meeting, approved the Society's efforts to keep its members out of improper activities, but registered serious reservations against the tendency of certain leaders to openly condemn "the general Proceedings of the People." He believed that Providence would overrule such of the popular measures as were contrary to God's word, and that Friends ought, therefore, to trust in Him, "and not suffer their Zeal to carry them beyond the Bounds of true Knowledge." Referring to the sentiment for abolition of the slave trade manifested by a segment of the Revolutionary party, Sansom asked, "if that only, or if that in some Degree, should be the happy Consequence of our present Difficulties, who is there among us who can say that the Hand of Providence is not in these Things?" All in all, he argued,

> The Zeal of Friends for the Support of our Testimony has been great, many Pieces of Advice & Caution have been written, printed, & dispers'd among the Society on various Occasions: The Yearly Meeting Epistle (which I much approve of) will be spread abroad, and will effectively invalidate any Imputation that Friends have joined as a People in the late general Measures[;] what then have we to do but be quiet? we are not forced to be active in these Measures, I pray that none may officiously & unnecessarily attempt to counteract them[. A]ll things I hope will work together for Good, and that a happy Union & Harmony may succeed our present Difficulties.[18]

Samuel Wetherill, who was later to be the leading spirit in the organization of the Free Quakers, also wrote to James Pemberton to voice his reservations concerning the Society's position. Noting that the Quakers were coming to be widely regarded as friends of the corrupt ministry and enemies of the people, Wetherill urged,

[18] Samuel Sansom to James Pemberton, 5/xi/74, PP, 27 : 9.

for the credit of the Society, that they act to change this impression. "I have thought with Respect to our society on this Publick affair, that we ought to be as Watchmen on the Walls, and that there is something due from us both to the King and to the Publick Cause, and altho we ought to treat all such whom Providence has seen meet to permit to Rule over us with the greatest Respect, yet when ever they deviate from the Righteous Law of Justice in which Kings ought to Rule, it is the Right of the People and their Duty to be Plain & Honest in letting them know wherein." He went on to suggest that, "a Decent & Dutyfull Petition to our Sovereign on this Occasion is in my opinion Very Requisite from us as a People."[19]

Such a petition would not in all likelihood have appeased the radicals in the Revolutionary party, but there were many of more moderate outlook who would have viewed it with considerably more sympathy than would be granted the diatribes the Society did issue. Moreover, it would have been well within the limits of doctrinal acceptability and consistent with Quaker tradition to have presented a remonstrance of the kind suggested by Wetherill. Indeed, the Society's pronouncements at the time alluded to the remonstrance of their ancestors against the injustice and oppression of the government, but the leaders failed to take the next step and issue a petition to the king on their own behalf.

Wetherill's letter offers an important clue as to why the Society did not in fact make any concessions to the Revolutionary movement in its public pronouncements. Apparently, he expressed his opinions in a session of the Philadelphia Quarterly Meeting, but felt that he had been misunderstood. "[I would]," he said, "have attempted to explain myself, but fearing that there might be some so impatient as to get a little disturbed themselves and then blame me as an unsettler of the Meeting, a fear of this kind sealed my mouth as to any further matter. There are some that I wish to be understood by, & take this means to make myself so to thy Self, as one of them."[20]

[19] 4/ii/75, *ibid.*, p. 67.
[20] *Ibid.*

Samuel Sansom's letter, it will be recalled, was also addressed to James Pemberton, who seems to have been at or near the center of Quaker opposition to the Revolutionary movement, as were his brother Israel, Abel James, and Henry Drinker.[21] While it is difficult to document concretely, there are strong indications in the tone and content of the epistles, in the glimpses we have had of the meetings in which current affairs were an issue (such as the session mentioned by Wetherill), as well as in the events of the preceding six or seven years, that the public denunciation of the Revolutionary movement by the Society was actually the expression of a relatively small group of Quaker politiques, and was imposed upon the Society through the force of their influence and their importance within the church organization. These men were, we remember, wealthy, conservative, socially influential, jealous of Quaker prerogative and privilege in Pennsylvania, distrustful of the background, methods, and outlook of many of the Revolutionary leaders and their supporters, and predisposed to involve themselves in the public affairs of the province in a vigorous and outspoken manner. Whereas the inclination of the reformers was to remain quiet and aloof from the turmoil of outward affairs, the politiques were unable to refrain from obtruding their public view and policies upon the Society, for the most part through their role in the Meeting for Sufferings.

Besides the hostility of the patriots and the misgivings of some of their brethren within the Society, as a result of the Testimony of January 24, the leaders of the Quaker opposition incurred the disapproval of Friends in England who had formerly commended their position. Dr. Fothergill cautioned them to "Mind your own business, and neither court unworthily the favr of your superiors on this side nor oppose with vehemence the party which steps forward in the protection of your libertys, which are all at stake."[22] Fothergill apparently was more in sympathy with the aims of the patriots than were his correspondents, for he acknowledged the importance of their stand for the liberties of Americans.

[21] Thayer, *Pennsylvania Politics*, p. 154.
[22] John Fothergill to James Pemberton, 17/iii/75, PP, 34 : 173.

David Barclay, another key correspondent in England, admonished the Pennsylvanians for their self-righteousness.

> I allude to the *Publications* of Friends wch are now made a handle of, to the disadvantage of ye Community—the language of the Court being that they have the Quakers Approbation of their Measures;—in particular the Testimony of the 24th 1st Mo, in wch we think there are some hard words that we could have wish'd had been omitted, as they seem to convey that which we hope is not in your hearts, an inclination to obtain favor at the Expence of *others*: The Declaration of our *religious* & peaceable principles every body must approve, & these (on that Ground) your best Friends wish you to *remain*; unless it is the inclination of the society generally to give up that *Palladium*, wch we have always understood to be (under providence) your great temporal advantage, beyond your Brethren on this side the Atlantic—Pray attend to this hint in your future Operations, & let nothing of a contrary Tendency be thrown before the public, who are so deeply interested in the Conduct of their fellow subjects———.[23]

The intensity of the censure evoked by the Testimony, together with the heightening of the prevailing sense of crisis, had a noticeable effect upon the Quaker attitude and behavior. The imprudence of voicing anti-Revolutionary sentiments was finally recognized, and was replaced for a time by caution and circumspection. Ironically, James Pemberton deplored the fact that some of his fellow Quakers were "unguarded and imprudent & give a handle to our adversaries," while overlooking his own part in the issuance of the epistles and the Testimony. Characteristically, he responded to the adverse situation by emphasizing the need for Quakers, then more than ever, to exercise prudence and patience and other Christian virtues, in order to show their reliance upon divine support.[24]

The news of the outbreak of hostilities went still further toward

[23] David Barclay to James Pemberton, 18/iii/75, *ibid.*, 27 : 101 (italics in the original).
[24] James Pemberton to ?, 6/v/75, PP, 27 : 138.

bringing about a change in the behavior of Quaker leaders. Christopher Marshall noted with satisfaction in his diary on May 7, 1775:

> It's admirable to see the alteration of the Tory class in this place, since the account of the engagement in New England. Their language is quite softened, and many of them have so far renounced their former sentiments as that they have taken up arms, and are joined in the association; nay, even many of the stiff Quakers, and some of those who drew up the Testimony, are ashamed of their proceedings. It is said that J[ames] P[emberton], who signed that paper, and had called the people rebels, now declares in favor of the opposition made to king and parliament.[25]

The Meeting for Sufferings was even moved to initiate a subscription for the assistance of "Our Dear Friends & others in New England." This financial assistance, not only for the Quakers, or for Boston, was followed up subsequently with a series of further contributions for the relief of sufferings brought on by the war.[26]

The significant change in the outlook of the Society's leaders is nowhere more evident than in a comparison of two letters from James Pemberton to his English correspondents, written ten months apart. On July 1, 1774, he wrote to Dr. Fothergill as follows: "and on ye whole it is satisfactory to observe that friends are much united but as we are Numerous, & the station & Age of our Members are various & their prospects different, it requires forbearance & patience to be extended towards the few who are drawn aside by ye popular Judgment."[27] The following May, he lamented to David Barclay, "[I] wish we could unite with you in promoting Conciliatory measures, but our hands are weak & influence small and we are become here a people disunited in sentem[ent] and Conduct."[28] The earlier confidence and sense of con-

---

[25] *Diary*, p. 23.
[26] PMS, 29/vi/75 *et seq.*
[27] EC, 2 : 68.
[28] 10/v/75, PP, 22 : 140.

trol over the situation had been replaced by an almost despairing sense of helplessness.

In September, 1775, the Yearly Meeting cautioned its members very carefully to make certain that their non-participation was motivated solely by conscience and the Christian spirit, and warned them not to give offense to those who did not profess with them.

Late in October, it came to the attention of the Meeting for Sufferings that the Assembly had received a petition for the establishment of a militia. The Meeting viewed this situation and the conditions which had given rise to it with great alarm, and the Society's leaders quickly moved to prevent the burdensome measure. Basing their appeal upon the guarantee of liberty of conscience under the charter and upon the historical position of Quakers in Pennsylvania, the Meeting for Sufferings formulated an earnest and quasi-legalistic address to the Assembly, expressing their concern at the prospect of the establishment of a militia, which they feared would be compulsory, without regard for religious scruples against the bearing of arms. Tactically, an appeal to the charter was extremely inopportune in an address to the patriot-dominated Assembly, for the charter was widely viewed as an instrument which preserved and perpetuated the hegemony of the wealthy eastern ruling class at the expense of the inhabitants of the western counties and the citizens of Philadelphia. It was to no avail to seek relief under a constitution which was one of the chief targets of those to whom the appeal was directed. The militia law was passed in November, requiring military service, or a financial payment in lieu thereof, of every male in the province between the ages of sixteen and fifty.

The last public effort carried out in the name of the Society to avert the prospect of a break with England was made on January 20, 1776, just a few days after the publication of *Common Sense* had all but precluded the possibility of a reconciliation.[29] Called "The Ancient Testimony & Principles of the People Called Quakers," the document was composed by a committee of the

[29] Thayer, *Pennsylvania Politics*, p. 176.

Meeting for Sufferings and was published in the *Pennsylvania Ledger* on January 27. The Testimony put forward again what had become, in effect, the official Quaker position regarding the state of public affairs: the present calamities and afflictions were a dispensation of Divine Providence for the sins and iniquities of the people. Pride, wantonness, luxury, profaneness, slaveholding, and forgetfulness of the goodness and mercies of God were everywhere prevalent; they called for the transgressor's reformation and subjection of self to divine wisdom, and the giving over of the selfish spirit of animosity and discord. An extended allusion to the glories of the province under Quaker founding and rule followed, with the consideration that this happy state was enjoyed under the king and his government, and that the connection ought therefore to be preserved.

Perhaps the most important aspect of the Testimony of 1776 was the first reference, made therein, to what was to become the charter of the Society's position for the duration of the Revolutionary period. This was a quotation from the Ancient Testimony of 1696 (as cited by Sewell in his history of the Quakers): "the setting up & putting down Kings and Governments, is God's peculiar Prerogative, for Causes best known to himself and . . . it is not our business, to have any hand or contrivance therein, nor to be busy bodies above our station, much less to plott and contrive the ruin, or overturn of any of them, but to pray for the King and safety of our Nation, and good of all Men: that we may live a peaceable and quiet Life, in all Godliness and honesty; under the Government which God is pleased to set over us."[30] Friends must abhor all writings and measures designed to break off the connection with Great Britain, the king, and those lawfully placed in authority under him.

The second Testimony is in certain ways a key to the orientation of the Society during the remainder of the war period. Unable to reconcile themselves to the behavior of the Revolutionary party and therefore to understand or sympathize with the true economic,

[30] PMS, 20/i/76.

social, and political issues at stake, the leaders of the Society fell back on an interpretation of the situation to which they did know how to react and with which they could cope. If the prevailing turmoil was God's judgment for the moral degeneracy of the people, the proper place of the Quaker was to see that his own behavior conformed to God's word and submit to His dispensations. All contrary behavior demanded the rigorous exercise of church discipline, for the results of deviation were costly and contributed to the suffering of others. The notion of "setting up and putting down governments" was a wide one, and, together with the fact that the country was at war, provided considerable latitude for the exercise of the Discipline. The fact that there was strong sentiment for the strengthening of the Discipline at the Yearly Meeting is evident throughout, although most explicitly in the annual epistle to the London Yearly Meeting. The leaders of the Society were disturbed by the lack of effect the various advices and cautions to stay out of the commotions had had on the members, and by the time of the Yearly Meeting they were prepared to increase the rigor of the Discipline.

By the end of 1775, one hundred sixty-three members of the Pennsylvania Society had been dealt with under the Discipline for activities connected with the Revolution: one hundred forty-four for military activities, six for accepting public office, and thirteen for both offenses. Of these, sixty-five were disowned, some acknowledged their transgression, and the remaining cases were carried over to the next year.[31] Because the overwhelming proportion, if not virtually all, of the infractions were in support of the colonial cause, the measures taken by the Society added to the growing store of animosity against the Quakers.[32] The prospect that this animosity might serve to intensify the persecution of Quakers for their noncompliance with Revolutionary measures was in no way a deterrent to those entrusted with the exercise of the Discipline. Suffering was a condition they knew how to deal with —even, paradoxically, welcomed and took comfort in—for it

[31] Mekeel, "The Quakers in the American Revolution," p. 91.
[32] Marshall, *Diary*, p. 270.

seemed to preclude self-interest and to suggest true religious dedication. Thus, the alienation of the Society of Friends from the political currents which flowed around it was confirmed well before independence was declared. How the Quakers' outlook affected their behavior during the Revolution is our next consideration.

X

REVOLUTION, REFORMATION,
AND A NEW
POLITICAL ROLE

If the Yearly Meeting of 1775 was a presage of the Society's accommodation to the Revolution, that of 1776 showed the policy in substantial outline. Using this Meeting as a springboard for the discussion of Quaker political behavior during the remainder of the war, let us consider the changes in policy and personnel which ultimately put the seal on Quaker withdrawal from the partisan arena and turned the Friends in Pennsylvania toward a new political role.

Of the measures taken by the Meeting, the most important was the following advice, directed primarily at members who were potential holders of office or other positions of authority under a Revolutionary government, but applicable to Friends in every station. "As the Lust of worldly Honour and Power hath been productive of the Calamities & Distresses to which we are now subjected, we are incited by a sincere Concern for the Welfare of our Brethren & in their Prosperity in the Truth, to entreat them, during the present Commotions, & unsettled State of public Affairs to decline from having any Share in the Authority, & Powers of Government, & to circumscribe themselves within plain & narrow bounds."[1]

---

[1] PYM to Quarterly Meetings and Monthly Meetings, 1776.

True, the Society had been issuing exhortations to decline worldly honor and power and to stay out of office regularly since 1756, with some, but far from complete, success. The effectiveness of the appeals was limited largely by the Society's lack of effective means of enforcement. From a practical point of view, it had not been feasible to disown officeholders on the grounds that they were parties to the suffering of fellow Friends who were conscientiously scrupled against paying mixed taxes; the latter constituted a very small minority, whose stand ran counter to long-established precedent, and, while many members supported their right to decline payment, a large number would have opposed disowning others on that basis.

Now, however, with the province in a state of armed rebellion, acceptance of a position in government implied a priori the most direct kind of support of measures and principles which undeniably violated the peace testimony and the injunction against involvement in setting up and putting down governments. Office-holding likewise led to calling upon other Friends to deviate from their profession and to being accessory to their suffering if they resisted. To cite a particularly cynical example of this last problem, a number of Quakers were appointed as tax collectors; when they declined the duty, they were fined by the government for their refusal.[2] The important point is that participation in the Revolutionary government afforded clear-cut and ample grounds for the full exercise of the Discipline.

The injunction at the end of the passage quoted earlier demands special attention: "and to circumscribe themselves within plain & narrow bounds." This goes beyond a mere exhortation to stay out of political office. It is, rather, a call to withdraw *completely* from active involvement in external affairs relating to government. Individual Friends had issued similar calls in the past, but this was the first instance of a call for complete withdrawal made in the name of the Society as a whole.

[2] PMS, 15/iv/79; Tract Association of Friends, *Biographical Sketches and Anecdotes of Members of the Religious Society of Friends* (Philadelphia, 1870), pp. 326–27.

Circumstances had advanced to the point where it was beyond the capacity of the Society to influence their course from the outside; at the same time, they were of such a nature that sincere Quakers could not participate from within. As Dr. Fothergill noted, only one alternative was consistent with the preservation of the Society, or rather, with the preservation of the peace testimony which had come to be the symbol of the Quaker profession: "Your part is a clear one. Be quiet, mind your own proper Business. If your Kingdom is *not* of this World, mind that *only* which we look for, and are taught by the highest Authority to seek. . . . The Kingdom we profess to see is not of this World—leave the World then to contend for its own—."[3]

The Revolutionary conditions of war and rebellion served to make issues other than officeholding more clear-cut. For instance, the Yearly Meeting of 1776 decreed that any member who paid a fine, penalty, payment, or tax in lieu of personal military service, or allowed his children, apprentice, or servant to do so, thus violated the peace testimony and separated himself from the Society by virtue of his action. In a like manner, compliance with the various test laws, which required abjuration of allegiance to the imperial government and an oath or affirmation of allegiance to the Revolutionary regime as a qualification for the enjoyment of one's civil rights, was proscribed on both of the above grounds.[4]

It is noteworthy, however, that refusal to render any overt form of allegiance to the Revolutionary government did not necessarily affect Quaker support for the more routine functions of government. Benjamin Kite, a Quaker schoolmaster in Bucks County during the war, records that

> . . . the inhabitants were generally friends and the Revolution raging with its utmost violence, their money-making schemes were suspended, and not having taken the qualification to the new government, of course they could have no public employment. some

[3] John Fothergill to James Pemberton, 24/iv/77, PP, 34 : 178 (italics in the original).
[4] PMS, 30/vi/78.

of the benevolent people . . . thought it would not do, to let their few paupers, and public roads suffer, because the revolutionary folk took no notice of such things——they therefore took counsel together, and formed what might be called a "Government within a Government," appointed Overseers of the Road and Guardians of the Poor, hunted up the old Duplicates, made out new ones, conformable to the old, and the inhabitants (to their honor be it spoken) almost one and all, cheerfully paid those Taxes, knowing they were for a useful purpose. I know what I say, for their Caucases, Elections &c, were all held in my School Room. . . .[5]

The once debatable question of the propriety of paying taxes for military purposes was no longer moot. To be sure, there were arguments raised in favor of rendering financial support to the Revolutionary government, but they were few and ineffectual. The principal instance was Isaac Grey's *Serious Address*, published in 1778.[6] The volume was in the main a compilation of various precedents and pronouncements from ancient history, the Bible, and the history of the Friends, which purportedly justified the payment of taxes to the new regime. Of these precedents and pronouncements, many were ambiguous, and the bulk of the others referred to the very early period in the church's history when the peace testimony had not yet been institutionalized. The arguments were easily refuted, or were at least countered with others; Grey himself was disowned for his activities on behalf of the Revolution.

The most ambitious formulation of the Society's position with regard to the taxes was the work of Samuel Allinson, a Burlington attorney and conveyencer, and sometime clerk of the Burlington Monthly Meeting. His "Reasons against War, and paying Taxes for its support," dated June 13, 1780,[7] is a lengthy essay which systematically confronted and disposed of all the major counter-arguments in legal fashion, and marshalled the positive arguments against compliance.

[5] "Memoir of the Early Part of his Life," 1834, Friends Historical Library, Swarthmore College, Swarthmore, Pa., pp. 4–5.
[6] *A Serious Address to such of the People Called Quakers . . . as Profess Scruples Relative to the Present Government* (Philadelphia, 1778).
[7] MS 968, Quaker Collection, Haverford College Library, Haverford, Pa.

Allinson's arguments against Friends paying taxes because they had always paid them are particularly interesting. Significantly, he cited the counterprecedent of John Churchman, John Woolman, and the others who had refused to pay mixed taxes in 1756 and thereafter, thus vindicating their difficult and controversial stand in retrospect. Again, along lines set out by Woolman, Allinson contended that tradition and precedent are not infallible; Friends must do what appears most consistent in a particular situation. The controlling factor must be that, if there is any reservation ("religious fear") in one's mind that voluntary compliance with a particular measure would not serve to uphold the light of the Gospel of Peace, or would be a stumbling block to others, it must not be carried through. A Quakers' first obligation is to be faithful to every manifestation of divine grace vouchsafed to him.

> It is not to be wondered at, or an argument to be drawn against a reformation in the refusal of Taxes for War at this Day, that our Brethren formerly paid them; Knowledge is progressive every reformation had its beginning. . . . Let none startle at this advancing in what is believed by some to be our indispensible duty as We find our minds touch'd with a concern so to do; one step makes way for another, even greater things and further advances may in future be required of us, if we are faithful to the discoveries of true knowledge, and happy will it be for us to be found worthy of divine Communications.[8]

This carries the idea of reliance upon God and obedience to His word to its logical limit, making Him the prime source of political influence, the center of the political environment, above even tradition or the Discipline.

The Society's advocacy of a policy of noncompliance naturally provoked the ire of the Revolutionary regime. Tolerance often is an early victim of revolution, its place soon being occupied by a rigorous "if you're not with us, you're agin' us" philosophy. Moreover, the Quakers had, over the years, accumulated a considerable number of political enemies who were now in the ascendancy.

[8] *Ibid.*, pp. 16–19.

Consequently, Friends who chose to abide by the policy of the Society were subjected to persecution and harassment, both legal and extralegal, including imprisonment, fines, distraints, destruction of property, and vituperation. The arrest and exile to a remote part of Virginia of twelve leading Quakers—namely, Israel, James, and John Pemberton, Thomas, Miers, and Samuel Fisher, John Hunt, Thomas Wharton, Edward Penington, Henry Drinker, Thomas Gilpin, and Samuel Pleasants, has often been recounted. The episode was conducted throughout in a most arbitrary and unjust manner, and was prompted largely by hysteria and vindictiveness. Although the group included outspoken and bitter critics of the Revolutionary program, the conduct of the affair was unnecessarily severe in light of the actual behavior, advanced age, and peaceful demeanor of the accused; they were denied even the right to hear and defend themselves against the charges raised against them.[9]

As one would expect, in reaction to the constant trials and tribulations to which Friends were subjected, the injunction of the Society's leaders to their brethren was to remain steadfast and suffer. Once again, the example of the First Publishers of Truth was held up to their descendents.

> And 'as it became him for whom are all things, & by whom are all things, in bringing many sons unto glory, to make the captain of their salvation perfect thro' sufferings,' Heb. 2, 10. Let us not be dismayed if we are now led in the same path—.
>
> As we keep in the Lords power and peaceable truth, which is over all & therein seek the good of all, neither outward sufferings, persecutions, nor any outward thing that is below, will hinder or break our heavenly fellowship in the light & Spirit of Christ. G. Fox's Epist. 1685.[10]

The Society united behind the sufferers, assisting them in their trials and gaining strength from their fortitude and perseverance.

[9] Thomas Gilpin, *Exiles in Virginia* (Philadelphia, 1848); Theodore Thayer, *Israel Pemberton: King of the Quakers* (Philadelphia, 1943), pp. 215–31.
[10] PMS, 20/xii/76.

The Yearly Meeting of 1776 urged that all Friends who had been favored with an increase in earthly possessions avoid all unnecessary expenditures and be ready to contribute to the relief of their suffering brethren and members of other societies as well. It is apparent that a sense of solidarity and spiritual integrity did in fact attend the Society in the face of, and largely because of, the mutual suffering endured by its members. By mid-1777, James Pemberton's discouragement of the previous year had changed to reassurance as he reported that Friends were presently in good harmony and union.[11] The Meeting for Sufferings wrote to its New England counterpart in February, 1778, "We are favoured to hold our Meetings in this City as usual, Friends generally have staid in their Dwellings, and maintain a Care to act consistent with their Religious principles, and are preserved in Love, and Harmony among themselves, tho' we have been and are subject to many Trials, Exercises, and Sufferings."[12]

Pains must be taken, however, to forestall the impression of total love and harmony conveyed by the above passage. The Meeting's description falls short of complete accuracy on a particularly important count. The severe external pressures imposed by the Revolution subjected the Friends who endured them to greater strains than they had ever experienced in the exercise of their religious profession in Pennsylvania. The "true seed," who were able to withstand the pressures, took justifiable pride in upholding the standard. At the same time, however, the Society proceeded with rigor against those members who deviated from the testimony. By the end of 1778, four hundred eighteen disownments had been carried out in Pennsylvania against Friends who participated in the Revolution or complied with its measures; by the end of the war, the figure would stand at nine hundred eight.[13]

In plain practical terms, the Society could not afford to condone any deviation from its program while the Revolution was in prog-

---

[11] James Pemberton to John Fothergill and William Dillwyn, 21/v/77, PP, 34 : 179.

[12] PMS to New England Meeting for Sufferings, 19/ii/78.

[13] Arthur J. Mekeel, "The Quakers in the American Revolution" (Ph.D. diss., Harvard University, 1939), pp. 91, 124, 143–44, 153.

ress. Only by maintaining absolute consistency was it possible to forestall or controvert the accusation, which many stood ready to make, that the Quakers' appeal to religious scruples in justification of their unwillingness to participate in or support the Revolution was really a mask for obstinacy, cowardice, or some other base motive. If known transgressors were allowed to remain in the Society, it would have appeared that Quaker religious principles were not in fact inconsistent with activity on behalf of the colonial cause.[14]

Although the exercise of the Discipline was supposed to be conducted in a spirit of loving concern for the spiritual welfare of the erring Friend, there is evidence of a high level of intolerance and excessive zeal on the part of the Meeting authorities, and of resentment and rancor on the part of the disowned members during the Revolution. Christopher Marshall voiced a common sentiment when he accused Friends of Discipline worship: "How formal in crying out the Discipline, the Discipline, yet how covetous . . . and uncharitable you are."[15]

As the war progressed, and their number increased, disowned Friends came to be viewed almost as a special group in the city, where the urban situation rendered them more conspicuous than elsewhere. A large majority of those disowned either were estranged from the Society to begin with or began to lose their identity as Quakers when they were expelled from the fold, but there were some among them whose roots in the church were too strong to break completely, despite their transgression of the Discipline. Wishing to retain their identification as Quakers and yet to participate in the Revolution, a number of these disowned Friends formed their own Society, called the Free Quakers, early in 1781.

[14] PMS, 18/xii/77 and 4/viii/78; Anthony Benezet to Samuel Neale, undated (ca. the end of 1777), in George S. Brookes, *Friend Anthony Benezet* (Philadelphia, 1937), p. 410.
[15] Mekeel, "The Quakers in the American Revolution," p. 270.

Reacting against the treatment they had received at the hands of the orthodox Quakers, the founders of the Society of Free Quakers provided that no one who joined with them would be disowned for any cause whatsoever. They maintained that it was better to practice freedom than to repress, to advise with an erring brother than to turn him away, and to labor for his reformation instead of casting him out in his hour of spiritual need. Furthermore, they held that all government was essentially a defensive war for the protection of the public peace, and that when government is threatened by domestic treason or foreign invasion, every man is duty-bound to come to its defense, even to the extent of waging defensive war, which, although extreme, would then be justified. The Free Quakers professed to have "no new doctrine to teach, nor any design of promoting schisms in religion. We wish only to be freed from every species of ecclesiastical tyranny, and mean to pay a due regard to the principles of our forefathers, and to their rules and regulations so far as they apply to our circumstances, and hope, thereby, to preserve decency and to secure equal liberty to all."[16]

The moving spirit of the Society of Free Quakers, and its first clerk, was Samuel Wetherill, a former minister who was disowned in August, 1779, for taking the test of allegiance and for "being concerned in publishing or distributing a book tending to promote dissension and division among Friends." When proceedings were instituted against him by the Society of Friends, he addressed a letter to Owen Jones, Isaac Zane, Edward Jones, James Pemberton, John Pemberton, and David Bacon, all prominent figures in the Philadelphia Monthly Meeting. The letter was written in defense of having taken the test, and to present his ideas "on the propriety of disowning such who may acknowledge themselves subjects of the present Government."[17] His arguments are of interest chiefly for the light they shed, by contrast, on the position of the orthodox Friends.

[16] Charles Wetherill, *History of the Religious Society of Friends, Called by Some the Free Quakers* (Philadelphia, 1894), p. 48.
[17] 1788, EC, 2 : 89.

Grounding his arguments in Hobbesian political theory, Wetherill subscribed to the view that the Revolution was justified and proper because the king and government of Great Britain had violated their obligation to protect the people, and had perverted their power through oppression. Therefore, rebellion was due; God had taken America out of the hands of king and Parliament to avenge the dishonor done to Himself by the oppressors. Viewing the Revolution as divinely sanctioned, Wetherill considered it his place to submit.

Apparently, John Pemberton had contested Wetherill's position, countering with the view that the throes of the Revolution constituted a chastisement from heaven for the sins of the people in England and in America. Wetherill dismissed Pemberton's objection, insisting that the contest between Great Britain and America concerned "a matter of right," which ought to be distinguished from a consideration of the morality or immorality of the parties involved, even though these may be of real concern to every Christian mind. Justice, he held, requires a distinction "between the immorality of the people & the rights of the people, for the impious have some rights which they ought to enjoy in common with the most virtuous."[18]

Even had the orthodox Quakers accepted Wetherill's argument, however, there would still have been the issue of the war to make them reject his over-all position. Nevertheless, Wetherill's statement serves to point up the degree to which the body of Friends was alienated from the thought and feelings of most of the other citizens, for the Quakers ignored the social, economic, and political basis of the War of Independence while gearing their own behavior to a strictly moral interpretation. As the Revolution wore on, there was even a tendency within the Society to consider the whole situation as relating specifically to the Quakers.[19] Before deploring

[18] *Ibid.*

[19] Anthony Benezet to James Pemberton, 28/i/78, in Brookes, *Friend Anthony Benezet*, 326–27; Thomas Millhouse to Henry Drinker, 22/iii/78, MS Letterbook RS 181, Philadelphia Yearly Meeting, Department of Records, Philadelphia, Pa., p. 23; PMS to LMS, 15/xi/81.

this collective myopia which helped to alienate the patriot element within and without the Society and which brought suffering down upon the heads of obedient Friends, it is essential to recognize that, irrespective of its correspondence to objective "reality," the orthodox Quaker view of the Revolution served vitally important ends within the church—namely, the attainment of the goals pursued by the reformers for more than two decades: the drawing inward of the membership away from the outside world, and its centralization around the meeting structure, accompanied by at least an outward purification of Friends' behavior along the lines set by the Quaker testimony. So thoroughgoing were the changes in the situation of the Society that by the end of the Revolutionary period the reformers believed the long-awaited reformation of the church at last showed a substantial promise of being achieved.

It is particularly instructive to trace the progress of the reformation through the Revolutionary period in the writings of George Churchman. Always a severe and tough-minded critic of moral delinquency and worldiness within the Society, Churchman's positive judgments on the righteous development of Friends are that much more worthy of attention. On the fifth of February, 1778, he wrote to John Pemberton: "The Subject of a Real Reformation in Life & Practice is now that which employs the Attention of many Friends in Pennsylvania. The Clearness & weight in which that Subject open'd & spread before the View of Friends who were Collected at our last Yearly Meetg was such that will not I believe be easily forgotten by many who were favour'd to attend there. And I have a Comfortable Hope the Work is coming forward . . . and a Considerable Number of Friends are deeply engaged . . . to labour to promote it both amongst themselves & their Brethren & Sisters."[20] During the following month, Churchman noted in his journal that the meetings at which he assisted were "attended with remarkable Solemnity," and that "We were appre-

---

[20] PP, 31 : 108.

hensive that the order of Truth is rather gaining ground in the City in this difficult time."[21]

Attending the Yearly Meeting of Ministers and Elders in September of 1780, Churchman recorded with growing satisfaction that the gathering was "large & solemn; may it not be said, 'The house of David grows stronger.' Surely the wisdom & power of truth is more prevalent in this meeting than in years past."[22]

Four years later, following a fruitful Yearly Meeting, Churchman wrote again to John Pemberton, expressing his thankfulness for "such a Meeting as I never saw, nor scarcely have heard of in our Country. . . . It was I believe a Season wherein was visible to discerning Eyes, the rising Glory of her who is coming out of the Wilderness in these latter Days, leaning on the Breast of her Beloved."[23]

Let us consider those changes in the composition or outlook of the church's membership which could have accounted for the kind of change in behavior to which Churchman attested. Perhaps the most obvious contributing factor was the departure from the Society, through disownment, of the mass of members who gave priority to the demands and exigencies of the external world at the expense of strict conformity to the Society's policies and Quaker principles. With reference to membership in the Society, the Revolution demanded an all-or-nothing commitment; it was no longer possible to participate in external political activities and yet retain one's membership, even nominally, in the church. Although most of the Quakers who had formerly been numbered among the worldly politicians relinquished or were deprived of their membership, there were some in whom the religious commitment prevailed when it came to the test. Edward Penington, for instance, had been prominent among the Quakers who bore arms against the Paxton Boys, and had played an active role in the anti-British agitation of the early and mid-1770s, but he found himself unable to support out-and-out revolution, and so was among the group of

[21] 21/iii/78 and 27/iii/78, GCJ, 3 : 23–24.
[22] 23/ix/80, *ibid.*, 4 : 7.
[23] 11/x/84, PP, 42 : 43.

Friends exiled to Virginia in 1778 for alleged opposition to the Revolutionary regime. Thomas Wharton also was among the Virginia exiles, although he had been an important and vigorous leader of the Quaker party through the 1760s.

In addition to the older worldly generation, the Society also lost the younger men who subsequently would have taken their places; disownments for military service, as opposed, say, to compliance with the test acts or participation in the Revolutionary government, involved principally youthful members.[24]

Disownment from the Society was not, of course, irrevocable. Some of the deviants who joined the colonial cause experienced second thoughts when the war was over and petitioned the meetings for readmission. Most notable among these were Richard Humphreys, captain of the company raised among the Philadelphia Quakers, and Owen Biddle, leading patriot and member of the Board of War of Pennsylvania.[25] Before these men could be received back into the Society, however, they had to acknowledge their former errors, and in a sense the pressure was on them thereafter to show themselves to be true and faithful Quakers, so that they would not compromise the Society in any way. In a like manner, those who joined the Society through convincement during and after the Revolution were held to the strict standards laid down by the testimony and the leaders of the church.[26]

Much space has been devoted in this work to the effect of a series of political crises upon the political outlook and behavior of the group of Quaker leaders we have designated politiques. These were men who were active and prominent in the affairs of the Society of Friends, and devoted, in their own view, to its prin-

---

[24] Christopher Marshall, 3–4/v/75, in *Extracts from the Diary of Christopher Marshall*, ed. William Duane (Albany, 1877), p. 22; Israel Pemberton to Edward Stabler, 3/vi/75, PP, 27 : 155.

[25] James Pemberton to John Pemberton, 10/xi/82 *et seq.*, PP, 37 : 93; 15/xii/82 *et seq.*, *ibid.*, 38 : 5; 22/i/83 *et seq.*, *ibid.*, p. 8; 19/vii/83, *ibid.*, 39 : 73; 14/v/84, *ibid.*, 41 : 7.

[26] PYM, 1781; PMS to LMS, 15/xi/81; PYM, 1791 and 1794; PMS, 17/ii/91.

ciples, but who were also, by virtue of their wealth and social position and their religious affiliation itself, engaged in the worldly public affairs of the province as well, in contradistinction to the reformers within the Society, who rejected such outward concerns. We have attempted to demonstrate that the effect upon the politiques of the succession of crises they encountered from the mid-1750s onward was to impel some of them at least toward the position of the reformers, away from the worldly political involvement which their position in the secular society ordinarily dictated.

In the situations dealt with thus far, however, the reorientation of the politiques was transitory, at times not even persisting for the duration of the crisis which prompted it. What is more, the leaders themselves reacted differently in particular situations; some expressed their disillusionment with public affairs in circumstances which left their compatriots undaunted, only to plunge into subsequent activities which raised doubts in the minds of others. To a degree, the succession of difficulties which the Society encountered in the political arena during the fifties and sixties did have a cumulative effect, in that the Society's statesmen grew progressively more circumspect in their worldly political affairs, but these affairs were never completely foresworn, as the reformers urged at every turn —that is, until the advent of the Revolution.

The Revolutionary period greatly exceeded, both in intensity and duration, any of the crises to which the Quakers had ever been subjected in Pennsylvania. It must be remembered that the Society began to withdraw in earnest from affairs connected with the Revolutionary movement around 1770, with the politiques relinquishing their attempts to stem the tide toward independence in 1776. Although pressures abated with the victory at Yorktown in 1781, and the war ended in 1783, Friends continued to suffer judicial penalties until 1789. This meant that the Quakers who submitted themselves to the Discipline and would not comply with the measures of the Revolutionary regime were the objects of harassment and ill-will for a period of almost twenty years, and of legal persecution for nearly fifteen, excepting only the brief interlude when Philadelphia was under British control. The war itself, which wore on for eight years, was a constant source of strain upon a people for whom peace was among the highest of religious values.

To summarize, then, from the viewpoint of the Society's faithful members, the Revolution was carried through by men of whom the Quakers were deeply suspicious, using methods of which they could not approve and over which they found themselves unable to exert any influence; it involved the breaking of political ties and patterns of government which the Quakers valued highly and their replacement by a regime which subjected Friends to penalties, harassment, and the deprivation of their civil rights. The events of the past two decades had primed the politiques for a disengagement from worldly political affairs, and the massive pressures of the Revolution sealed their withdrawal. Let us document this crucial change in detail.

John Reynell, as often before, may serve as an example. This important Quaker, we recall, was a leading figure in both non-importation campaigns, and certainly was cognizant of at least the economic grievances of the colonists in their disputes with Great Britain. Yet, by mid-1778, he was voicing the orthodox moralistic-reformist theory that the Revolution was intended "to teach the Inhabitants to learn Righteousness,"[27] and resigning himself to the protection of the Divine Arm. "Its best for us to have our Trust & Confidence in the Lord, who is able to preserve & protect us under every power, & I very much desire my dependence may be more & more fixed upon him & come to know a total resignation To the divine will in all things."[28]

Henry Drinker was another prominent Quaker, a man who had been actively involved in the campaign for a change of government and in the non-importation efforts. In 1779, he expressed satisfaction with the measures which deprived Quakers of the civil privileges related to voting and officeholding, and rejoiced in the afflictions and sufferings which paved the way for the Friends'

[27] John Reynell to Elias Bland, 12/viii/78, JRLB, 1774–84.
[28] John Reynell to Mary Groth, 16/vi/78, *ibid.*

deliverance.[29] At the end of the war, he recorded with gratification his own personal success in having borne the trials of the Revolution "without bringing a blemish on the testimony & precious cause," meaning, in effect, that he was able to resist the inclination to become engaged in the political tempests of that period.[30]

But the example, *par excellence*, of the reorientation in outlook of a Quaker politique is revealed in the correspondence of James Pemberton. Here was a man who was an activist to the core, always in the forefront of political activities or undertakings which affected his church, from the early 1750s onward. His long and energetic career made his subsequent reversal all the more striking. Not only did he withdraw personally, but he disclaimed any familiarity with the postwar political scene and considered it a great advantage that Friends were excluded from government and thereby insulated from partisan contention. He even went so far as to express the conviction that the deprivation of their civil rights was itself "a providential Security" for the Quakers and tended to the preservation of the Society.[31] Most remarkable of all, Pemberton saw the entire history of Quakerism as manifesting proof of the advantages of trusting virtuous behavior for the preservation of religious liberty rather than relying upon conventional political means to secure a liberty which could only be nominal.[32] This was nothing less than an implicit repudiation of his own past political career, and it indicated how truly fundamental a reorientation he had undergone.

To establish a disinclination toward external political involvement on the part of the Quaker politiques during and immediately after the Revolution is not, of course, to prove that they continued to remain aloof once the severe pressures of the Revolutionary period began to abate. Indeed, this very problem was a source of

[29] Henry Drinker to David Barclay, 12/i/79, MS Letterbook RS 181, Philadelphia Yearly Meeting, Department of Records, Philadelphia, Pa. p. 27.

[30] Henry Drinker to Samuel Neale, vii/84, HDLB, p. 53.

[31] James Pemberton to John Pemberton, 13/x/82 and 7/x/84, PP, 37 : 61 and 43 : 34; James Pemberton to William Matthews, 9/iii/85, *ibid.*, 43 : 64; James Pemberton to William Dillwyn, 9/xi/85, *ibid.*, 44 : 130.

[32] James Pemberton to John Gough, 21/xii/84, *ibid.*, 42 : 123.

considerable concern to the leaders of the Society during the post-war years. They were gratified and exalted by the reformation which the Society had undergone, and anxious that Friends "not be unguardedly seduced into a bewildering Pursuit of, and unwarrantable Confidence in, Things visible & uncertain."[33] The problem was compounded by circumstances surrounding the partisan alignments which emerged from the Revolution in Pennsylvania, for both the Presbyterian and Anglican parties (as they were seen by the Quakers) courted the support of the Friends to add strength to their respective forces. James Pemberton warned that this situation required as much watchfulness on the part of the Quakers as had the more obvious difficulties just past. Proof that "no Confidence is to be placed in the *friendship of the men of this World*, or of those who are actuated by its unstable Spirit," lay ready at hand.

In the late session of our assembly, the party who profess themselves advocates for moderate measures, and friends to our society had long been Concerned of the Justice & propriety of repeal of the Test Law, and declared they would embrace the first favourable opportunity to effect it became the greatest opposers when the motion for its repeal was brought on by the other Side. Each of whom we find were governd in their Conduct by Some political view wch at that Juncture presented, so the matter was postposed wch [though ?] an unjust determination is rather a [benefit ?] than an Injury to us—.[34]

When the Test Law was finally repealed, in 1787, fears were once again renewed that Friends would seek the offices from which they had been barred for so long.[35] This concern prompted the Yearly Meeting to advise the membership against mixing in external politics. A letter from James Pemberton to Moses Brown, discussing the need for advice of this tenor, indicates how wary and circumspect the Society's leaders had in fact become with reference to public affairs.

[33] PYM to LYM, 1783.
[34] James Pemberton to William Rotch, 6/iv/84, PP, 40 : 147 (italics in the original).
[35] James Pemberton to John Pemberton, 7/iv/87, *ibid.*, 48 : 8.

... Divers were precipitatedly drawn in to Sign petitions to the assembly towards the close of their session in the ninth month to promote a Speedy Election of Delegates for the State Convention, wch proceeded from inattention and I believe many have been Since convinced of the impropriety of what they did in that matter from which the people who are active in these concerns may have taken occasion to represent the Judgment of our Society to be favorable to their cause, but an Election for Delegates in the proposed State Convention has been lately held in the city, and other parts, and I do not find that the members of our Society intermeddled, except a few ———— young persons and others who will follow their own wills without due consideration and run with the multitude. . . .[36]

The convention alluded to in the letter was the Constitutional Convention, held to deliberate the proposed new federal constitution. This was clearly a matter which affected Quakers and all other citizens equally, and for individual Quakers to have taken a stand on the constitution issue would not have compromised the Society as such, even if their position had been attributed to their brethren by members of the general public. The lesson drawn by Quaker leaders from past experience, however, was to stay clear of any partisan issue on which Quaker principle did not clearly indicate that a stand be taken.

Pemberton's letter hinted at another cause for concern within the Society, the prospect that the body's youth would be seduced into worldly pursuits to the detriment of the Society's reputation. This was a problem which had beset the church since the First Professors began to bear offspring, but in the period immediately following the Revolution it was complicated by an additional factor. The generation of leaders which had guided the Society through the turbulence of the fifties, the sixties, and all or part of the Revolutionary period was being severely thinned by death, thus occasioning deep concern among those of their compatriots who remained. Daniel Stanton, Mordecai Yarnall, Benjamin Ferris,

[36] James Pemberton to Moses Brown, 16/xi/87, *ibid.*, 49 : 6.

John Smith, and John Woolman all died in the early 1770s. Between 1775 and 1784, the Society lost John Churchman, Isaac Andrews, Aaron Ashbridge, Joseph White, John Hunt, Israel Pemberton, Josiah White, Anthony Benezet, and John Reynell. In addition, other pillars of the church—notably John Pemberton and Samuel Emlen—went abroad on religious missions when the war ended. The guiding presence of all these mainstays of the Society was especially missed in the middle and late 1780s, when the crisis of the years just past no longer served as a means of bolstering the spirit of discipline and reformation.[37]

What the survivors perhaps could not see from their perspective was that they had less to fear with regard to the next generation than their predecessors had. The most rebellious among the succeeding generation of Quaker youth had left the Society during the Revolution.[38] A few, most notably Nicholas Waln and William Savery, underwent a spiritual transformation and went on to become valued leaders of the church. Those who remained in the Society, it must be remembered, were socialized during a period in which the spirit of reformation pervaded Quaker education, and in which the influence and efforts of the Society were devoted to effecting a withdrawal by Quakers from worldly politics. Furthermore, the prelude to their assumption of positions of responsibility was the war itself, which drove home most convincingly the lessons of the past two decades.

The result, then, was that a highly capable generation of new leaders came to the fore within the Society to replace those who had departed. This much was noted by contemporaries, as in the following: "I was glad to hear that you had So fine appearance of Young Ministers Now when many of the ancients are gone off the Stage of this World or far advanced in the decline of life."[39] It

---

[37] James Pemberton to John Pemberton, 14/v/84, *ibid.*, 41 : 7.

[38] Marshall, *Diary*, p. 22; Israel Pemberton to Edward Stabler, 3/vi/75, PP, 27 : 155.

[39] Joshua Robinson to Israel Pemberton, 26/v/75, PP, 27 : 151; John Reynell to Mary Groth, 21/xi/74, JRLB, 1774–84; George Churchman to John Pemberton, 5/ii/78, PP, 31 : 108; Henry Drinker to Samuel Neale, 14/vi/84, HDLB, pp. 42–43.

was not yet evident to the older Friends that the new leaders would be far less engaged in worldly political affairs than they themselves had been, or that the rest of the membership of the Society would also remain more aloof in the years to come.

It would, however, be misleading to give the impression that virtually no Quakers succumbed to the lure of worldly office after the removal of the barriers against them in 1789, for a small handful did in fact take up places in government as soon as the way was clear, and their doing so was unquestionably a source of concern to the Society.

The problem was more than just a violation of Quaker behavioral norms; there was a larger issue involved, although it was not a new one. In laying the legislative foundation for the new republic, congress included a militia law which provided exemption for conscientious objectors on payment of two dollars a year toward defraying the expenses of civil government. Payments of this type were inconsistent with the testimony, and Friends were enjoined from complying with the provision. This gave rise to a situation which paralleled that of the late fifties and after with regard to the withholding of mixed taxes: Quakers who held positions in government were thereby exposed to becoming parties to the legal persecution of their conscientious brethren, in violation of their liberty of conscience. Their participation in government also weakened the arguments made against the militia by the rest of the Society. The Yearly Meeting of 1791 accordingly revived the minutes and advices of 1758, 1762, 1763, 1764, and 1770, recommending them to the observation of the quarterly and monthly meetings and of Friends in general, and the Meeting for Sufferings in 1795 advised the monthly meetings to work with those of their members who persisted in office despite the sufferings of their co-religionists.[40]

Still, for several reasons, the degree of concern which the office-holders aroused was insignificant compared to the intensity of the debate evoked by the same issue in the prewar years. Besides the

[40] PMS, 16/iv/95.

simple factor of much smaller numbers, the reaction against office-holding was tempered by the fact that the secular political power of the Quakers was no longer a public issue as it had been before the Revolution; the partisan spectrum had shifted to the extent that none of the opposing elements felt threatened by the Quakers in the political arena. It was clearly apparent to all concerned that for the most part the Friends desired to remain aloof from partisan involvement, maintaining their disengagement even in the face of attempts by both major parties to woo their allegiance. Precisely because the Quakers had rendered themselves so innocuous in this regard, they were spared situations in which the Society and the "reputation of Truth" came under attack for political reasons, and thus could afford to spare themselves an intense, all-out effort against the few transgressors within the Society. Moreover, the strong sense of internal cohesion and solidarity which characterized the Society after the ordeal of the Revolution served to ease any fears which may have been held of the prospect of a wholesale return to worldly political involvement. Before the Revolution, a real cleavage existed within the Society on the issue of political behavior, but in the postwar period the situation was rather one of a small number of deviants from the norm upheld by a well-disciplined and homogeneous body.

The pursuit of moral reformation in the midst of a Revolution, although it cost the Society strong and concentrated effort and was attended with considerable suffering and tribulation, was not an end in itself. It was instead an instrumental goal: "we in much brotherly Affection intreat that we may be vigilant in our several Stations, and faithful in the discharge of our respective duties; *that thus our lights may shine before Men, who seeing our good Works may glorify God in the Day of Visitation.*"[41]

This short statement is a major key to the public behavior of the Quakers during the Revolution and in the years which followed.

[41] PYM to Quarterly Meetings and Monthly Meetings, 1776 (italics added).

179

On the surface, the entreaty might appear to indicate a desire for "the honor of men," against which the reformers so constantly inveighed, and thus to indicate a disparity between profession and practice. It must be emphasized, however, that the glory being sought was not worldly honor for worldly behavior, but glory to God through obedience to His word. Furthermore, the responsibility to God and the testimony came first, and was fixed; if men could be brought to honor the Lord through the behavior of Friends, well and good, but the testimony was not to be compromised in the pursuit of the good will of outsiders.

More important, however, the outlook implicit in the passage introduced a positive element into the Quakers' political behavior vis-à-vis the larger society. As was emphasized earlier, a program directed at securing the withdrawal of Friends from particular modes of political behavior formerly shared by them with the general community, though negative, nevertheless constituted a form of political behavior in its own right. But in this case the Society was tending toward the substitution of a different kind of behavior, which was equally and wholly political as well. Here again, this may not be apparent to those accustomed to thinking of political behavior in terms of partisan involvement or the pursuit of office; participation in the functions of government was a minor and subordinate aspect of the program suggested by the Society's exhortation. Instead, within the context in which it was made, the statement held forth an alternative to the conventional modes of political involvement.

It will be remembered that the early Quakers were strongly imbued with a sense of being the chosen instruments of God, entrusted with the mission of bringing the rest of mankind into the universal Quaker fold in order to build a kingdom attentive to the will of God and governed by His word.[42] Politics in the conventional sense would obviously have no place in this heavenly kingdom. Instead, political behavior, in the sense of behavior aimed at realizing the public goals of society, would have consisted

[42] Thomas G. Sanders, *Protestant Concepts of Church and State* (New York, 1964), pp. 136–37.

of obedience to God's word through adherence to its standard. The entreaty made by the Yearly Meeting of 1776 marked the first step on the part of the entire Society toward a return to the mission of the First Professors after nearly a century of entanglement in worldly government in the Quaker colony of Pennsylvania. Anthony Benezet expressed the Friends' new mission thus: "As a people we are called to dwell alone, not to be numbered with the Nations content with the comfortable necessities of life; as Pilgrims & Strangers; to avoid all incumbrances, as was proposed to Israel of old, to be as a Kingdom of Priests, an Holy Nation, a peculiar people to show forth the praise of Him that hath called us, in our plain innocent, self-denying lives."[43]

While a uniform adherence to the behavioral standards of the church was a prerequisite of the post-Revolutionary program, the desire to attract the attention of others suggested the usefulness of being alert to opportunities for doing so. In 1780, for instance, the Meeting for Sufferings petitioned the Committee of Grievances of the Pennsylvania Assembly for relief from the oppression of measures which infringed upon Friends' liberty of conscience. The committee responded with a series of leading questions aimed in part at getting the Society to acknowledge the political, social, and economic issues at stake in the Revolution, and to admit the propriety of recognizing and submitting to the new regime. The Meeting's reply presented the standard arguments, but, judging from the Meeting's own description of the exchange, the leaders of the Society attached more significance to the situation than was apparent on the surface: "altho' it [the reply] may not be productive of Relief, we hope [it] has a tendency to elucidate & bring into view the Grounds of our religious Principles, and particularly our christian Testimony against War." This statement of principle was considered important in itself, regardless of its immediate results, because it served to bring the testimony to the attention of others.[44]

[43] Anthony Benezet to Morris Birkbeck, 16/x/81, in Brookes, *Friend Anthony Benezet*, pp. 360–61.
[44] PMS to LMS, 15/vi/80.

Sensitivity to "openings" for bringing the testimony to the attention of the outside world was, in effect, an extension of the kind of awareness which was supposed to characterize the spiritual state of all properly religious Quakers. During the stressful period of the Revolution especially, Friends were closely attuned to the direction afforded them by Divine Providence as they experienced ever more difficulty in relating to the worldly events around them. The Yearly Meeting of 1780 exhorted Friends "strictly to attend to the Monitions of divine Grace, and carefully guard against suppressing them either in themselves or others, so that they may be preserved in a Conduct consistent with our holy Profession . . . not at all doubting that he to whom appertains the Kingdom and the Power, and who is wonderful in working, will in his own Way and appointed Time carry on and prosper his blessed Cause of Peace in the Earth."[45] How better to ensure that one was acting in accordance with the Quaker profession than to look for occasions to bring the testimony before others, to pave the way for the blessed cause of peace on earth? If the Society in its corporate capacity undertook to perform this task, it would redound to the credit of the church and all its members, as well as of their profession.

From one point of view, the post-Revolutionary period as a whole represented an opening for the diffusion of the Quakers' social message. The war was followed, as all revolutions must be, by a time of considerable social ferment, as society sorted itself out and people exercised their new political awareness. The tenor of the times was apparent to the Quaker leadership, and it gave impetus to the Society's program. Responding to a letter from Moses Brown, the prominent Quaker leader from Rhode Island, James Pemberton wrote with much insight:

> I agree with thee that it is not a time for us to be idle, and neglect the present opportunity of using the means put in our powers to diffuse the knowledge of Truth among the people in many of whom there appears a desire for information and enquiry

[45] PYM, 1780.

"who shall shew us any good," more prevalent than heretofore and if friends were more attentive to prospects of duty, they might be instrumental in promoting the good of Mankind more extensively than we are; at the same time recommending the excellency of our Christian profession & principles by a Correspondent Conduct, & Conversation—.[46]

Notwithstanding the general openness of the times, however, and the receptivity of the people, the great mass of the Quakers' corporate activity in the closing decades of the eighteenth century was concentrated upon a small number of concerns. Certain issues, for reasons shortly to be discussed, were in the forefront of the Quakers' political consciousness, and the natural tendency was for openings to proliferate in those areas. The ensuing discussion will concentrate on activities in three of these areas—namely, concern for public morality, opposition to slavery, and efforts on behalf of the Indians.

[46] 25/i/86, PP, 45 : 29.

XI

THE QUAKERS AND PUBLIC MORALITY

A concern for public morality was apparent in the political behavior of at least a segment of the Quakers long before the outbreak of the Revolution, and in large part the Society's postwar activities were a continuation of earlier efforts. If anything, the strict moralism of the Quakers had grown stricter with the hardening of the Discipline during the war years, although the heady social atmosphere of the postwar period was hardly conducive to the abatement of the moral tendencies the Society deplored. James Pemberton's letters to his brother John, who was on an extended mission to Europe after the Revolution, are a chronicle of the Friends' ongoing moral anxiety; such developments as the spread of dramshops and the popularity of stage plays were held to be at the root of the spread of vice and profanity among the people.[1] "Occasions still offer," he wrote in 1785, "and I may Say rather encrease for the exercise of attentive care among ourSelves as a religious Society as also to manifest our Concern for the general good & the suppression of evil wch is Sorrowfully prevailent."[2]

Part of the Quaker program involved direct attacks on vice and immorality through lobbying against theatrical entertainments and

[1] 30/viii/85 and 29/xi/85, PP, 44 : 75, 148; 26/vii/88, *ibid.*, 50 : 122; and 12/xi/88 and 15/ii/89, *ibid.*, 51 : 67, 175.
[2] 29/xi/85, *ibid.*, 44 : 148.

dramshops. Because it was mainly in Philadelphia that these iniquities flourished, the memorials and petitions against them came mostly from the monthly meetings in the city itself.[3] Because other religious groups shared the Quakers' views on these matters, Friends were able on occasion to pool their efforts with others in the campaign against vicious and irreligious entertainments, even though they retained their sense of themselves as moral leaders throughout. The fact that others joined in was taken as an indication that the Quakers' policy of promoting the testimony through their "conduct and conversation" was having the desired effect.[4]

The campaign for public virtue, however, was motivated by a higher impulse than the suppression of immorality for its own sake, important as this motive may have been. The period following the Revolution was a time when the efforts and attention of Americans were focused on the building of new governments and new social orders, and the Quakers, among other members of the commonwealth, were particularly concerned about public morality in the conviction that, "unless there is an increase of Virtue among the People, all the efforts of human wisdom, & policy will avail little to promote their real happiness and welfare."[5] By the same token, however, the Quakers believed that it was the duty of government to encourage and promote virtue by all means at its disposal; this was the other half of the equation of public happiness and welfare. On this level, the concern was promoted by the highest bodies in the Society, the Yearly Meeting and the Meeting for Sufferings.

The corporate stance of the Society was set as early as 1781, with the first major public statement being prompted, appropriately enough, by the Quakers' reaction to the festivities occasioned by the victory at Yorktown, which marked the beginning of the end of the war. Enjoined by religious principle to remain outwardly aloof from public celebrations, the Quakers refused to illuminate their houses and close their shops during the festivities,

[3] PMS, 29/xi/85, 26/vii/88, and 12/xi/88.
[4] James Pemberton to John Pemberton, 15/ii/89, PP, 51 : 175.
[5] James Pemberton to John Pemberton, 20/ix/87, *ibid.*, 48 : 152.

which aroused the ire of some of the more ardent patriots and provoked the last outburst of patriot violence and resentment against them. The Meeting for Sufferings responded by appointing a committee to prepare a statement concerning the vandalism perpetrated against the Quakers. The address was to be presented to the president and Executive Council of the Pennsylvania Assembly, not "from a Desire to complain of the Injury sustain'd, or to apply to human Power for Redress; but rather from a Sense of it's being *an Opening & call publickly to give a Reason of the Hope that is in us, and to labour for the spreading & propagation of the Gospel of Peace among our fellow Citizens, Countrymen, & mankind in general.*"[6]

Explaining why members of the Society were unwilling to participate in the victory observances, the authors of the address declared, "we can neither really worship, nor put on any part of the Appearance thereof, merely in Conformity to the Injunctions of human Authority, believing it our Duty rather to *shew our Neighbours by our practice* that in this gospel Day, the holy Spirit hath led us out of the Formality of public Fasts."[7] The statement thus complemented the Quakers' exemplary behavior; it was the "conversation" to accompany the "conduct."

Having stated their own position and explained their behavior, the authors went on to bring the implications of the situation home to the members of government.

> We are not incited by party Views or vindictive Motives in this Representation, but to awaken your cool & dispassionate Attention to our multiplied Sufferings, & the Abuses we have received, knowing that Magistracy is intended for a Terror to Evil doers, and an Encouragement to the virtuous; but where the necessary Care & Exertions are not used for the Prevention and suppression of Prophanity, Tumults & Outrage, and . . . Part of the Community are oppressed & insulted, the true End of Government is neglected and Anarchy, confusion, Contempt of Authority & Insecurity to persons & Property will succeed: And altho' public Fasts may be

[6] PMS, 16/xi/81 (italics added).
[7] *Ibid.*, 22/xi/81 (italics added).

proclaimed, and Days under the Name of Humiliation recommended and appointed and Confession of Sin & Transgression verbally made; yet unless there be a true and sincere fasting from Ambition, Strife, Ill will, Animosities, Infidelity, Fraud, Luxury, Revelling, Drunkeness, Oppression & all Manner of Evil, it cannot be a Fast or acceptable Day to the Lord, nor can we have a well grounded Hope that the Scourge with which the Inhabitants have been visited will be removed, & days of Peace & Tran-Quility restored.[8]

For the remainder of the period under review, the Society continued to press for the position that "the true foundation and wholesome order of civil government" depended upon the attentiveness of those in power and authority to the promotion of piety and virtue through personal behavior and public policy, and to the righteous suppression of vice, infidelity, and irreligion.[9]

Besides their public interest, of course, there was also a clear measure of self-interest in the Quakers' efforts to promote public virtue and morality. In terms of their view of the Revolution from its earliest stages, the decline in public morality had gone hand-in-hand with increasing inroads on their liberty of conscience. Persecution of the Quakers was symptomatic and productive of a more general moral decline, and the best hope of securing liberty of conscience and freedom from oppression was therefore the promotion of general virtue among the populace and the securing of public protection for the conscientiously moral and godly. This, then, was the general tenor of the Society's appeals on behalf of the free exercise of conscience, whether occasioned by mob violence, as in 1781, or by militia laws, with which they could not comply during the remainder of the eighteenth century; a desire to contribute to the support and promotion of the public weal was coupled with the hope of securing liberty of conscience for themselves.[10]

[8] *Ibid.*
[9] PMS to Pennsylvania Assembly 16/ii/86; PYM to LYM, 1789; PYM to George Washington, 1789; PMS to Pennsylvania House of Representatives, 2/xii/93.
[10] PMS, 22/xi/86; PYM to George Washington, 1789; PMS, 18/ii/90.

The political role of moral lobbyists was one which suited the Quakers particularly well. One of its more important advantages, not previously mentioned, was that it provided an avenue for their continued leadership in the political affairs of Pennsylvania even after the sweeping developments of the sixties and seventies had deprived them of their former hegemony over its affairs. For, despite all the efforts and resolutions to abjure worldly activity and public affairs, the solid and immutable fact that Pennsylvania had been founded by Quakers and for Quakers, and that it had been administered by Quakers as a haven and refuge for others, could not be forgotten. Indeed, it was kept in the forefront of the Quakers' consciousness by the very fact that their circumstances were so altered that it was possible for the descendents of those to whom they had granted religious liberty to curtail their own free exercise thereof.[11]

But the political role which the post-Revolutionary Quakers retained for themselves was sharply curtailed in comparison with the diverse and wide-ranging political activities of Pennsylvania Friends in earlier years. Whereas Quakers had formerly provided leadership in every political sphere, the Friends of the eighties and nineties restricted themselves to limited, non-partisan issues which could protect the testimony and display it to good advantage, and which would not lead to compromise by members of the Society or attacks by outsiders.

The campaign for moral improvement conformed admirably to these qualifications. Gratifyingly, members of other denominations displayed a willingness to join the Quakers in their fight against immorality, and did so in such a way that the Friends retained the sense of being the movement's leaders. In February of 1789, for example, a group of Friends joined with members of other denominations in a united effort against the play actors in the city. The combined group, numbering about twenty, with Episcopal Bishop White at its head, waited on the Assembly and presented the representatives with an address formulated by the Quakers.[12]

11 PMS, 22/xi/81 and 16/ii/86.
12 James Pemberton to John Pemberton, 15/ii/89, PP, 51 : 175.

Whether or not the others acknowledged the Quaker leadership was beside the point, as long as the Quakers themselves saw their policies being vindicated.

A strong symbolic reinforcement of the Quakers' self-assumed position in the body politic came about in response to an address presented to George Washington by the Yearly Meeting in 1789, on his assumption of the presidency under the new Constitution. James Pemberton reported that the message was "adopted with as great unanimity as any matter I can Remember & many friends have acknowledged that the solemnity attending the meeting was more prevalent than at any other Sitting." In his ever-practical manner, Pemberton added, "it will, I hope . . . be productive of some good effects & open the way for our future applications to those in authority of which occasions will doubtless offer."[13]

Finally acknowledging their acceptance of the Revolution as a *fait accompli*, permitted by God to succeed, and paying their compliments and respects to Washington, the Friends, as members of the body politic, expressed their hope that he would be devoted to God's service and would act as His instrument in the suppression of vice, infidelity, irreligion, and every species of oppression on the persons and consciences of men, so that righteousness and peace might prevail. Washington's gracious reply, from which a passage is quoted below, was the best kind of recognition the Quakers could have wished to receive.

> While Men perform their social Duties faithfully they do all that Society or the State can with propriety demand or expect and remain responsible only to their Maker for the religion or mode of Faith which they may prefer or profess.
>
> Your principles and conduct are well known to me and it is doing the People called Quakers no more than Justice to say that (excepting their declining to share with others the burthen of the common defense) there is no Denomination among us who are more exemplary and useful Citizens.[14]

[13] James Pemberton to William Dillwyn, 20/x/89, *ibid.*, 52 : 104.
[14] PYM, 1790.

XII

THE CAMPAIGN AGAINST
THE SLAVE TRADE

It is often useful to look to the timing of a political act for an indication of its significance. This tactic, in fact, takes us right to the heart of the political role of the Pennsylvania Quakers in the post-Revolutionary period, for the Society's first approach to the Continental Congress after the close of hostilities opened a campaign which absorbed a second major portion of the Quakers' political energy in the years that followed. The issue to which the Society addressed itself in its petition to Congress was the abolition of the slave trade.

The "opening" for the address was a clear one. Although the war had brought the slave trade to a standstill, the cessation of fighting revived the demand for slaves, and with it the trade in procuring and selling them. It was noted at the Yearly Meeting of 1783 that the English Quakers had taken occasion "to represent to the Rulers in that Nation the crying Iniquity of the Traffic," and, "this Meeting being renewedly affected with a grateful Sense thereof, and a Solicitude prevailing that we may not on our Part fail of Faithfulness in our Endeavours to co-operate with the Openings which are or may be divinely afforded for the further advancement of this interesting Branch of universal Righteousness," a committee was appointed and drew up the following petition, which was signed by 535 members at the Yearly Meeting and presented to the Congress, sitting in Princeton, New Jersey:

Being through the favour of divine Providence met as usual at this Season in our annual Assembly to promote the Cause of Piety & Virtue, we find with great Satisfaction our well meant Endeavours for the Relief of an oppressed Part of our fellow Men have been so far blessed, that those of them who have been held in Bondage by Members of our religious Society, are generally restored to Freedom, their natural and just Right.

Comiserating the afflicted State into which the Inhabitants of Africa are very deeply involved by many Professors of the mild & benign Doctrines of the Gospel, and affected with a sincere Concern for the essential Good of our Country, we conceive it our indispensable Duty to revive in your View the lamentable Grievance of that oppressed People, as an interesting Subject evidently claiming the serious Attention of those who are entrusted with the Powers of Government, as Guardians of the common Rights of Mankind & Advocates for Liberty.

We have long beheld with Sorrow the complicated Evils produced by an unrighteous Commerce which subjects many thousands of the human Species to the deplorable State of Slavery.

The Restoration of Peace, and Restraint to the Effusion of human Blood, we are persuaded excite in the Minds of many of all Christian Denominations Gratitude & Thankfulness to the allwise Controuler of human Events; but we have grounds to fear that some forgetful of the Days of distress, are prompted by avaricious Motives to renew the Trade for Slaves to the African Coasts, contrary to every humane & righteous Consideration, and in Opposition to the solemn Declarations, often repeated, in favour of universal Liberty; thereby encreasing the too general Torrent of Corruption and Licentiousness & laying a Foundation for future Calamities.

We therefore earnestly solicit your christian Interposition to discourage & prevent so obvious an Evil, in such Manner as under the Influence of divine Wisdom you shall see meet.[1]

The question may arise of why, if the antislavery campaign was so important to the Quakers in the postwar period, it has not been discussed at all up to this point. The principal reason is that before

[1] PYM, 1783.

the Revolution the matter of slavery was not a political issue for the Quakers in the dimension being treated in this study. From an analytical point of view, as far as the political engagement of the Quakers was concerned, the antislavery efforts of the fifties, sixties, and seventies were apolitical, for they were directed within the Society, by one segment against another, and only to a very limited extent to society at large.

From time to time before the 1750s, Quaker consciences were troubled by lone voices raised against the moral and spiritual dangers of slavery in the Caribbean and North American colonies. George Fox, Edmundson, Southeby, Morgan, Pyle, Hepburn, Burling, Coleman, Sandiford, and Lay all criticized the institution forcefully, but their efforts were of no avail, either in inducing Friends as a body to abandon the practice voluntarily, or in moving the Society to take corporate action against it. Slavery simply was too widespread and generally accepted, and too many influential Quakers—such as many substantial members of the Newport Quaker community—were slaveholders themselves, not to mention slave traders.

With the advent of the reform movement within the Society, however, the tenor of the antislavery campaign underwent an important change. In the minds of the reformers, the practice of holding men in bondage, of living off the labor of others, became a symbol of an avaricious attachment to the cumbers of this world, as well as an embodiment of the weak-spirited willingness to compromise with principle, for slaves were taken by violence and bloodshed. The most vigorous reformers—men like John Woolman, John Churchman, and Anthony Benezet—led the Society's attack on slavery because they were against all worldliness and spiritual decline.

Their efforts, particularly those of Woolman, began to bear fruit in 1754, when the Yearly Meeting progressed to the point of advising its members against purchasing or keeping slaves. No measures were prescribed against those who refused to heed the advice, but the following year the Meeting decreed that Friends who imported or purchased slaves were to be admonished. The new set of queries instituted in 1755 included the following (number 10): "Are Friends clear of importing or buying Negroes and do they use those well which they are possessed of by Inheritance or otherwise endeavouring to train them up in the Principles of the Christian Religion?"[2]

When the crisis brought on by the Indian wars burst upon Pennsylvania, the moral issues facing the Society of Friends were heightened, with the peace testimony as their focal point. Not surprisingly, the slavery problem was linked with the horrors of war and the shame of moral decline. John Churchman was in Philadelphia in the winter of 1756, when a band of aroused frontiersmen brought in the bodies of some victims of an Indian raid and paraded them through the streets. "Standing at the door of a Friends' house as they passed along," he wrote,

> my mind was humbled and turned inward, and I was made secretly to cry, What will become of Pennsylvania? for it felt to me that many did not consider that the sins of the inhabitants, pride, profane swearing, drunkenness, with other wickedness, were the cause why the Lord had suffered this calamity and scourge to come upon them. The weight of my exercise increasing as I walked along the street; at length it was said in my soul, This land is polluted with blood, and in the day of inquisition for blood, it will not only be required at the frontiers and borders, but even in this place where these bodies are now seen. I said within myself, How can this be? since this has been a land of peace, and as yet not much concerned in war; but as it were in a moment my eyes turned to the case of the poor enslaved Negroes. And however light a matter they who have been concerned in it may look upon the purchasing, selling, or keeping those oppressed people in slavery, it then appeared plain to me, that such were partakers in iniquity, encouragers of war and the shedding of innocent blood, which is often the case, where those unhappy people are captivated and brought away for slaves.[3]

---

[2] *Ibid.*, 1755.

[3] *An Account of the Gospel Labours and Christian Experiences of ... John Churchman*, The Friends' Library, vol. 6 (Philadelphia, 1842), p. 236.

Further confirmation of the centrality of the slavery issue to the reformist position is afforded by the actions of the Yearly Meeting of 1758. This Meeting, which was notable for the decision to exclude persistent officeholders from "the service of truth," applied the identical sanction against any Friend guilty of purchasing or selling slaves; it also appointed a committee of five earnest reformers—John Woolman, John Churchman, John Scarborough, John Sykes, and Daniel Stanton—to visit the slaveholders within the Society and treat with them concerning the evils of the institution. By 1762, the committee had made sufficient progress to ask to be relieved of its duty, but buying, selling, or keeping slaves still had not been completely eliminated from the Society, nor did any of these practices yet constitute sufficient grounds for disownment.

The Society took the final and conclusive steps to rid itself of the taint of slavery as part of the heightened push to purify the church during the Revolution. As early as 1770, when the movement toward the Revolutionary crisis of later years was in its beginning stages, John Woolman began warning his brethren of the bloody judgment which was coming, and which he, like Churchman before him, attributed in part to the guilt of slaveholders: "When Blood shed unrighteously remains unatoned for, and the Inhabitants are not Effectually purged from it; when they do not wash their hands in Innocency, as was figured in the Law in the case of one being found slain, Deut. xxi. 6; but seek for gain arising from scenes of Violence and Oppression, here the land is polluted with blood."[4] Two years later, when Woolman departed for England on a lengthy mission (from which he did not return), he repeated his warning, but by that time the point had all but been won.[5]

In 1774, in response to a request from two of the quarterly meetings for stronger antislavery measures than those provided by the minute of 1758, which suspended buyers or sellers of slaves from

[4] John Woolman, *The Journal and Essays of John Woolman*, ed. Amelia Mott Gummere (London, 1922), p. 458.
[5] *Ibid.*, p. 487.

195

participation in the Society's business meetings, the Yearly Meeting finally instituted disownment for these offenses, except in cases where a slave was purchased as a preliminary to manumission. Then, as if to underscore the turning point in the Society's history, and to signal the success of the reformation within the church, slaveholding itself was prohibited, and the decision was buttressed with a new query: "Are Friends clear of importing, purchasing, disposing of, or *holding* mankind as slaves? And do they use those well who are set free and necessarily under their care, and not in circumstances, through nonage or incapacity, to minister to their own necessities? And are they careful to educate and encourage them in a religious and virtuous life?"[6]

Thus, by 1783, as the Quakers themselves pointed out, they were amply qualified to undertake a campaign against slavery in the outside world, having first won the battle within their own Society. Moreover, there were excellent reasons why the issue was a particularly appropriate one for the Quakers to confront in the public arena. To a degree, the address of 1783 constituted a gesture of reconciliation with the victorious patriots, in that it affirmed the Society's commitment to the principles of liberty; it showed the patriot government that the Quakers valued at least this important ideological foundation of the Revolution. At the same time, however, as in the various Quaker demands that full liberty of conscience be accorded to all, the petition put pressure on the new government to make good its professed principles by granting justice to the Negroes. This argument had been used before, and at the beginning of the Revolution by individuals,[7] but it was now brought to bear by the Society itself.[8] Then too, the address afforded the Society an opening to underscore its own virtues in this regard: "Thus may our Lights so shine before Men, that thou-

---

[6] PYM, 1774 (italics added).

[7] Anthony Benezet to Richard Shackleton, 6/vi/72, in George S. Brookes, *Friend Anthony Benezet* (Philadelphia, 1937), p. 294; Samuel Allinson to Patrick Henry, 17/x/74, MS 968, Quaker Collection, Haverford College Library, Haverford, Pa.

[8] PMS to United States Congress, 19/x/86.

sands afar off may be brought to confess it is through the Love of God shed abroad in our Hearts, and under the Authority thereof, that we labour to promote Peace on Earth & universal good-Will to Men, that we are afflicted with the Afflictions of the Poor, and oppressed by the Oppression of the Stranger among us."[9]

Perhaps the most beneficial aspect of the antislavery campaign, from the point of view of the Quakers' place in post-Revolutionary American society, was the fact that others, including "various religious denominations" and "The Clergy both of the Church of England & Dissenters," shared their opposition to slavery and were willing to join with Friends in their efforts to eradicate the institution.[10] It was undoubtedly this willingness, manifested even before the outbreak of the war, and strongly in evidence after it was over, which induced the Quakers to take up the public campaign when the fighting ended.[11]

The high regard they were shown was particularly gratifying to the Quakers because the support and praise of others in a political area in which they felt they had taken the lead amounted to a vindication of their political program; honor paid to them for their actions, they believed, was really honor given to the Divine Author of the testimony and principles which guided their behavior. Here, for example, is the praise of Patrick Henry: "I cannot but wish well to a People, whose system imitates the Example of him whose Life was perfect.—And believe me I shall honour the Quakers in their noble Effort to abolish Slavery. It is equally calculated to promote moral and political Good."[12]

The Quakers were thus reinforced in their commitment, and were eager to continue the campaign. "And as we perceive the Light of Truth in this respect is gradually taking place in the Minds of many who do not make religious profession with us, it is a subject worthy the consideration of all who desire the advancement of the Kingdom of righteousness & peace, to unite in pro-

[9] PYM to LYM, 1784.
[10] Anthony Benezet to Robert Pleasants, 8/iv/73, in Brookes, *Friend Anthony Benezet*, p. 299; PMS, 22/iv/73; PMS to LMS, 17/vii/83; PMS, 16/x/88.
[11] PMS to LMS, 17/vi/83.
[12] Brookes, *Friend Anthony Benezet*, p. 443.

moting it, carefully guarding against every thing tending to retard or prevent its progress."[13]

After the initial formulation of the Yearly Meeting address of 1783, the management of the antislavery campaign passed to the Meeting for Sufferings, which appointed a standing committee to remain vigilant for opportunities to advance the cause. For the most part, the committee concentrated on the problem of the slave trade as it was raised in the original petition, recalling this document to the attention of Congress at intervals.[14]

In Pennsylvania itself, for all practical purposes, the slave trade had been brought to an end by a series of high import duties imposed in 1761 as the result of a Quaker petition, duties which were renewed in 1768 and made even more prohibitive in 1773.[15] In 1780, largely because of the indefatigable lobbying of Anthony Benezet, the state had also passed a law for the gradual abolition of slavery. The major remaining concern was the fitting out of slave ships in Philadelphia, and this constituted the target of Quaker efforts until effective measures were imposed by the legislature in 1788.[16] In order to make the Pennsylvania measures still more effective, the Meeting for Sufferings also lobbied for similar prohibitions in the neighboring states of Delaware, Maryland, and New Jersey, with the active aid of members of other religious societies.[17]

At the end of the decade, the Yearly Meeting itself stepped back into the campaign. The original petition of 1783 had been addressed on behalf of the Society to the representative body of the new American nation, the Continental Congress. In 1789, with government about to convene under the new Constitution, the Meeting took occasion to submit a new appeal against slavery to the president, Senate, and House of Representatives of the United States. Earlier, before the Constitution had been ratified, some

---

[13] PMS to LMS, 21/xi/76.

[14] See, for example, PMS, 21/xii/86.

[15] Thomas E. Drake, *Quakers and Slavery in America* (New Haven, Conn., 1950), p. 86.

[16] *Ibid.*, p. 96.

[17] PMS, 15/v/88, 22/v/88, and 16/x/88.

Quaker leaders had expressed disapproval of the document on the grounds that it condoned the continued existence of slavery,[18] but after ratification the Quaker effort was directed at securing an amendment abolishing the slave trade immediately instead of postponing it for twenty years. A Yearly Meeting appeal to this effect was taken to New York in the fall of 1789 by a committee which included Nicholas Waln, James and John Pemberton, Henry Drinker, and Samuel Emlen. The plea stirred up a storm in Congress, provoking heated southern opposition, and was the earliest major battle fought on sectional grounds within the new national government. It was, however, ultimately unsuccessful.

With the failure of the Quaker attempt to induce Congress to abolish the slave trade once and for all in 1790, the Society's corporate efforts declined in intensity, for there was little more it could hope to accomplish in the North, and little hope of accomplishing anything at all in the South.[19] Although Friends, together with like-minded non-Quakers, continued to work privately in a practical way to improve the lot of the Negroes around them (principally through the agency of the Pennsylvania Abolition Society), in the 1790s the Society's corporate concern was turned in another direction, toward the Indians. To be sure, this was one of the oldest concerns of the Society in Pennsylvania, and the one with which we began this study, but it is also an appropriate one on which to end it. In the fifties, the Indian question was one which pointed up the political divisions among Quakers and between Quakers and others around them; in the nineties it symbolized the unity of the group and the culmination of half-a-century of political reorientation toward a new and harmonious role in the political society of Pennsylvania.

[18] James Pemberton to John Pemberton, 20/iv/88, PP, 50 : 30; James Pemberton to James Phillips, 4/v/88, *ibid.*, p. 28.
[19] Sydney James, *A People Among Peoples* (Cambridge, Mass., 1963), p. 298.

XIII

NEW EFFORTS AMONG THE INDIANS

Although the Indians had ceased to be a major factor in the political environment of the Quakers by the mid-1760s, the connection and contacts between the groups had merely lapsed, not ended. The Indians continued to pay their respects to the Quakers whenever their business, state or otherwise, brought them to Philadelphia, and they were always cordially received by the Friends. Joseph Oxley, a visiting English minister, reported an instance of such a meeting in October, 1770, between a group of Indians who were in Philadelphia to hold a treaty with the governor and a group of Friends who had gathered at the house of John Pemberton. In the course of his remarks to his Indian guests, Pemberton told them: "Brothers, we are not men concerned in the management of the affairs of government, and therefore cannot do much to serve the Indians on that account. But when any of them are sent down on business to the governor we are glad to see them, and shall be willing to do them any kindness we can."[1]

In 1773, possibly as the result of repeated Indian requests for Quaker teachers, the venerable Zebulon Heston, accompanied by John Parrish, decided to visit the Quakers' old friends the Delawares, who had by then moved beyond the Ohio.[2] Being careful

[1] Joseph Oxley, *A Journal of the Life and Gospel Labours of Joseph Oxley* (London, 1837), p. 323.
[2] PMS to LMS, 22/iv/73; PMS, 8/vii/73.

not to antagonize the governor or to infringe on his prerogative, a delegation of Friends waited on him to secure his approval of the plan and to ask if he had any message to transmit to the Indians. The governor seemed to think well of the project, and raised no objection to the Quakers' proposal. During the journey, the Indians' request for teachers was repeated to the two emissaries, but the Quakers were preoccupied with difficulties of their own in those years, and the Revolution soon precluded any effort to assist the Indians which might otherwise have developed.[3]

The American-British settlement of the Revolution left unsettled the position of the Indian tribes that had served as allies to the British, and for the most part they were left to shift for themselves when the war ended. The Treaty of Paris was followed by more than a decade of violence and unrest on the frontiers, as the native inhabitants of the western lands tried to stave off the influx of settlers from each of the Ohio. For much of this period, government-Indian diplomacy, like the fighting, was confined largely to the frontier itself, and the Quakers were not involved.

In 1790, however, two important developments occurred which led to a resumption of Quaker contacts with the Indians and a strong revival of interest in their condition and affairs. The first of these was the settlement of the United States capital at Philadelphia, which made the city a focal point for the management of Indian affairs, for these were now in the hands of the national government. The second occurrence, a consequence of the first, was the arrival in Philadelphia of three Seneca chiefs—Cornplanter, Big Tree, and Half Town—who had traveled down to the capital to assist in a peace settlement. Cornplanter, possibly at Washington's suggestion, asked the Society to provide instruction in the white men's ways for three Seneca boys, including his own son.[4] The Meeting for Sufferings notified Cornplanter of its will-

---

[3] Rayner W. Kelsey, *Friends and the Indians, 1655–1917* (Philadelphia, 1917), p. 34.

[4] Merle Deardorff and George S. Snyderman, "A Nineteenth Century Journal of a Visit to the Indians of New York," *Proceedings of the American Philosophical Society*, 100 (1956) : 584; PMS, 19/v/91.

ingness to undertake the teaching, but further developments on the frontier prevented the offer from being accepted at the time.

With their interest in the Indians rekindled, the Quakers were all the more dismayed by the increase in hostilities on the frontier and by the apparent lack of firm prospects for peace. In an epistle to the president and to both houses of Congress, the Meeting deplored the war with the Indians and voiced the hope that the government would "pursue such pacific measures as have been heretofore experienced to be salutary and effectual in securing Peace and Friendship with the original Owners of this Land, whose religious instruction and civilization if rightly promoted, may tend to this desirable end."[5] To the Meeting's satisfaction, the epistle received a respectful hearing, and it was recorded that "the performance of our duty therein tends to the satisfaction & peace of our own minds, apprehending a concern should excite us on all occasions to unite our Endeavours for the promotion of the peaceable Kingdom of Christ and prevent the effusion of human blood."[6]

The next occasion had, in fact, already presented itself. Fifty Iroquois sachems arrived in Philadelphia on March 13 for a council with the administration. In response to this "opening," the Meeting for Sufferings was prompted to institutionalize a program for taking advantage of such opportunities; the Meeting decided that,

> when any of the Natives of the Wilderness comes to the City to transact business with the Government, it is thought advisable to continue the Custom that has long subsisted of shewing our friendly regard to them, to inculcate on their minds the value and benefit of a peaceable disposition, and to remind them of the Cordiality and friendship which early commenced between their Ancestors & ours on the first settlement of Pennsylva, and continued uninterrupted through many years; on which occasions they have always expressed their pleasure & Satisfaction.[7]

[5] PMS, 15/xii/91.
[6] PMS to LMS, 15/iii/92.
[7] *Ibid.*

As a result of the Iroquois' visit to Philadelphia, several members of the tribe agreed to serve as emissaries to the western Indians, carrying a proposal for peace talks with the United States government. The proposal won the day. It was agreed that hostilities would be suspended for the winter of 1792/93 and that peace talks would be held the following Spring, whereupon the Iroquois notified Washington of the prospects for a council and took the initiative of asking expressly that "some Friend, or Quaker," accompany the government commissioners to the talks.

For its own part, the Yearly Meeting had already appointed a committee to unite with the Meeting for Sufferings to consider means by which the Society might help to promote peace with the disaffected tribes. Once again, the Quakers chose to manifest their concern in the form of an address to the president and Congress: "Our Minds have been brought into a religious Concern, that the Rulers of this Land may pursue such Measures as may tend to the Promotion of the Peace and Happiness of the People. We are sensible that the Lord's judgments are in our Land, and being deeply affected with the distressed Situation of the Frontier Inhabitants, we desire a solid & careful enquiry may be made into the Cause. And we are firmly persuaded, that if the Counsel and Direction of the holy Spirit is waited for and followed, the divine Blessings will crown the Labours of those who uprightly engage in the Work of Peace."[8] Expressing their approval of the administration's disposition to promote pacific measures with the Indians, the Society pledged the compliance of Friends with the government policy, which had always been their own, of keeping settlers off the lands that had not been fairly purchased from the natives. The epistle concluded with the following highly significant and suggestive statement:

> We feel cautious not to move out of our proper Line but being interested in the Welfare of this Country, & convinc'd of the Expedience of the further Endeavours being used to encourage the Indians to come forward with a full Representation and Statement

[8] PYM, 1792.

of their Grievances, and that every just Cause of Uneasiness in their Minds may be fully investigated and removed, we apprehend it our Duty again to address you on this affecting and important Occasion; under a Belief that nothing short of strict Justice will ever be a Basis of solid and lasting Peace.[9]

What is particularly striking about both of the Quakers' messages is the close similarity they bore to the approach of the Friendly Association for Regaining and Preserving Peace with the Indians by Pacific Measures during the Indian crisis of the 1750s. As against the similarity, however, one need only contrast the assertiveness and partisan political objectives of the earlier venture with the caution, deference, and circumspection of the later one to realize how far the Quakers had come politically in three-and-a-half decades. The Quakers of the 1790s were in an entirely different position from that of their brethren in the fifties. They had no stake in any partisan position relative to the Indians, and no place in government to vindicate and protect. Nor were they troubled by deviance and opposition from within the Society. Thus their professed goals of advancing the peace testimony and serving the welfare of their country were in no danger of being compromised in the public eye by their own or other Quakers' actions, as their predecessors' efforts had been.

Despite their caution "not to move out of our proper Line," the Quaker leaders were more than pleased when the administration notified them of the Iroquois' request for their presence at the ensuing treaty; the request was an implicit acknowledgment of their special position in Pennsylvania. Although any work with the Indians involved complicity with the government, the Society's leaders apparently believed that the church had been solidified and purified from within to the extent that involvement in government, in the way that was opening to them, would not endanger their spiritual gains or lead them into corrupt and worldly practices; instead, it would yield benefits to all concerned. Thus, after long years of actively dissociating itself from government, the

[9] PMS, 17/xi/92.

205

Society as a corporate body was, at the end of 1792, on the verge of becoming directly involved in government affairs. In terms of the history of Quaker political development in the eighteenth century, the significance of this situation would be difficult to overestimate.

In response to the Indians' request, and with Washington's consent, six Friends expressed a willingness to undertake the arduous mission of attending the forthcoming conference, held at Sandusky in the summer of 1793.[10] These men—John Elliott, John Parrish, William Savery, Jacob Lindley, Joseph Moore, and William Hartshorne—traveled under individual concern, as was customary, with certificates from their respective monthly meetings; in the address which was prepared for them by the Meeting for Sufferings, all concern with the management of the affairs of government was expressly disclaimed.[11] The disclaimer notwithstanding, the Friends' participation in the Indian talks took place under the auspices of the government and with its express approbation.[12] Moreover, the six delegates themselves expressed an awareness that the reputation of their religious society would be bound up with the success or failure of their mission.[13] In 1770, when John Pemberton told the Indians that the Quakers were "not men concerned in the management of affairs of government," the statement was a fair one, and was soon to become even more accurate. In 1793, exactly the opposite was the case.

For reasons which have been dealt with by others at considerable length, the council at Sandusky was a failure from a diplomatic point of view, and the Quakers who attended could not help but be affected by this negative outcome and the prospect of renewed warfare which it raised. The council did, however, afford them a valuable opportunity to renew their acquaintance with former

---

[10] Francis R. Taylor, *The Life of William Savery of Philadelphia, 1750–1804* (New York, 1925), p. 70; PMS, 21/iii/93.

[11] PMS, 19/iv/93.

[12] Taylor, *Life of Savery*, p. 70.

[13] *Ibid.*, p. 71.

friends among the Indian tribes, and to establish contact with others. In addition, they had ample occasion to expound their pacific principles to all concerned in the negotiations, and this brought satisfaction in its own right. In their report to the Meeting for Sufferings upon their return, they summed up their reactions thus: "Notwithstanding the desirable Object of Peace was not obtained we have not a doubt of the Rectitude of our submitting to go on the arduous & exercising Journey, we believe it tended to renew the antient Friendship with the Indian Natives; and altho' we were not admitted to see them in full council, yet have reason to believe they were all made acquainted with our Motives & friendly Sentiment towards them."[14]

Even more gratifying perhaps, and the source of considerable encouragement, was the high regard expressed by others for the Quakers' benevolent efforts. Governor Simcoe, for example, of the Canadian government, told the Quaker emissaries that their undertaking did their Society great honor.[15] And despite their objections against the drinking of toasts, the six Friends were pleased by the pledge proposed by a group of British officers at Detroit: "Success to the Quakers in their present honorable and disinterested undertaking."[16] It was precisely this quality of disinterestedness which distinguished the Quakers' policy and approach to the Indians from that of the Friendly Association, and which brought praise to the Society instead of censure.

The Quakers themselves were cognizant of the contrast between their present situation and the stormy career of the Friendly Association a generation earlier. Even though their perspective was understandably somewhat distorted and they imputed the change to alterations in the character of the government rather than to changes in the behavior of Friends, they recognized clearly the preferability of maintaining amicable relations with the government and were deeply gratified by manifestations of official cordiality and high regard. The following is an illuminating reflec-

[14] PMS, 19/xii/93.
[15] Taylor, *Life of Savery*, p. 74.
[16] *Ibid.*, p. 84.

tion recorded by James Emlen, a Quaker delegate to a subsequent treaty (discussed later in this chapter).

> At the invitation of Colonel Pickering (sole Commissioner from the United States to treat with the Indians) we went to dine with him at his Lodgings at the house of Thos. Morris, where we were kindly entertained, he manifesting a friendly deportment towards us; indeed it is cause of humble admiration to reflect on the contrast between those who formerly executed Government in Pennsylvania & the present rulers of the United States, the former impelled by that selfish jealousy which a dark & covetous policy inspires, were violently opposed to the attendance of friends at the Indian Treaties, notwithstanding which our predecessors actuated by a regard to their own safety as Members of civil Society & a love of humanity & justice overcame all opposn.—whilst the latter, on the contrary, endued with a spirit of more liberality & well knowing the influence which the exercise of benevolence hath gained our Society over the minds of the Indians, are rather solicitous that friends should attend.[17]

With the collapse of the talks at Sandusky, the western tribes renewed the battle for their lands against the American soldiers and settlers. In addition, the New York Iroquois, who had been counted on the side of the American interest in 1793, began to show disturbing signs of an inclination to join their hostile brethren a year later. In order to counteract British influence in stirring up Indian hostility, the government, in the late summer of 1794, called for a treaty conference with the Six Nations, which would be held later that fall. As before, the Iroquois desired that Quakers assist at the negotiations, and to this the government added its own encouragement for their participation.[18] Both parties apparently valued the disinterested good offices of the Friends, the Indians seeing them as fair and honest advisers, and the government acknowledging them as capable mediators and establishers of rapport with the natives.

[17] James Emlen, "The Journal of James Emlen Kept on a Trip to Canandaigua, New York," ed. William N. Fenton, *Ethnohistory*, 12 (1965) : 292.
[18] PMS, 21/viii/94 and 8/ix/94.

The decision to comply with the joint request of the administration and the Indians was made by the Meeting for Sufferings, acting in concordance with the Yearly Meeting committee appointed in 1792 to consider the Society's Indian policy, under a sense of obligation that "what is incumbent on us . . . in contributing to the removal of any just Causes of Uneasiness remaining as Obstructions to a solid Pacification with those People, may not be omitted."[19]

Four men—William Savery, John Parrish, David Bacon, and James Emlen—offered to attend the treaty, to be held at Canandaigua in New York State. Two of the Friends, Savery and Parrish, were well known to the Indians, having assisted at Sandusky the year before.

Although the treaty proceedings, which convened at the end of September, were marked with the slowness, wrangling, frustration, and tactical jockeying for advantage which customarily attended such negotiations, they ultimately produced a settlement, for which an important measure of the credit went to the efforts of the Friends in attendance. They enjoyed the confidence of the Indians and the commissioners alike,[20] and served as vital mediators in a crisis which threatened to disrupt the treaty just as it was on the verge of being concluded.[21] Significantly, they declined to sign the treaty as witnesses—though requested by both parties to do so—because of conscientious reservations against being direct parties to a settlement which confirmed white possession of land that had been acquired by conquest, and for which they believed the Indians were being inadequately compensated. At the same time, however, they did not feel it to be their place to disrupt a settlement in which the two parties concurred, and they welcomed the conclusion of a peace, which was their principal desire.[22] They

---

[19] *Ibid.*, 8/ix/94.

[20] William Savery, *A Journal of the Life Travels, and Religious Labours of William Savery*, ed. Jonathan Evans (London, 1844), pp. 81, 90 (hereafter cited as *Journal*).

[21] Taylor, *Life of Savery*, pp. 142–43.

[22] Savery, *Journal*, pp. 87, 97; Emlen, "Journal," p. 329.

were obliged by their position to remain disinterested parties with regard to the form of the settlement, and they did so.

Still, although they could not intercede on behalf of the Iroquois in the working out of the treaty, the Quakers found themselves earnestly concerned for the Indians' future welfare. William Savery recorded their thoughts as the negotiations progressed.

> This evening Friends being quietly together, our minds were seriously turned to consider the present state of these six nations, and a lively prospect presented that a mode could be adopted by which Friends and other humane people might be useful to them in a greater degree than has ever yet been effected; at least for the cause of humanity and justice, and for the sake of this poor declining people, we are induced to hope so. The prospect and feelings of our minds were such as will not be forgotten, if we are favoured to return home. The happy effects of steady perseverance in the cause of the Africans, is an encouraging reflection, and may serve as an animating example in this.[23]

Without questioning the integrity of the Quakers' motives in working for the aid of the Negroes or the Indians, we may remind ourselves that one of the "happy effects" of the efforts on behalf of the enslaved Africans to which Savery alluded was the granting of public honor to the Society and to their benevolent principles; we have identified this, in fact, as the principal political goal of the Quakers in the post-Revolutionary period. It becomes apparent that the Indian work was undertaken for substantially the same reasons, although plain humanitarian motives were certainly important in immediate terms. The Quaker role at Sandusky and Canandaigua had already elicited the high regard of outsiders, and by the close of the latter treaty there was evidence of a strong inclination on the part of the Friends to devote more intensive efforts to the cause of Indian welfare.

Moreover, a promising direction for these efforts had been indicated years before. For several decades the Society had been receiv-

---

23 *Journal*, p. 75.

ing requests from various tribes for assistance in the form of instruction and training in the arts of civilization; the request was revived at Canandaigua. "Sagareesa, or the Sword Carrier [a Tuscarora chief], visited us; he appears to be a thoughtful man, and mentioned a desire he had, that some of our young men might come among them as teachers; we supposed he meant as schoolmasters and artizans. Perhaps this intimation may be made use of in a future day, that great good may accrue to the poor Indians, if some religious young men of our Society could, from a sense of duty, be induced to spend some time among them, either as schoolmasters or mechanics."[24] In 1773, when a like request was first made, no young Quakers felt the call of duty, but by the mid-1790s the situation had altered.

On their return from Canandaigua, the four travelers conveyed their impressions and suggestions to the Meeting for Sufferings,[25] and by the time of the next Yearly Meeting the Society was ready to act upon them. A special committee, appointed for the purpose of considering what might be done in this regard, brought in a recommendation that the Society undertake "to promote amongst [the Indians] the Principles of the Christian Religion, as well as to turn their attention to School Learning, Agriculture, and useful Mechanic Employments," and that a liberal subscription be raised to finance the undertaking.[26] To carry the decisions into effect, a large new committee was set up. This body, to which additions were subsequently made, was known as the Indian Committee, and from the perspective of this study its establishment was the culmination of the entire period under review.

The Indian Committee was a unique body within the Society of Friends at the time of its establishment. Within a year of its founding, it was constituted as a permanent standing committee and was designated as a meeting of record which would coordinate the Society's work in a particular and restricted social area. Its nearest analogue was the Meeting for Sufferings, and it is note-

24 *Ibid.*, p. 79.
25 PMS, 20/xii/94.
26 PYM, 1795.

worthy in this connection that these two bodies, together with the extrasocietal and abortive Friendly Association, represented the only instances of structural innovation during the entire course of political change described in this study; all other developments must be accounted for in terms of changes in the content of *existing* institutions or of the redistribution of personnel through individual changes in attitude or outlook. This is a dimension which seems especially pertinent to comparative investigation, for some cases have been documented in which institutional discrepancies have grown out of the development of *new* structures and *new* institutions to meet the demands of novel situations in which earlier expectations and responses do not apply or in which they are not relevant.[27] Here too, of course, the incompatibility of institutions may not become overtly apparent so long as it is possible for situational separation to be maintained.

The Meeting for Sufferings, like the Indian Committee, was a permanent offshoot of the Yearly Meeting and a meeting of record, but it had a wider area of competence; it was delegated, in effect, to represent the Yearly Meeting and the whole Society during the remainder of the year when the Yearly Meeting was not in session. Moreover, the Meeting for Sufferings was established as a *defensive* political arm of the Society in Pennsylvania, which functioned in large part to cover the Friends' gradual withdrawal from worldly political involvement and to defend their rights and principles against outside attack while the reformation went on within. The Indian Committee, on the other hand, was a product of that reformation. It represented the Society's direct assumption of the role of coordinator of a positive political *offensive* undertaken in the name of the church as a whole, an offensive based on, and strictly limited by, approaches and principles which were products of the reformation. Let us examine its operations in more detail.

As we have said, the ostensible purpose of the Indian Committee was to coordinate the Society's aid to the Indians, and this it

[27] See, for example, A. L. Epstein, *Politics in an Urban African Community* (Manchester, 1958), pp. 229–40.

212

did, beginning in 1796 with the establishment and operation of a mission to the Oneidas which lasted for something less than two years, and then moving on to conduct a similar program among the Allegheny Seneca on the Cornplanter grant. There are numerous accounts describing the missionary efforts, the details of which need not concern us here.[28] Suffice it to say that the bulk of the volunteer missionaries' energies were devoted not to proselytizing, but to inducing their charges to give up their excessive use of alcohol and to take up agriculture as practiced by the whites—that is, in family groups on individual holdings rather than by women alone on land controlled by the matrilineages. The point which requires emphasis is that the missionary work among the Indians, like the other benevolent undertakings of the Society, had an essentially political foundation. It afforded an opening for the exercise of the Quakers' "professed principles of Peace and good will to Men" in a sphere of affairs which affected the whole country, and therefore gave rise to an avenue by which the excellence of those principles could be demonstrated before men in the interests of society at large.

Adding to the significance of the Indian work was the fact that in undertaking it the Quakers were performing what was actually the work of the government, for Indian affairs, and responsibility for the condition of the natives, belonged within the precinct of the administration. The "apparent friendly disposition of Government toward [their] desirable Object" was one of the factors which encouraged the Quakers to undertake their work among the Indians in the first place.[29] Furthermore, it was necessary to secure the formal consent of the government for the actual initiation of the project. Happily, the Quakers were well known to the two officials in the administration with whom they had to deal. Timothy Pickering, then secretary of state, had been a government commissioner at the treaty of Canandaigua and remembered the good offices which Friends performed there. Pickering had also been at

[28] See Anthony F. C. Wallace, *The Death and Rebirth of the Seneca* (New York, 1970), and the references therein.
[29] PYM, 1795.

Sandusky the year before, and thus had double knowledge of the disposition of the Quakers. Israel Chapin, superintendent of the Six Nations, was the son of the elder Israel Chapin, who also had represented the government at Canandaigua. Both men, therefore, were "friendly disposed toward the concern, and willing to aid the Committee in the promotion thereof."[30] Pickering wrote letters to accompany the circular letter sent out by the Indian Committee —one to the Indians, one to the interpreter Jasper Parrish, and one to Chapin, in which he stressed the disinterestedness of the Quakers' benevolence. These letters, copies of which are in the files of the Indian Committee, attest to the success of the Friends' political design. Describing the project to the chiefs and warriors of the Six Nations, Pickering wrote:

> Now Brothers I have the great pleasure to inform you that your good friends the Quakers have formed a wise plan, to show your young Men and Boys the most useful practices of the white people. They will chuse some prudent good Men to instruct them. These good men will do this only for the love they bear to you their Fellow-men as Children of the Great Spirit, whom they desire to please and who will be pleased with the good they do to you.[31]

To Chapin, he wrote: "The Society of Friends have formed a plan to instruct the Indians of the Six Nations in husbandry, and the most necessary arts of civil Life. The goodness of the design, and the disinterestedness of the motives, must recommend it to the favour and Support of all who wish the happiness of their fellow-men."[32]

The setting up of the Indian Committee, then, and the initiation of its labors, meant that the Society had institutionalized, within its corporate structure, an agency which was political in two respects. On the one hand, the work of the committee, like the Society's work on behalf of public morality or in opposition to the

[30] Indian Committee, 3/viii/96, Papers of the Indian Committee, Box I, Philadelphia Yearly Meeting, Department of Records, Philadelphia, Pa.
[31] *Ibid.*
[32] *Ibid.*

slave trade, was actuated by a desire to influence the social policies of society at large and to bring sound practice and divine approbation to the country through the exercise of the distinctive Quaker testimonies. On the other hand, the Indian Committee represented the taking over of a function of government by the Society in its corporate capacity. The fact that this should have come about as the culmination of a long process of political reorientation, a goodly portion of which was devoted to getting individual Quakers *out* of government while proclaiming the Society's detachment from worldly political engagement, is as appropriate as it is striking, and it provides an excellent standpoint from which to review and analyze the process itself and bring the study to a close.

XIV

CONCLUSION

Max Weber has written that "every religiously grounded un-worldly love and indeed every ethical religion must, in similar measure and for similar reasons, experience tensions with the sphere of political behavior."[1] The Pennsylvania Quakers were one of Weber's cases in point, and, although his knowledge of the case was less than adequate, there is no questioning the appropriateness of citing them in this connection, for the key to the development of Quaker politics in Pennsylvania, as traced in the foregoing pages, was the contradiction between the kinds of behavior and outlook associated with involvement in worldly politics on the one hand, and the demands of consistent compliance with the testimonies of Quakerism on the other.

During the first half of the eighteenth century, it is evident that the character of Quaker involvement in the political community of Pennsylvania was not without a considerable element of compromise, expediency, assertiveness, contentiousness, and general reliance upon the human agency, which ran directly counter to the Quaker prescription of meek and selfless submission to the agency and protection of the Almighty. It is also true, however, that the religious standards of the Society were sufficiently relaxed and the

---

[1] *The Sociology of Religion*, trans. Ephraim Fischoff (Boston, 1963), p. 223.

217

worldly political style so firmly entrenched that, as long as no issue was made of this state of affairs, it posed no real difficulty for any but a few pious souls, and generated no recognizable conflict within the Society. We have noted a few signs of a lack of fit between active political engagement and a properly religious life —the 1710 minute of the Yearly Meeting cautioning against deviation from Quaker principles in office, Israel Pemberton's attempt to set up a more strictly pacifist slate for the Assembly election of 1744, John Churchman's refusal of office in 1748, John Pemberton's admonitions to his more worldly brothers in the early 1750s—but the adoption of birthright membership, and the economic prosperity, religious and political freedom, and lack of outside pressures for Quakers in Pennsylvania all had contributed to a loosening of religious bonds within the Society to the extent that worldliness and compromise could be accommodated without visible strain.

Then, around mid-century, the situation began to change, both within the Society and in the political environment, with the emergence of the reform movement, the growth of the anti-Quaker opposition, and the inception of a period of imperial warfare which had important colonial repercussions. Quaker legislators in Pennsylvania had long since worked out means of rationalizing appropriations for military defense, but, in 1755–56, for the first time there was warfare within the borders of Pennsylvania itself, and a formal declaration of war was issued by the governor. In consequence, and also because of the growing strength of the opposition, the demands on the Quaker Assembly for military measures were more vigorous and urgent than ever before, as was the denunciation of Quakers for failing to provide them. Added to these forces was the public emergence within the Society of the movement for religious reform, calling not merely for a holding of the pacifist line but for a return to the rigorous standards of the church in the early years of its history, before the decline into worldliness had weakened its purity and diluted its moral strength. The combined effect of these factors was to precipitate a major cultural crisis within the Society of Friends in Pennsylvania in the sense suggested by Turner, Swartz, and Tuden, namely, "a momentous juncture or turning point in the relations between components of a political field—at which apparent peace becomes overt conflict and covert antagonisms become visible."[2] In the case of the Quakers, the crisis was precipitated not so much by breaching a norm as by bringing out into the open a conflict between norms— political and religious—concerning which no loud and public concern had formerly been voiced. The principal focus of this investigation has been upon the consequences of the conflict for the Quakers as individuals and for the Society of Friends as an organization in the decades which followed.

To speak of the incompatibility of the compromise, pursuit of self-interest, contentiousness, and general worldliness of partisan politics with the steadfastness, suppression of self, humility, and dependence upon divine guidance of the pure Quaker faith is to speak first of all of a conflict between the behavioral expectations inherent in institutions. Institutions, of course, are analytical abstractions, and cannot themselves be in conflict; rather, the conflict is manifested by conflicting role expectations and is localized, when it occurs, within those individuals who are subject to the discrepant but simultaneous demands of those institutions.

It has been pointed out by analysts of role conflict that one way of coping with—in fact, neutralizing—conflict of this kind is to subordinate one set of expectations to the other, or decline altogether to be bound by them, opting, in effect, for the consistency of one set of role demands.[3] This was the aveune followed by those factions of politically relevant Quakers we have designated the *worldly politicians* and the *reformers.*

From this point of view, the politicians were those Friends who, when confronted with the necessity of choosing, opted for their political roles at the expense of their religion, refusing to accept the contention of the meeting leadership that wholehearted en-

[2] Victor Turner, Mark Swartz, and Arthur Tuden, *Political Anthropology* (Chicago, 1966), p. 33.

[3] Theodore R. Sarbin and Vernon R. Allen, "Role Theory," in *The Handbook of Social Psychology*, vol. 1, *Systematic Positions*, ed. Gardner Lindzey and Eliot Aronson, 2nd ed. (Reading, Mass., 1968), p. 542.

gagement in worldly politics was incompatible with being a Friend. To be sure, it was not incompatible in the technical sense of membership in the Society of Friends, for the politicians remained members, despite their behavior, and attended meetings for worship, but we will get to this point later. For the politicians, the Society was as much—or even more—a political power group as a religious organization, and their principal concerns were the partisan issues of the day, such as public finance, military defense, or a change to royal government. They were subjected to pressure by the meeting leadership, in which they themselves took no part from the mid-fifties to the Revolution, in order to avoid compromising the Society and its doctrines, but they refused to accede to the Society's demands and remained fixed upon the partisan arena.

The reformers related to the conflict between institutions in the same way as the politicians, but at the opposite pole, for they subordinated all other demands to those of the Quaker faith. Their goal was to re-establish the religious purity of the Society of Friends, and they looked for guidance not to the electorate but to God, whose leadings could be discerned within one's own spirit or in the disposition of outward events. Their religious commitment predisposed the reformers strongly against partisan politics, and they desired and labored for the disengagement of Friends from that sphere. As we have stressed repeatedly throughout the study, however, this does not mean that the reformers were disengaged from politics, that they engaged in no political behavior themselves, for it is just as political to endeavor to change someone else's political behavior as it is to engage wholeheartedly in partisan politics oneself. Moreover, in the functional sense in which politics is understood in this work, the reformers had a positive political program and strategy of their own. We have defined as political all behavior which is aimed at influencing the setting and pursuit of public goals, which for the reformers involved doing their religious duty as Quakers, thereby serving as moral guides to society at large and intercedents for mankind before God.

Thus, for two of the three political types we have identified among the Pennsylvania Quakers, the incompatibility between religion and politics was not productive of role conflict, for neither group recognized the legitimacy of both sets of role expectations. It was the third type, the *politiques*, who experienced the role strain which interests us here.

The fundamental allegiance of the politiques, we have pointed out, was to the reputation and integrity of the Society of Friends and its religious testimony. These men, however, were wealthy and powerful, socialized and habituated to secular political power and influence. As it appeared to them, the source of the stress upon the Society lay in the hands of their political adversaries, and because they were used to dealing in the political arena they endeavored to defend the church by worldly political means— through involvement in electoral politics, lobbying, and other pressure tactics with partisan overtones. It is here that we find the potential core of role conflict, the pursuit of religious ends by worldly means, for it is here that conflicting role expectations are brought together in a single sphere of activity. The aspect of potentiality must be stressed, however, because it is quite clear that, for the most part, the politiques pursued their efforts on behalf of their church believing in all good faith that their means —the outlook and methods to which their historical and social position and their upbringing called them—would serve their ends. Role strain, in the sense of felt difficulty in fulfilling role obligations,[4] arose only intermittently. This in turn suggests that the politiques had recourse to some other adjustive strategy in order to lessen its occurrence.

The strategy they employed was twofold. One means of forestalling conflict derived from the means-ends nature of the incompatible elements in their chosen course of political action. By giving cognitive primacy to their religiously oriented political goals and subordinating the worldly means by which they pursued them, the politiques provided themselves with grounds for viewing their behavior as properly religious, and their association with the

[4] William J. Goode, "A Theory of Role Strain," *American Sociological Review*, 25 (1960) : 483.

221

reformers within the meeting structure helped to sustain this view. The other components of their adjustive strategy, more important because of the difficulties they encountered in maintaining it, rested upon an attempt to segregate the civil from the religious spheres by pursuing their active political offensives outside the formal structure of the Society. This motive was clearest in the activities of the Friendly Association, which was explicitly described as an undertaking of Friends in their "civil" capacity, but it was also present in their activities as individuals, such as taking a public stand on the issue of a change to royal government, returning to public office, etc. The implicit assumption, of course, and one which would have been unacceptable to the reformers, was that there were separate standards for behavior in each sphere, and what may have been unacceptable within the framework of the Society of Friends was legitimate outside its formal organizational structure.[5]

Relying upon the compensatory strategies we have outlined, the politiques pursued their political program on behalf of their religious society from the mid-1750s almost through the sixties, involving themselves in the Friendly Association, the campaign for a change to royal government, the first non-importation campaign, and even returning to public office when political gains by the Presbyterians raised fears of an eventual Presbyterian takeover of the province. The basic flaw in the politiques' program was that it could not succeed, for reasons which they could not foresee or fully understand. They were attempting to uphold the place and reputation of the Quakers in Pennsylvania during just that period when the numerically superior members of other groups were attaining a sense of their own power and becoming intent upon democratizing the government of the province, thereby challenging the hegemony of the wealthy, eastern ruling class—mostly Quakers or of Quaker extraction. There simply was no way that

[5] Cf. A. L. Epstein, *Politics in an Urban African Community* (Manchester, 1958), pp. 229–40.

attacks on the Society could be forestalled, for the opposition leaders saw no point in distinguishing between the Quaker politicians and the Quaker politiques; both were clearly opposed to their own political ambitions, so there was no point in being concerned about such irrelevancies as the stronger or weaker commitment to Quakerism of either faction. Continued stress, then, and recurrent failure were all but inevitable for the politiques, given the nature of the political environment within which they had to operate. It was at those times when the stress became especially heavy, when their stratagems failed, when a particular course of action seemed to bring down even stronger attacks, that the unstable role compromise they had worked out for themselves gave way; individual politiques were driven to question the course they had chosen and to reflect that perhaps they had been too worldly after all, that peace and ultimate vindication might be attained by withdrawing altogether from the worldly arena. The reformers, of course, were ever ready to reinforce this view. It was stress from the environment, then, which was the precipitating cause of role conflict when it did occur. When the stress eased again and the crises passed, however, the politiques turned back to the worldly arena and took up their former ways, for those were the ways they knew best how to pursue.

The second non-importation campaign, however, beginning in Pennsylvania in 1769, marked a turning point beyond which this process could no longer operate. Prior to that time, whatever compromise was entailed in participating in partisan politics was at least a kind of compromise which Quakers had been able to come to terms with during the history of the province and which the politiques had been socialized and habituated to accept. As long as it was possible to carry on in traditional ways, a kind of equilibrium could be maintained, even though partisan conflict was endemic.

From the 1740s onward, however, new political forces were developing in Pennsylvania which in many fundamental ways were opposed to the political role of Quakers in the province. These forces, in the forefront of the movement toward revolution, were given to mass action, public meetings, coercion, and an ever-increasing disdain for moderation, all of which were anathema to the Quaker leaders and simply beyond the limits of political conduct which the politiques felt they could employ as Friends. By the time of the second non-importation campaign, the politiques finally realized that the political arena had changed to the extent that the prospect of there no longer being any room for them to participate on terms which they could accept had become very real. By mid-1774, this prospect had become the reality, and, although they continued to issue anti-Revolutionary statements up until 1776, their withdrawal from direct participation in public affairs was sealed two years earlier.

For the Quaker politiques, as for all Americans, the Revolution brought about a fundamental restructuring of political life, although it is somewhat ironic that the struggle which opened the way for fuller political involvement for great numbers of citizens served to constrict severely the sphere of participation of the politiques, whose forebears had welcomed the non-Quakers to Pennsylvania. Already alienated by the ascendency of the Revolutionary party, the outbreak of actual warfare and the institution of the Test Act and of tax measures for military finance sealed the final withdrawal of politiques from worldly political engagement. No longer able to cope with the worldly political arena, they fell back, as in other crises, on the reformers' perspective, viewing the trials of war and disruption as divine judgments for moral decline, and maintaining the necessity of Friends remaining wholly apart from the turmoil in order to devote themselves entirely to the integrity of the church and its testimony. So drastic and protracted was the war experience that those politiques who survived it never returned to their former ways; the Revolution drove them back within the sheltering boundaries of the Society. This time, when they withdrew to the position which had enabled the reformers to cope all along, they stayed there. By finally giving up their engagement in worldly politics, the politiques were able during the Revolution to write an end to the role conflict which had burdened them off and on for more than thirty years.

We have to this point been concentrating our attention on conflict within individual Quakers—that is, role conflict—because that is where conflict theory directs us under conditions of institutional incompatibility. At the same time, however, we have been neglecting another dimension—namely, conflict between Quakers, which we know to have been a feature of the Quaker experience during this same period, and one grounded in the same incompatibility between a pure Quaker life and involvement in worldly politics which divided the Society into opposing factions.

Social conflict is not something we would ordinarily expect in a case of this kind, for institutional incompatibility is generally held to generate conflict within individuals, and "group conflicts are at their strongest, are most likely to develop and least easily dissipated when no conflict is felt within the person."[6] Studies like Lloyd Fallers' *Bantu Bureaucracy*, for example, have been concerned to demonstrate how conflict engendered within individuals by the discrepant demands of different institutions in the political sphere "does *not* divide persons into intransigently opposed groups."[7] The question is, how does incompatibility between institutions make for conflict between sets of individuals as well as within individuals?

Let us first review the structure of the conflict with which this study is concerned. We recall that there was on either ideological side of the politiques a segment of the Society which opted for one or the other set of conflicting expectations—the reformers for pure religion and the politicians for worldly politics. Moreover, the politiques understood themselves to be allied ideologically with the reformers, inclining to this extent toward their goals rather than their means. Both the politiques and the reformers were concerned with defending the reputation of the Society and its testimony, so they made common cause against the politicians, whose actions they considered were having the opposite effect. Their base of operation was the formal meeting structure, the con-

[6] James S. Coleman, "Social Cleavage and Religious Conflict," *Journal of Social Issues*, 12, no. 3 (1956) : 46.

[7] 2nd ed. (Chicago, 1965), p. 246.

trol of which, as the members of the Society most concerned with religious affairs, they shared—the reformers because of their intense spiritual dedication, the politiques because of their social influence.

From this base within the meeting structure, the reformers and politiques took the ideological offensive against the politicians, who were the most passive parties to the conflict in the sense that they manifested their opposition to their more religious brethren simply by refusing to accede to their demands and going about their political business. The efforts of the more religious faction involved minutes and advices against officeholding and later against active involvement in the Revolutionary movement, thereby dissociating the Society from the activities of the politicians, and direct personal efforts to change the politicians' ways.

Given the control of the meeting structure by the reformers and politiques, what is notable about the conflict within the Society is the fact that it remained within the Society; despite the fact that those in control considered the behavior of the politicians to be in violation of the pure testimony of the church, despite the fact that the meetings had the power to invoke disciplinary measures against religious offenders—and such measures were explicitly threatened—no one was disowned from the Society of Friends in Pennsylvania on grounds relating to political behavior up to the time of the Revolution.

It is difficult to account for this circumstance with any certainty, although a number of possible contributing factors may be suggested. First of all, in terms of the total membership of the Society of Friends in Pennsylvania, the reformist position was, during the fifties and sixties, unquestionably a minority one, and a relatively small minority at that. Despite their prominence in the leadership of the Society, the active reformers were relatively few in number, and it is likely that the membership at large was not hostile to the continuation of their co-religionists in office. The precedent of history was on their side, and partisan sympathies naturally favored Quakers over non-Quakers, especially Presbyterians. Moreover, the reputation of the testimony, of which the meeting leadership made such an issue, was not seriously threatened except in those periods surrounding the crises of 1755–56, 1763, and to a lesser extent 1769. Finally, it is clear that the politiques themselves, with whom the reformers shared the positions of leadership, did not fully reject the validity of participation in worldly politics, including the holding of office, until approximately 1770, although they deplored such activity as brought difficulty to the Society. Whatever the cause, however, the net effect was that the politicians were able to retain their membership in the Society, and internal conflict persisted up to the Revolution.

The Revolution altered the balance within the Society by shifting the ground of political engagement in the political system at large. Whereas formerly no grounds had been found for taking disciplinary action against the politicians, the Revolution not only provided ample grounds for doing so, but it affected the religious leaders of the Society in such a way that they were especially strongly motivated—all but compelled in fact—to use them. War and rebellion clearly were disownable offenses, and any Quaker who accommodated himself to the demands of the Revolutionary regime to any extent—by paying taxes, taking the oath of allegiance, joining in military activities, or accepting political office— was held to be in violation of the Discipline. The choice between strict religious compliance and engagement in worldly politics became absolute; any position short of complete disengagement from the Revolution implied support, however mild or passive, of the Revolutionary course. The politicians had been estranged for too many years from the demands of the Quaker testimony to accept the all-or-nothing compliance which the Society's leaders demanded of them. At the same time, the meeting leadership could not afford to tolerate any compromise on this issue, for to do so would have left them open to the accusation that their own refusal to submit to the demands of the regime was grounded not in absolute religious principle but in selfish policy. The result, then, was the disownment of that segment of the Society which placed political concerns above religious compliance. Those who remained were more strongly united around their religion and more submissive to the Discipline than ever before, and the decades of conflict within the Society were brought to a close. The intense crisis of the Revolution made possible what the best efforts of the reformers throughout the fifties and sixties had failed to achieve, a united and politically homogeneous Society of Friends in Pennsylvania.

Having attained this state of unity and centralization, it remained for the Society to develop a program in which the political energies of Friends could be employed. Although they had been compelled by internal and external factors to withdraw from active political involvement during the war, those Friends who remained in the Society were not prepared to relinquish all public influence in a province which was founded by Quakers as a Quaker colony. The problem was to find a political program which would not conflict with their religious testimony as had the earlier activities of the politicians and politiques.

The elements of a new perspective on society at large and their place within it had begun to emerge among Friends in Pennsylvania during the years prior to the Revolution. As they witnessed the course of what they considered the decline of public morality, the leaders of the Society began to tend gradually toward the original Quaker role of moral models; they would show their countrymen the way, just as the reformers had assumed the role of intercedent and model for their own co-religionists several decades earlier.

Although the Quakers' moral view of the movement for independence served to alienate them from the rest of American society as the Revolution progressed, their general perspective and strategy enabled them to emerge from the Revolution in a position of considerable consistency and strength, for it brought the remaining members of the Society together and impelled them to greater religious zeal. By the end of the war, the members' attention and efforts were centered within the meeting structure, and the impulse toward engagement in the partisan arena was no longer felt. At the same time, the roots of a program which opened the way back into the good graces of their countrymen and back to a position of influence, however lessened, in the body politic, lay ready at hand. Moreover, the program posed no contradictions with respect to religion, for it was calculated to redound to the glory of God and the Society of Friends. By remaining attentive to openings for the furtherance of selected issues which were devoid of partisan content and self-interest and acceptable to non-Quakers as well, and by pursuing the openings as a corporate effort through the organization of the Society, the Friends could hope to influence the politics and course of society at large, while winning credit for their church, its testimony, and most important, for the Divine Author who had vouchsafed them the testimony to bear. In this way, the Pennsylvania Quakers were able to reconcile the need to bear a role in the public affairs of their province with that of remaining true to the tenets of their religion, even to the extent of bringing their Indian work under the auspices of government. Freed of the contradictions of their earlier role, the Quakers in Pennsylvania, like the founders of their church, became worthy of the tribute the English philanthropist Thomas Clarkson extended to their Society:

> They have shown and established . . . a proposition, which seems scarcely to be believed if we judge by the practice of statesmen, but the truth of which ought for ever to be insisted upon, that the policy of the Gospel is superior to the policy of the world.[8]

[8] *A Portraiture of Quakerism*, 3 vols. (London, 1806), 3 : 318.

Appendix I

THE ORGANIZATION OF
THE SOCIETY OF FRIENDS

The following is an outline of those features of Quaker organization which are pertinent to the present study. Although cast in the present tense, it should be understood as referring to the period under review—namely, the second half of the eighteenth century. Key terms are underlined for reference purposes. For additional information, the reader may wish to consult the following sources, all of which were used in preparing the accompanying outline: Howard H. Brinton, *Guide to Quaker Practice*,[1] L. Hugh Doncaster, *Quaker Organisation and Business Meetings*,[2] and the Pennsylvania Historical Survey's *Inventory of Church Archives: Society of Friends in Pennsylvania*.[3]

The basic structural unit of the Society of Friends, and the unit of individual membership, is the *Monthly Meeting*, the sessions of which consist of a meeting for worship, supposedly attended by all members, and separate men's and women's meetings for business. The Monthly Meeting concerns itself with such matters as receiving applications for membership, recording births and deaths, issuing certificates of marriage and removal (for Friends moving to an area under the jurisdiction of another Meeting), managing the group's financial affairs, superintending the affairs of the weekly meetings for worship, and seeing to the general welfare of its members. The term "Meeting" refers both to the actual gather-

[1] (Wallingford, Pa., 1952).
[2] (London, 1958).
[3] (Philadelphia, 1941).

231

ing and to the corporate group which conducts it and for which it acts.

One of the most important functions of the Monthly Meeting is the administration of the *Discipline,* as contained in the *Book of Discipline,* the formal compendium of Quaker principles of belief and practice, which consists of a series of topically arranged extracts from major doctrinal writings and past decisions taken by the Society. The Book of Discipline is compiled by the Yearly Meeting and is expanded and amended as important new policies are made. When a Friend behaves contrary to the Discipline, a committee is appointed to treat with him in a spirit of love and to induce him to acknowledge his transgression. Failing this, the committee recommends his *disownment* from the Society. A disowned Friend may subsequently be readmitted to membership, provided the proper acknowledgment of error is forthcoming and a disposition toward reform is evident. Or, if he believes he has been wrongly judged by the Monthly Meeting, he may appeal its decision to a higher body. In any event, he may continue to attend meetings for worship after his disownment, for these are open to all, but only acknowledged members may "engage in the service of truth"—that is, participate in meetings for business.

Another important function of the Monthly Meeting is the recognition and certification of *ministers.* From the beginning, the Quakers have employed no paid or trained clergy; every member has the right to address the Meeting. They do, however, follow the practice of formally acknowledging the special gift of individuals whose preaching is generally recognized as being particularly instructive and inspiring. Those who achieve this recognition, either men or women, are ministers. The Monthly Meeting issues certificates to those ministers who feel a concern to visit other meetings in their ministerial capacity, and receives the certificates of traveling ministers from other meetings. The Meeting also designates a body of *elders,* both men and women, to aid, counsel, and encourage the ministers, and give spiritual advice and guidance to their other brethren as well. This group of select and weighty Friends also serves to open and close meeting sessions. The ministers and elders participate jointly in a series of monthly, quarterly, and yearly meetings that parallel the hierarchy of Quaker business meetings, but are exclusively concerned with the spiritual welfare of the Society.

The *Quarterly Meeting* for business is comprised of several adjacent Monthly Meetings, all of whose members are eligible to attend and participate in Quarterly Meeting sessions. In actual fact, however, many members do not attend, leaving the business to be conducted primarily by the representatives chosen by the respective Monthly Meetings together with such other members as wish to take part. The functions of the Quarterly Meeting include the "setting up" or "laying down" of Monthly Meetings, the consideration of appeals against measures taken by the Monthly Meetings, and, most important, the concentration, aggregation, and transmission of information from the Monthly Meetings to the Yearly Meeting, and the dissemination in turn of minutes and advices from the Yearly Meeting to the subordinate meetings.

The highest unit of Quaker organization is the *Yearly Meeting*, which is made up of all the Quarterly Meetings within its delimited area. It, too, is open to participation by all members within its province, but, as in the case of the Quarterly Meeting, it is attended by a much smaller number—that is, by appointed representatives from the various quarters and by such other members as feel a concern to participate. It is held annually at the end of September and the beginning of October.

All Quaker business meetings employ the committee system to a greater or lesser extent to facilitate the conduct of business, but the committees are relied upon especially heavily in the Yearly Meeting, because of the scope of its affairs and the large numbers in attendance. Among the chief functions of the Yearly Meeting are maintaining contact with other Yearly Meetings, serving as the court of last resort for appeals against the decisions of subordinate meetings, gathering together the answers to the *Queries* (a set of questions to be answered by all Monthly Meetings concerning their organizational and spiritual state), and, in general, considering all problems of relevance to the Society as a whole and issuing *advices* and directives outlining policy to the membership and the meetings as such.

Records are kept of the proceedings of all Quaker business meetings, which is to say that they are *meetings of record*. The keeping of the *minutes* is one of the duties of the *clerk*, who is named to the position by the meeting at large. This functionary also presides over meeting sessions, brings up the items of business to be considered, coordinates the discussion, appoints committees, and sees that decisions are implemented. Although the position is one of great importance and responsibility, the clerk is not supposed to influence the meeting, or impose his own views upon the membership, but is expected to conduct his functions with complete impartiality, subservient always to the will of the meeting.

The Quaker method of reaching decisions is a special feature of Quaker organization and requires additional comment. With regard to decision-making, Hugh Doncaster has summarized the underlying rationale thus: "Belief in the universal nature of the Light of Christ, the Light given in measure to every man, implies both an immediate individual apprehension of the will of God, and also an understanding of his will mediated through the insights of others."[4] The goal of the Quaker meeting, then, is the discovery of God's will with reference to each matter of concern, and is based upon the conviction that His will will emerge through corporate attendance upon Him and be recognized as such when it is given expression. Proper attendance upon the Light, therefore, ultimately will lead to a unified *sense of the meeting*, although long and often painful deliberation may be required before unity is reached. It is the duty of the clerk to endeavor to discern the emergent sense of the meeting and cast it in the form of a minute for the approval of the assembled membership. Assent to a minute, however, does not necessarily imply its universal acceptance as the ultimate and immutable truth, but is best thought of as recognition of what is right for the particular group at a particular time.

[4] *Quaker Organisation and Business Meetings*, p. 63.

Appendix II

CAPSULE BIOGRAPHIES

The following biographical résumés are presented as a supplement to the discussion in Chapter IV of the characteristics of the three political types which prevailed among Pennsylvania Quakers in the years between the crisis of 1755 and the Revolution. The figures have been chosen on the basis of their status as politically relevant Quakers who exemplify the essential characteristics of the reformers, the politiques, and the worldly politicians.

REFORMERS

Anthony Benezet (1713–84)

Anthony Benezet was a member and elder of the Philadelphia Monthly Meeting. After rejecting a mercantile career, he taught in Friends' schools throughout his adult life, living very plainly and testifying frequently against a life of riches. A highly active participant in the affairs of the Yearly Meeting, he was also a longtime and energetic member of the Meeting for Sufferings. He was among the subscribers to the Epistle of Tender Love and Caution in December, 1775, and a member of both the 1758 and 1764 committees which issued advices against officeholding. Much of his energy was devoted to philanthropic works, especially on behalf of the Negro, but he also served as a manager of the Pennsylvania Hospital and acted for many years as John Reynell's almoner. Benezet was the author of a large number of papers, books, and tracts, many of which were polemics against slavery, and he was a close friend and associate of John Woolman in the effort to eradicate this institution. He conducted an extensive correspondence with many eminent Quakers and non-Quakers, and was widely loved and admired.

George Churchman (1730–1814)

George Churchman, the son of John Churchman, was a member and elder of the Nottingham Monthly Meeting in Chester Quarter (later in Western Quarter). He served as clerk of the Western Quarterly Meeting from 1758 to 1768, and of the Yearly Meeting in 1767, was generally active in meeting affairs, and was, by his own admission, strongly concerned with upholding the Discipline. He participated in the systematic visiting of Friends' families undertaken by a number of reformers between 1757 and 1760 under the auspices of the Yearly Meeting, and was a member of the 1758 committee which advised against officeholding by Friends. Churchman was also the founder of a Quaker school in 1763 which was subsidized by Israel Pemberton.

John Churchman (1705–75)

John Churchman was a member of the Nottingham Monthly Meeting in Chester Quarter (later transferred to Western Quarter). He records that he was visited by the Lord's Spirit at eight years of age, becoming an elder at the early age of twenty-five, and a minister three years later. He was an active participant in the Yearly Meeting, for several years a member of the Meeting for Sufferings, and is noted as having been useful in carrying out the Discipline. His name appears among the subscribers to the Epistle of Tender Love and Caution. Churchman, who had been abroad in the ministry, accompanied Samuel Fothergill to America in 1755, and was a close associate of the English minister during the latter's stay in the colonies. He was also an intimate friend of John Woolman, and an active opponent of slavery. His rejection of the office of justice of the peace in 1749 and his actions and sentiments relating to the Indian wars have been recounted in the text. Churchman was a member of the 1758 and 1764 committees which advised Friends to reject public office, and of the group of reformers engaged in visiting Friends' families between 1757 and 1760.

Samuel Emlen, Jr. (1730–99)

Samuel Emlen was a member and minister of the Philadelphia Monthly Meeting. He was also a member of the Meeting for Sufferings, and acted as its clerk from 1762 to 1764. Emlen served an apprenticeship in the counting house of James Pemberton, but inherited a fortune and retired without entering business on his own. Despite his ample means, he was noted for dressing very plainly, and for being a close reprover of those who shunned the cross and followed the vain fashions and customs of the world. Regarding his own spiritual experience, Emlen stated that he was visited with the temptations of Satan at an early age, but was preserved by visitations of the Holy Spirit. He was especially noted for his powerful, almost mystical, insight into the character of people with whom he came in contact, and there were numerous testimonies to the strength and effect of his spiritual vision.

John Pemberton (1727–95)

John Pemberton was a member of one of the wealthiest families in Pennsylvania, the youngest son of the elder Israel Pemberton, a grandson of Phineas Pemberton, who accompanied William Penn to the province, and the brother of Israel and James Pemberton. In 1750, he journeyed to England in the company of John Churchman and William Brown, ostensibly for reasons of business and health, but once abroad he elected to accompany Churchman in the ministry, and realized the gift of the ministry in himself. Throughout his life he was one of the most energetic Friends in the service of his church, serving as clerk of the Philadelphia Quarterly Meeting (1755–57), clerk of the Yearly Meeting of Ministers and Elders (1766–82), and member and clerk of the Meeting for Sufferings (1764–77). He signed the Epistle of Tender Love and Caution, and was engaged with a number of his fellow reformers in promoting the reformation by visiting Friends' families between 1757 and 1760. He is noted as having been useful in supporting the Discipline and zealously concerned with upholding Friends' testimonies and the good order of the church.

Daniel Stanton (1708–70)

Daniel Stanton, a joiner by trade, was a minister of the Philadelphia Monthly Meeting. He participated actively in the affairs of the Yearly Meeting, and was a long-term member of the Meeting for Sufferings. Among his particular concerns was the need for general moral reform in the province, and he campaigned assiduously against the evils of horseracing, stage plays, and drunkenness. He was also noted for his opposition to slavery, and as a great encourager of the religiously inclined among the younger generation. Stanton was among the signatories to the Epistle of Tender Love and Caution and took part in the reformers' visitation program between 1757 and 1760. He was a close friend of Israel Pemberton and died in the latter's house.

James Thornton (1727–94)

James Thornton was a resident of Bucks County and a member of the Byberry Monthly Meeting. He confessed to having consorted with loose and vain company as a youth, but was saved by being favored with heart-tendering visitations of the Divine Spirit, and became a minister at the age of twenty. He was known as a benevolent and hospitable Friend, but was also noted as being fervently engaged for the Discipline of the church. Thornton was a frequent participant in the Yearly Meeting and a member of the visiting committees in the late 1750s. He was, in addition, a member of the Meeting for Sufferings for many years.

John Woolman (1720–72)

John Woolman was a widely loved and revered minister who resided all his life in Mt. Holly, New Jersey, in the Burlington Quarter. Well on his way to achieving considerable prosperity as a tailor, merchant, and farmer, he purposefully cut back his trade and elected to live a life of simplicity and self-denial. Perhaps best known for his tireless and selfless work on behalf of the enslaved Negroes, Woolman also campaigned against the snares and dangers of wealth among Friends, and was considered very useful in treating with transgressors against the Discipline. In common with other reformers, he was concerned for the proper education of the younger generation of Friends and accordingly founded a school for Quaker youth in Mt. Holly. Woolman was very active in the affairs of the Yearly Meeting, a signer of the Epistle of Tender Love and Caution, and a member of the 1758 committee which warned against the dangers of officeholding by Friends. He also participated in the reformist project of visiting Friends' families between 1757 and 1760.

POLITIQUES

Aaron Ashbridge (1712–76)

Aaron Ashbridge was a well-to-do farmer who belonged to the Goshen Monthly Meeting in Chester Quarter, both of which he served as clerk. He was a justice of the peace from 1749 until 1757, when he refused to attest recruits for the Indian wars and tried to dissuade them from entering the king's service. He took an active part in the affairs of the Yearly Meeting, serving on a 1760 committee which advised Friends against officeholding. Ashbridge was also a member of the combined committee, part of which issued the Epistle of Tender Love and Caution in 1755, but his name does not appear among the signers of the document.

William Callender (1703–?)

William Callender, a wealthy Philadelphian, represented the city in the Assembly from 1753 until 1756, when he and five other Quakers resigned their places because of conscientious reservations concerning the provincial war policy. He was a member of the Meeting for Sufferings and a trustee of the Friendly Association.

Abel James (1724–90)

Abel James was a wealthy Philadelphia merchant, who served as a member of the Meeting for Sufferings and as clerk of the Friendly Association. He was also a member of the inner circle of the Quaker party, and was elected to represent Philadelphia City in the provincial Assembly of 1770 and 1771. James was one of the tea agents who was forced by a mob to resign his commission in December, 1773.

Owen Jones (1711–93)

Owen Jones, the independently wealthy grandson of the leader of a group of Welsh Quakers who settled at Merion in 1682, moved his residence to Philadelphia and became an elder of the Philadelphia Monthly Meeting. For many years he held the position of treasurer of the Province of Pennsylvania. Within the Society of Friends, he participated actively in the Yearly Meeting, serving on the 1758 and 1764 committees which advised Friends against the dangers of officeholding. He was, in addition, a trustee of the Friendly Association, and a member of the Meeting for Sufferings from its inception until the time of his death. He was one of the prominent Philadelphia Friends exiled to Virginia in 1777 for purported acts against the Revolutionary government.

Israel Pemberton (1715–79)

Israel Pemberton was the oldest son of Israel Pemberton, Sr., and the brother of James and John Pemberton. He was prominent in business, and one of the wealthiest men in the province. His extensive undertakings and influence, and his vigorous, assertive manner, earned him the sobriquet "King of the Quakers." Pemberton was a founder and patron of the Pennsylvania Hospital and of many of the city's other public institutions. He served only one term in the Assembly in 1750–51, but enjoyed a considerable degree of influence in the Quaker party for a number of years. From 1750 to 1759, he was clerk of the Yearly Meeting, and he served on the 1758 and 1764 committees which concerned themselves with Friends in office. He was an active member of the Meeting for Sufferings, and a founder, trustee, and moving spirit of the Friendly Association. He died not long after his return from Virginia, whence he had been exiled by the Revolutionary government as an enemy of the cause.

James Pemberton (1723–1809)

James Pemberton, the brother of Israel and John Pemberton, was a highly successful and influential Philadelphia merchant. He was very active in public life, a founder and manager of the Pennsylvania Hospital, a burgess of the city of Philadelphia, and one of the inner circle of the Quaker party. He was elected to the Assembly from Philadelphia County in 1755, but resigned his seat in 1756 because of scruples against the provincial war policy. In 1765, he stood again for the Assembly, this time from Philadelphia City, to help counteract the rising power of the Proprietary party, and was subsequently elected to five terms in the House. Within the church, he was an elder, clerk of the Philadelphia Quarterly Meeting from 1756 to 1777, clerk of the Yearly Meeting from 1761 to 1766, 1768 to 1776, and 1778 to 1781, and clerk of the Meeting for Sufferings from its inception until the beginning of 1762, during which time he also served on a large number of committees. In addition, he was one of the trustees of the Friendly Association. Together with his brothers, he was among the Quaker exiles to Virginia in 1777.

John Reynell (1708–84)

John Reynell, born of a prominent English family, was educated at Exeter, where his uncle was mayor. He came to Philadelphia from Barbados in 1728, and became very successful in shipping and trade. He was one of the founders, treasurer, and president of the Pennsylvania Hospital and of the Friendly Association. During the mid-1750s, he was appointed Indian commissioner, and during the following decade he played a leading part in both Non-Importation campaigns, serving as head of the Non-Importation Committee in 1769. Reynell participated actively in the affairs of the Society, and held the position of elder. He attended numerous Yearly Meetings and was on the 1758 and 1764 committees which dealt with Quakers in office. He participated in the proceedings which led to the issuance of the Epistle of Tender Love and Caution, although he did not sign it. He was also an active member of the Meeting for Sufferings. For many years, Reynell allotted one-third of his substantial expenditures for the relief of the poor, with Anthony Benezet as his almoner.

Isaac Zane (1710–94)

Isaac Zane was the father-in-law of John Pemberton, and an elder of the Philadelphia Monthly Meeting. He took an active role in the proceedings of the Yearly Meeting, signed the Epistle of Tender Love and Caution, and was a member of the Meeting for Sufferings for almost four decades. Zane was a trustee of the Friendly Association, and was sent by the provincial Assembly in 1758 to supervise the building of a new village for the Delawares in the Wyoming valley, a project financed by the Quaker organization. The problem of Friends' education was another of his major concerns.

Politicians

Joseph Fox (1709–79)

Joseph Fox was a prominent Philadelphia merchant, landowner, and mortgage holder. An adherent of the Quaker party, he represented the city, and later the county, in the Assembly for more than twenty years, serving as Speaker from 1764 to 1767. His period in office included the crucial years from 1756 to the early 1760s, when many of his fellow Quakers withdrew from the House. He was barracks master to the Moravian Indians who were quartered in Philadelphia during the Paxton affair, and was later prominent in the non-importation campaigns.

John Mifflin (1714–59)

John Mifflin, a wealthy Philadelphian, was a supporter of the Proprietor who served the county as a justice of the peace and the province as a member of the Provincial Council. He was one of the commissioners appointed by the Assembly in November, 1755, to spend the sixty thousand pounds raised by the militia bill.

Thomas Mifflin (1744–1800)

Thomas Mifflin was a member of a prominent Quaker family in Philadelphia. After attending the University of Pennsylvania, he entered business as a merchant and emerged as one of the leaders of the radical faction in the Revolutionary movement. He was active in the second non-importation campaign, was elected to the Assembly from Philadelphia City (1772–78), and, while serving in the House, was designated one of the Pennsylvania representatives to the first Continental Congress. During the war, he was quartermaster general of the Revolutionary army, a member of the Continental Congress from 1782 to 1784, and president of that body in 1783 and 1784. From 1785 until 1787, he represented the county of Philadelphia in the Assembly and was a delegate to the federal Constitutional Convention; from 1790 until 1799, he served as governor of Pennsylvania. For his role in the Revolution —"being active in the promotion of military measures"—he was disowned from the Society on July 28, 1775.

Charles Norris (1712–66)

Charles Norris was the younger son of Isaac Norris, Sr., and the brother of Isaac Norris, Speaker of the House. He was a prominent and wealthy merchant in Philadelphia and an influential member of the Quaker party. His public activities included service as a trustee of the General Loan Office of Pennsylvania, membership on the Philadelphia Common Council, and terms as manager and treasurer of the Pennsylvania Hospital.

Isaac Norris (1701–66)

Isaac Norris, son of the senior Isaac Norris, and the elder brother of Charles Norris, was a merchant and large landholder. He was elected to the Philadelphia Common Council in 1727, appointed a magistrate in 1730, and served in the Assembly from 1734 to 1764. From 1751 to 1764, he was Speaker of the House and the leader of the Quaker party. His pro-defense position has been discussed in the text. He was, for a time, clerk of the Philadelphia Quarterly Meeting.

Samuel Rhoads (1711–84)

Samuel Rhoads was a wealthy master carpenter and investor in trade and real estate. He was elected to the Philadelphia Common Council in 1741, served as an Indian commissioner in 1762, and held a seat in the Assembly from 1762 to 1764 and again from 1771 to 1774. He represented Pennsylvania at the first Continental Congress, and became mayor of Philadelphia in 1774. He was also a manager of the Pennsylvania Hospital and served as its President in 1780 and 1781.

Thomas Wharton (1731–84)

Thomas Wharton, a very wealthy merchant, land promoter, and speculator, was a member of the inner circle of the Quaker party. He was a close associate of Galloway and Franklin, and a co-founder and owner, with Galloway, of *The Chronicle*, established in 1766 as the Quaker party organ. He was also a manager of the Pennsylvania Hospital, and its treasurer from 1769 to 1772. Originally a supporter of the Revolutionary cause, he withdrew his support when the movement entered the stage of armed conflict, and was exiled to Virginia in 1777.

LIST OF ABBREVIATIONS

EC   Etting Collection, Family Papers

GCJ   George Churchman Journal

HDLB   Henry Drinker Letterbook

INLB   Isaac Norris Letterbooks

JRLB   John Reynell Letterbooks

LMS   London Meeting for Sufferings

LYM   London Yearly Meeting

PMS   Minutes of the Philadelphia Meeting for Sufferings

PP   Pemberton Papers

PQM   Minutes of the Philadelphia Quarterly Meeting

PYM   Minutes of the Philadelphia Yearly Meeting

Smith
Corresp.   John Smith Correspondence

In accordance with Quaker usage, dates in the footnotes are given in the following form: day (Arabic numerals)/month (Roman numerals)/last two digits of year (Arabic numerals). Thus, 11/iv/62 refers to April 11, 1762, 12/vii/64 to July 12, 1764, etc.

BIBLIOGRAPHY

Meeting Records

Department of Records, Philadelphia, Pa. Philadelphia Yearly Meeting.
Minutes of the Philadelphia Meeting for Sufferings.
Minutes of the Philadelphia Quarterly Meeting.
Minutes of the Philadelphia Yearly Meeting.
Papers of the Indian Committee of the Philadelphia Yearly
Meeting.
Haverford College Library, Haverford, Pa. Quaker Collection, Philadelphia Yearly Meeting Book of Discipline, 1762 version.

Manuscript Collections and Personal Papers

Department of Records, Philadelphia, Pa. Philadelphia Yearly Meeting.
Manuscript Letterbook RS 181.
Friends Historical Library, Swarthmore College, Swarthmore, Pa. Benjamin
Kite, "Memoir of the Early Part of his Life," 1834.
Haverford College Library, Haverford, Pa. Quaker Collection.
Samuel Allinson to Patrick Henry, 17/x/74, MS 968.
Samuel Allinson, "Reasons against War and Paying Taxes for its
Support," 1780, MS 968.
George Churchman, Journal, 1759–1813, 10 vols., MS 975C.
James Pemberton to Jonah Thompson, 25/iv/56, MS 325.
James Pemberton to several Friends in London, 1/vii/74, MS 325.
John Pemberton *et al.* to Friends in Pennsylvania, 16/vii/74
(Epistle of Tender Love and Caution), MS 851.
Historical Society of Pennsylvania, Philadelphia, Pa.
Coates and Reynell Papers, John Reynell Letterbook.
Henry Drinker Papers, Henry Drinker Letterbook.
Family Papers, Etting Collection.
Norris Papers, Isaac Norris Letterbooks, 2 vols.
Pemberton Papers, 70 vols.
John Smith Correspondence.

Published Works

Bailey, F. G. *Stratagems and Spoils.* Oxford: Blackwell, 1969.

Beals, Alan R., and Siegel, Bernard J. *Divisiveness and Social Conflict: An Anthropological Approach.* Stanford, Calif.: Stanford University Press, 1966.

Beatty, Edward C. O. *William Penn as Social Philosopher.* New York: Columbia University Press, 1939.

Boulding, Kenneth. *The Image: Knowledge in Life and Society.* Ann Arbor: University of Michigan Press, 1956.

Braithwaite, William C. *The Second Period of Quakerism.* 2nd ed. Cambridge: At the University Press, 1961.

Bridenbaugh, Carl and Jessica. *Rebels and Gentlemen: Philadelphia in the Age of Franklin.* 2nd ed., paperback. New York: Oxford University Press, 1962.

Brinton, Howard H. *Guide to Quaker Practice.* 2nd ed. Wallingford, Pa.: Pendle Hill Pamphlets, 1952.

Bronner, Edwin B. *William Penn's "Holy Experiment."* New York: Columbia University Press, 1962.

Brookes, George S. *Friend Anthony Benezet.* Philadelphia: University of Pennsylvania Press, 1937.

Churchman, John. *An Account of the Gospel Labours and Christian Experiences of . . . John Churchman.* The Friends' Library, vol. 6. Philadelphia, 1842.

Clarkson, Thomas. *A Portraiture of Quakerism.* 3 vols. London: Longman, Hurst, Rees & Orme, 1806.

Coleman, James S. "Social Cleavage and Religious Conflict." *Journal of Social Issues,* 12, no. 3 (1956) : 44–56.

Crosfield, George. *Memoirs of the Life and Gospel Labours of Samuel Fothergill, with Selections from his Correspondence.* Liverpool: D. Marples, 1843.

Deardorff, Merle, and Snyderman, George S. "A Nineteenth Century Journal of a Visit to the Indians of New York." *Proceedings of the American Philosophical Society,* 100 (1956) : 582–94.

Doncaster, L. Hugh. *Quaker Organisation and Business Meetings.* London: Friends Home Service Committee, 1958.

Dove, David. *The Quaker Unmask'd.* Philadelphia, 1764.

Drake, Thomas E. *Quakers and Slavery in America.* New Haven, Conn.: Yale University Press, 1950.

Dunbar, John R. *The Paxton Papers.* The Hague: M. Nijhoff, 1957.

Easton, David. *A Framework for Political Analysis*. Englewood Cliffs, N.J.: Prentice-Hall, 1965.

———. *A Systems Analysis of Political Life*. New York: John Wiley, 1965.

Emlen, James. "The Journal of James Emlen Kept on a Trip to Canandaigua, New York." Edited by William N. Fenton. *Ethnohistory*, 12 (1965) : 279–342.

Epstein, A. L. *Politics in an Urban African Community*. Manchester: Manchester University Press, 1958.

Evans-Pritchard, E. E. *Social Anthropology and Other Essays*. New York: Macmillan, Free Press, 1964.

Fallers, Lloyd. *Bantu Bureaucracy*. 2nd ed., paperback. Chicago: University of Chicago Press, 1965.

Gilpin, Thomas. *Exiles in Virginia*. Philadelphia: Published for the Subscribers, 1848.

Gluckman, Max. *Order and Rebellion in Tribal Africa*. London: Cohen & West, 1963.

Goode, William J. "A Theory of Role Strain." *American Sociological Review*, 25 (1960) : 483–96.

Greene, Jack P. "Changing Interpretations of Early American Politics." In *The Reinterpretation of Early American History: Essays in Honor of John Edwin Pomfret*, edited by Ray Allen Billington, pp. 151–84. San Merino, Calif.: Huntington Library, 1966.

Grey, Isaac. *A Serious Address to such of the People Called Quakers . . . as Profess Scruples Relative to the Present Government*. Philadelphia, 1778.

Hallowell, A. Irving. *Culture and Experience*. Philadelphia: University of Pennsylvania Press, 1955.

Hanna, William S. *Benjamin Franklin and Pennsylvania Politics*. Stanford, Calif.: Stanford University Press, 1964.

Hazard, Samuel, ed. *Register of Pennsylvania*. 16 vols. Philadelphia: Printed by W. F. Geddes, 1828–36.

Hobling, Margaret B. *The Concrete and the Universal*. London: Allen & Unwin, 1958.

James, Sydney. *A People Among Peoples*. Cambridge, Mass.: Harvard University Press, 1963.

Jones, Rufus M. *The Later Periods of Quakerism*. 2 vols. London: Macmillan & Co., 1921.

Kelsey, Rayner W. *Friends and the Indians, 1655–1917*. Philadelphia:

Associated Executive Committee of Friends on Indian Affairs, 1917.

Ketcham, Ralph L. "Conscience, War and Politics in Pennsylvania, 1755–1757." *William and Mary Quarterly,* 20 (1963) : 416–39.

Lloyd, Arnold. *Quaker Social History.* New York: Longmans, Green, 1950.

Logan, James. "James Logan on Defensive War." *Pennsylvania Magazine of History and Biography,* 6 (1882) : 402–11.

Marshall, Christopher. *Extracts from the Diary of Christopher Marshall.* Edited by William Duane. Albany, N.Y.: J. Munsell, 1877.

Mekeel, Arthur J. "The Quakers in the American Revolution." Ph.D. dissertation, Harvard University, 1939. Typescript in the Haverford College Library, Haverford, Pa.

Neale, Mary. *Some Account of the Life and Religious Exercises of Mary Neale, formerly Mary Peisley.* Dublin, 1795.

Oxley, Joseph. *A Journal of the Life and Gospel Labours of Joseph Oxley.* London, 1837.

Parrish, Samuel. *Some Chapters in the History of the Friendly Association for Regaining and Preserving Peace with the Indians by Pacific Measures.* Philadelphia: Friends' Historical Association, 1877.

Pennsylvania Historical Survey. *Inventory of Church Archives: Society of Friends in Pennsylvania.* Philadelphia: Friends' Historical Association, 1941.

Phillips, Catherine. *Memoirs of the Life of Catherine Phillips.* Philadelphia, 1798.

The Quakers Assisting to Preserve the Lives of the Indians in the Barracks Vindicated, no. 2. Philadelphia, 1764.

Rothermund, Dietmar. *The Layman's Progress.* Philadelphia: University of Pennsylvania Press, 1961.

Sanders, Thomas G. *Protestant Concepts of Church and State.* New York: Holt, Rinehart & Winston, 1964.

Sarbin, Theodore, and Allen, Vernon R. "Role Theory." In *The Handbook of Social Psychology,* vol. 1, *Systematic Positions,* edited by Gardner Lindzey and Eliot Aronson, pp. 488–567. 2nd ed. Reading, Mass: Addison-Wesley, 1968.

Savery, William. *A Journal of the Life, Travels, and Religious Labours of William Savery.* Edited by Jonathan Evans. London: C. Gilpin, 1844.

———. *Political Leaders of Provincial Pennsylvania.* Philadelphia: Macmillan, 1919.

Sharpless, Isaac. *A History of Quaker Government in Pennsylvania.* 2 vols. Philadelphia: T. S. Leach & Co., 1898–99.

Smith, M. G. *The Plural Society in the British West Indies.* Berkeley and Los Angeles: University of California Press, 1965.

Smith, William. *A Brief State of the Province of Pennsylvania.* London, 1865.

————. *A Brief View of the Conduct of Pennsylvania for the Year 1755.* London, 1756.

Swartz, Marc; Turner, Victor; and Tuden, Arthur. *Political Anthropology.* Chicago: Aldine, 1966.

Taylor, Francis R. *The Life of William Savery of Philadelphia, 1750–1804.* New York: Macmillan, 1925.

Thayer, Theodore. *Israel Pemberton: King of the Quakers.* Philadelphia: Historical Society of Pennsylvania, 1943.

————. "The Quaker Party of Pennsylvania, 1755–1765." *Pennsylvania Magazine of History and Biography,* 71 (1947) : 19–43.

————. *Pennsylvania Politics and the Growth of Democracy, 1740–1776.* Harrisburg: Pennsylvania Historical and Museum Commission, 1953.

Tolles, Frederick H. *Meeting House and Counting House.* 2nd ed. New York: Norton, 1963.

Tract Association of Friends. *Biographical Sketches and Anecdotes of Members of the Religious Society of Friends.* Philadelphia, 1870.

Votes and Proceedings of the House of Representatives of the Province of Pennsylvania. Harrisburg: Pennsylvania Archives, 8th series, 1931–35.

Wallace, Anthony F. C. *King of the Delawares: Teedyuscung.* Philadelphia: University of Pennsylvania Press, 1949.

————. *The Death and Rebirth of the Seneca.* New York: Alfred A. Knopf, 1970.

Weber, Max. *The Sociology of Religion.* Translated by Ephraim Fischoff. Boston: Beacon Press, 1963.

Wellenreuther, Hermann. "The Political Dilemma of the Quakers in Pennsylvania, 1681–1748." *Pennsylvania Magazine of History and Biography,* 94 (1970) : 135–72.

Wertenbaker, Thomas J. *The Golden Age of Colonial Culture.* 2nd ed. Ithaca, N.Y.: Cornell University Press, 1959.

Wetherill, Charles. *History of the Religious Society of Friends, Called by Some the Free Quakers.* Philadelphia: Printed for the Society, 1894.

Williamson, Hugh. *The Plain Dealer: Or, a Few Remarks upon Quaker Politics.* Philadelphia, 1764.

Woolman, John. *The Journal and Essays of John Woolman.* Edited by Amelia Mott Gummere. London: Macmillan, 1922.

————. *The Journal of John Woolman and A Plea for the Poor.* New

York: Citadel Press, Corinth Books, 1961.

Zimmerman, John J. "Benjamin Franklin and the Quaker Party, 1755–1756." *William and Mary Quarterly*, 17 (1960) : 291–313.

INDEX

Allen, William, 8–9
Allinson, Samuel, 162–63
American Revolution, 127–58, 159–77, 179, 181, 190, 196, 224, 227–28
Amherst, Lord Jeffrey, 107–8
Andrews, Isaac, 177
Anglicans, 8, 58, 175, 197
Ashbridge, Aaron, 119, 177, 239–40

Bacon, David, 167, 209
Barclay, David, 153–54
Beals, Alan, xi
Benezet, Anthony, 41, 50, 56–67, 76, 93, 100, 119, 146, 177, 181, 193, 198, 235–36
Biddle, Clement, 146
Biddle, Owen, 146, 171
Big Tree, 202
Boston Resolves, 131
Boulding, Kenneth, 36
Brown, Hinton, 123
Brown, Moses, 175, 182
Brown, William, 54, 76
Byran, George, 123

Callender, William, 26, 80–81, 92, 240
Canandaigua, Treaty of, 209–11, 213–14
Chapin, Israel, 214
Chapin, Israel, Jr., 214
Chew, Benjamin, 110
Child, Isaac, 119
Churchman, George, 56, 62, 64, 120, 122, 124–25, 169–70, 236
Churchman, John, 12–17, 41–42, 45, 47, 50, 51, 92, 119, 129, 163, 177, 193–95, 218, 236–37
Clarkson, Thomas, 229
Common Sense, 155
Conestoga massacre, 109
Conflict: role, x–xii, xiv, 26, 63–64, 68–69, 81, 84–85, 94, 97–101, 121, 124–25, 171–74, 219–24; social, xi–xii, 9–11, 44–64, 69–72, 103, 105–7, 114, 117–18, 147, 151–52, 154, 157, 165–68, 170–71, 220, 225–28
Congress, Quaker petitions to, 199, 203–4
Constitution, Quaker efforts to amend, 198–99
Constitutional Convention, 176

Continental Congress, 146–47, 191
Cornplanter, 202, 213

Defense. *See* Peace testimony
Delawares, 79, 86–87, 91, 95–96, 108, 111, 201
Denny, William, 79, 85–90, 97
Discipline, 44, 55, 56, 69, 71, 106, 144, 147, 157, 160, 166, 227–28
Disownment, 165–67, 170–71
Drinker, Henry, 117, 134, 152, 164, 173, 199

Easton treaties, 79, 85–92
Elections, 3, 6, 7, 24, 26–27, 104, 106–7, 122, 135
Elliott, John, 206
Ellwood, Thomas, 75
Emlen, James, 208, 209
Emlen, Samuel, Jr., 61, 76, 120, 177, 199, 237
Epistle of Tender Love and Caution, 30, 45, 56, 70
Epstein, A. L., xiv
Evans-Pritchard, E. E., xvi

Fallers, Lloyd, xiv, 225
Ferris, Benjamin, 176
Fisher, Miers, 164
Fisher, Samuel, 164
Fisher, Thomas, 164
Fothergill, John, 96, 98, 123, 131, 135, 149, 152, 154, 161
Fothergill, Samuel, 25, 29, 33, 40–41, 42–43, 45–46, 57, 63–64
Fox, George, 129
Fox, Joseph, 61, 243
Franklin, Benjamin, 24, 26, 84, 110, 116–17, 123, 127
Free Quakers, 150, 166–69
Friendly Association for Regaining and Preserving Peace with the Indians by Pacific Measures, 77–101, 109, 112–14, 205, 207–8, 212, 222

Galloway, Joseph, 110, 123
German Reformed Church, 8
Germans, 2, 21, 81, 110
Gilpin, Thomas, 164

255

INDEX

Pennsylvania provincial charter, 5, 84, 117, 134, 155
Pennsylvania Provincial Council, 87–88, 96, 110
Peters, Richard, 86–88, 91
Peters, William, 26
Philadelphia City Corporation, 138–39
Philadelphia Meeting for Sufferings, 73–76, 77, 81, 91–92, 97, 106, 113, 120, 127–30, 136–37, 142–43, 147–48, 152, 155–56, 165, 178, 181, 186–87, 198, 202–4, 206–7, 209, 211–12
Philadelphia Monthly Meeting, 110, 133, 136, 167
Philadelphia Quarterly Meeting, 67–69, 136, 150, 151
Philadelphia Yearly Meeting, 10, 44, 65–73, 74, 81–82, 104, 107, 112, 118, 129, 133, 135–36, 144–46, 150, 155, 157, 159–61, 165, 175, 178, 181, 182, 186, 190, 191, 193–96, 198–99, 204–5, 209, 211–12, 218; Indian Committee of, 211–13
Pickering, Timothy, 208, 213–14
Pleasants, Samuel, 164
Political behavior: defined, xii–xiii, 17; Quaker modes of, 12, 54–55, 70–71, 138–39, 180–81
Politiques, 48, 59–64, 67–72, 75–76, 80–85, 93–94, 97–101, 114, 121–25, 133–34, 138–39, 143–44, 152, 171–74, 221–27, 239–43
Pontiac's War, 107
Presbyterians, 8, 9, 41, 58, 109, 112–13, 114–16, 122–24, 131, 175, 197, 222, 226
Proprietary party, 8, 21–24, 83–84, 91, 105, 122–23
Proprietors. See Penn family

Quaker belief and practice, development of, 36–41. See also Society of Friends
Quaker party, 8, 22, 26–27, 58, 60, 83, 105, 111, 113, 122–23
Quakers, political role of, 2–3, 43, 47–48, 97, 104–5, 118–19, 135, 143–44, 147, 156, 159–63, 176, 178–83, 189, 197, 201, 210, 212–15, 217–29. See also Politiques; Reformers; Worldly politicians

Reformers, 15–16, 32–33, 48–58, 70–72, 75–76, 93–94, 97, 99–100, 119–20,

122, 124, 129–30, 152, 169, 219–20, 223–27, 235–39
Reform movement, 28, 33, 35–46, 169–70, 179, 193–95, 218. See also Reformers
Revere, Paul, 141
Reynell, John, 67, 76, 80–81, 92, 113, 115–16, 119, 121, 127, 132, 173, 177, 242
Rhoads, Samuel, 61, 244
Richardson, Joseph, 80
Roberts, George, 142
Role conflict. See Conflict, role
Role strain. See Conflict, role
Royal government, campaign for, 84, 89, 116–18, 122–23, 127, 134

Sagareesa (Sword Carrier), 211
Sandusky, Treaty of, 206, 209, 214
Sansom, Samuel, 150, 152
Savery, William, 177, 206, 209–10
Scarborough, John, 195
Sharpless, Isaac, 128
Shoemaker, Benjamin, 61
Siegel, Bernard, xi
Simcoe, Governor, 207
Slave trade, 150, 191–99, 210
Smith, John, 78, 93, 115, 177
Smith, Samuel, 78
Smith, William, 21–22, 105
Social conflict. See Conflict, social
Society of Friends, organization of, 231–34. See also Quaker belief and practice
Spavold, Samuel, 57
Stamp Act, 127–30
Stanton, Daniel, 176, 195, 238
Strettel, Amos, 132
Swartz, Marc, 219
Sykes, John, 195

Teedyuscung, 85–87, 90–91, 95–96
Thomas, George, 5–7
Thornton, James, 238–39
Tolles, Frederick, 39
Townshend Acts, 130–32
Tuden, Arthur, 219
Turner, Victor, 219

Virginia, exile of Quakers to, 164, 171

Walking Purchase, 86, 91, 96
Waln, Nicholas, 61, 177, 199
Warder, Jeremiah, 80

257

INDEX

Washington, George, 190, 203, 206
Weber, Max, 217
Weiser, Conrad, 78, 87
Wetherill, Samuel, 150–51, 167–68
Wharton, Thomas, 61, 142, 164, 171, 245
White, Bishop, 189
White, Joseph, 129, 177
White, Josiah, 177
Whitefield, George, 9
Willing, Thomas, 110

Wilson, Christopher, 26–27
Wistar, Richard, 80
Woolman, John, 51–52, 53, 54, 56, 70, 100, 119, 129, 163, 177, 193, 195, 239
Worldly politicians, 48, 58–59, 82, 84, 99, 106, 170, 219–20, 225–27, 243–45
Worral, Peter, 26, 80, 119

Yarnall, Mordecai, 76, 176

Zane, Isaac, 76, 80, 92, 121, 167, 242

THE JOHNS HOPKINS PRESS
Composed in Garamond text and display
by Monotype Composition Company
Printed on 60 lb. Sebago Offset
by Halliday Lithograph Corporation
Bound in Columbia Riverside Linen RL-3963
by Moore and Company, Inc.